Early Modern Literature in History

General Editor: **Cedric C. Brown**
Professor of English and Dean of the Faculty of Arts and Humanities,
University of Reading

Advisory Board: **Donna Hamilton**, University of Maryland; **Jean Howard**,
University of Columbia; **John Kerrigan**, University of Cambridge; **Richard
McCoy**, CUNY; **Sharon Achinstein**, University of Oxford

Within the period 1520–1740 this series discusses many kinds of writing, both
within and outside the established canon. The volumes may employ different
theoretical perspectives, but they share an historical awareness and an interest
in seeing their texts in lively negotiation with their own and successive cultures.

Titles include:

Anna R. Beer
SIR WALTER RALEGH AND HIS READERS IN THE SEVENTEENTH CENTURY
Speaking to the People

Cedric C. Brown and Arthur F. Marotti (*editors*)
TEXTS AND CULTURAL CHANGE IN EARLY MODERN ENGLAND

Mark Thornton Burnett
CONTRUCTING 'MONSTERS' IN SHAKESPEAREAN DRAMA AND EARLY
MODERN CULTURE

Martin Butler (*editor*)
RE-PRESENTING BEN JONSON
Text, History, Performance

Jocelyn Catty
WRITING RAPE, WRITING WOMEN IN EARLY MODERN ENGLAND
Unbridled Speech

Dermot Cavanagh
LANGUAGE AND POLITICS IN THE SIXTEENTH-CENTURY HISTORY PLAY

Danielle Clarke and Elizabeth Clarke (*editors*)
'THIS DOUBLE VOICE'
Gendered Writing in Early Modern England

James Daybell (*editor*)
EARLY MODERN WOMEN'S LETTER-WRITING, 1450–1700

John Dolan
POETIC OCCASION FROM MILTON TO WORDSWORTH

Henk Dragstra, Sheila Ottway and Helen Wilcox (*editors*)
BETRAYING OUR SELVES
Forms of Self-Representation in Early Modern English Texts

Sarah M. Dunnigan
EROS AND POETRY AT THE COURTS OF MARY QUEEN OF SCOTS AND
JAMES VI

Elizabeth Heale
AUTOBIOGRAPHY AND AUTHORSHIP IN RENAISSANCE VERSE
Chronicles of the Self

Pauline Kiernan
STAGING SHAKESPEARE AT THE NEW GLOBE

Ronald Knowles (*editor*)
SHAKESPEARE AND CARNIVAL
After Bakhtin

James Loxley
ROYALISM AND POETRY IN THE ENGLISH CIVIL WARS
The Drawn Sword

Anthony Miller
ROMAN TRIUMPHS AND EARLY MODERN ENGLISH CULTURE

Arthur F. Marotti (*editor*)
CATHOLICISM AND ANTI-CATHOLICISM IN EARLY MODERN ENGLISH
TEXTS

Jennifer Richards (*editor*)
EARLY MODERN CIVIL DISCOURSES

Sasha Roberts
READING SHAKESPEARE'S POEMS IN EARLY MODERN ENGLAND

Mark Thornton Burnett
CONSTRUCTING 'MONSTERS' IN SHAKESPEAREAN DRAMA AND EARLY
MODERN CULTURE

MASTERS AND SERVANTS IN ENGLISH RENAISSANCE DRAMA AND CULTURE
Authority and Obedience

The series Early Modern Literature in History is published in association with
the Renaissance Texts Research Centre at the University of Reading.

Early Modern Literature in History
Series Standing Order ISBN 0–333–71472–5
(*outside North America only*)

You can receive future titles in this series as they are published by placing a standing order.
Please contact your bookseller or, in case of difficulty, write to us at the address below with
your name and address, the title of the series and the ISBN quoted above.

Customer Services Department, Macmillan Distribution Ltd, Houndmills, Basingstoke,
Hampshire RG21 6XS, England

Language and Politics in the Sixteenth-Century History Play

Dermot Cavanagh

Lecturer in English
University of Northumbria

First published 2003 by
PALGRAVE MACMILLAN
Houndmills, Basingstoke, Hampshire RG21 6XS and
175 Fifth Avenue, New York, N.Y. 10010
Companies and representatives throughout the world

PALGRAVE MACMILLAN is the global academic imprint of the Palgrave
Macmillan division of St. Martin's Press, LLC and of Palgrave Macmillan Ltd.
Macmillan® is a registered trademark in the United States, United Kingdom
and other countries. Palgrave is a registered trademark in the European
Union and other countries.

ISBN 1–4039–0132–5

This book is printed on paper suitable for recycling and made from fully
managed and sustained forest sources.

A catalogue record for this book is available from the British Library.

Library of Congress Cataloging-in-Publication Data
Cavanagh, Dermot, 1963–
    Language and politics in the sixteenth-century history play / Dermot Cavanagh.
        p.   cm. — (Early modern literature in history)
    Includes bibliographical references and index.
    ISBN 1–4039–0132–5
    1. English drama—Early modern and Elizabethan, 1500–1600—History and
    criticism.   2. Politics and literature—Great Britain—History—16th century.
    3. Literature and history—Great Britain—History—16th century.   4. English
    language—Early modern, 1500–1700—Style.   5. Historical drama, English—
    History and criticism.   6. Political plays, English—History and criticism.
        I. Title.   II. Early modern literature in history (Palgrave Macmillan (Firm))

    PR649.P6C38 2003
    822'.051409358—dc21   2003051967

10   9   8   7   6   5   4   3   2   1
12   11   10   09   08   07   06   05   04   03

Printed and bound in Great Britain by
Antony Rowe Ltd, Chippenham and Eastbourne

To my parents

Contents

Acknowledgements

This book has benefited from the good counsel and practical assistance of many people, but its most unselfish and encouraging reader has been Jennifer Richards. I am also indebted to: Jeremy Gregory, Tim Kirk, Mike Pincombe, Alison Thorne, David Walker and Greg Walker. The late Gareth Roberts was a good friend and an inspirational scholar; I will miss, among many other things, his response to this book.

A Research Award from the Arts and Humanities Research Board enabled the completion of this study; its progress was also assisted by Small Research Grants from the University of Northumbria. I am grateful to the staff of the University Library at Northumbria, especially its Inter-Library Loans section, and to the Humanities librarian, Jane Shaw. I have also benefited from the expertise of the staff and from the resources provided by the National Library of Scotland, the British Library, and the Robinson Library at the University of Newcastle, especially its Special Collections. The School of English at the University of Newcastle generously allowed me access to their Renaissance Resources Room. Earlier versions of Chapter 1 and Chapter 5 have appeared in, respectively, *English Literary Renaissance* and *Shakespeare Studies*. I am grateful to the editors and publishers concerned for permission to publish revised versions of this material. Some of the ideas expressed in Chapter 4 were also raised in an essay for *Shakespeare Yearbook*; these are presented in an entirely new version here.

Abbreviations and Conventions

A & M	John Foxe, *Actes and Monuments* (1563)
ELH	*English Literary History*
ELR	*English Literary Renaissance*
HJ	*Historical Journal*
Holinshed's Chronicles	*Holinshed's Chronicles* (1587), ed. Henry Ellis, 6 vols (London, 1807–8; repr. 1965)
LP	*Letters and Papers, Foreign and Domestic, of the Reign of Henry VIII*, ed. J. S. Brewer *et al.* (21 vols, 1862–1932)
P&P	*Past and Present*
Rackin	Phyllis Rackin, *Stages of History: Shakespeare's English Chronicles* (1990)
RenD	*Renaissance Drama*
RES	*Review of English Studies*
SEL	*Studies in English Literature, 1500–1900*
ShaksS	*Shakespeare Studies*
SP	*Studies in Philology*
SQ	*Shakespeare Quarterly*
TRP	*Tudor Royal Proclamations*, ed. P. L. Hughes and J. F. Larkin, 3 vols (1964–9)

In quotations from original texts, I have not modernized apart from expanding contractions and adopting modern conventions for u / v and i / j; diagonals have also been replaced.

Introduction

Shakespeare and the form of the sixteenth-century history play

What is a history play? This book examines some of Shakespeare's works that everyone agrees are exemplary instances of Elizabethan historical drama. It also deals with some earlier plays that might be seen as, at best, tangentially historical, or, at worst, not historical at all. Examining these works together as if they belonged to a common category of dramatic composition requires, therefore, some justification. For many critics, this approach threatens to conflate theatrical forms and contexts that should remain distinct. It is not simply that Shakespeare's plays differ radically in quality and kind from previous historical drama, but rather that any substantive concept of the genre originates with his work.[1] Hence, the three non-Shakespearean plays included in this study are better interpreted in terms of other categories: the political morality play, Senecan tragedy, romance drama. On this view, the history play 'proper' is a Shakespearean or, at least, an Elizabethan genre and such plays are concerned with 'English dynastic politics of the feudal and immediately post-feudal period' and are 'usually about tensions between central government and the barons'.[2] This form of theatre addresses itself to the audience's own national experience as it is located in an intelligible past. It is doubtful whether Bale's polemical morality play, *King Johan*, accords with these aims: dynastic politics are barely visible here in comparison to Shakespeare's *King John*; the former seems more concerned with a timeless spiritual conflict than a historically specific one. Norton and Sackville's *Gorboduc* is equally uncongenial to this definition, being both tragic in mode and set in a remote and pagan 'Britain'. Most flagrantly, Robert Greene's *The Scottish History of James the Fourth* might be accused justly of not being set anywhere historically intelligible at all.

1

This study suggests, however, that our approach to the history play would benefit from being more hospitable to its seemingly immature or otherwise imperfect representatives. It argues that attending to a shared interest of such drama – its representation of socially disruptive speech – enriches our sense both of Shakespeare's work and that of his predecessors and contemporaries. Furthermore, exploring this common thematic concern helps to extend consideration not only of the many distinct dramatic forms in which historical material appeared throughout the sixteenth century but also their theatrical richness and political subtlety. It is also in relation to the role of language in political conflict that historical drama adopts some important and shared formal characteristics. The most significant aspects of these will be analysed here as a key point of contact between Shakespeare's work and that of other historical dramatists.

This emphasis on dramatic form and its elaboration of a major political topic provides an alternative to some influential definitions of the genre. In his important study of *The English History Play in the Age of Shakespeare* (1957; revised 1965),[3] Irving Ribner presented this kind of drama as a steadily evolving tradition. In contrast, this book emphasizes the history play's successive moments of birth and rebirth within a variety of theatrical spaces; these include the Great Hall, the Inns of Court, as well as multiple appearances upon the stages of the Elizabethan public playhouses. It is important to understand these works in their own terms, and in relation to their historical contexts, without assuming that they are ideologically crude, artistically rough-hewn or somehow rendered inherently deficient by their chronological priority to Shakespeare, or their authorship by other hands.[4] Similarly, there is a need to be wary of claims that Tudor history plays articulate a consensus within the period concerning the function of history. In Ribner's view, 'a history play was one which fulfilled what Elizabethans considered the purposes of history'; it drew upon chronicle sources that were assumed to be true in the interests of satisfying one fundamental intention: 'to use the past for didactic purposes'.[5] In fact, historical material was dramatized for a variety of ends; a homiletic objective was certainly a powerful constituent of these, but it did not preclude other motives. More recent analysis has emphasized the complexity of historical consciousness in the period: what was assumed to be true requires careful analysis and the uses of history were both manifold and subject to dispute.[6] Any assurance concerning the nature (or even the existence) of Shakespeare's didacticism or of the period's 'orthodox' values is now far less easily composed.

Conceiving of the history play as a consistent 'kind' of drama is problematic; all retrospective definitions will be subject to a degree of arbitrariness that reflects the eclecticism of contemporary theatrical practice. Yet the idea of the history play as a sixteenth-century genre is worth resuscitating and this book proposes a new starting-point for this. Primarily, it needs to be understood as ideologically various, theatrically diverse, and as committed to political enquiry as much as to sermonizing. Consequently, this study makes no great claims concerning an immutable, defining essence shared by all such dramatic works. Initially, any play that attempts both to reconstitute a past world and to retrieve its political implications for the present will be admitted for consideration. Such plays can also be distinguished by their interest in 'the life of the state' – that is, the key personal and/or institutional embodiments of authority – and how this undergoes a crisis. As Alexander Leggatt puts it, this drama is concerned with 'ordering and enforcing, the gaining and losing, of public power in the state'.[7] This process can result in either a fortuitous or a catastrophic outcome – a conclusion that is not generically prescribed – but both kinds of plot expose authority and the challenges it faces to intense forms of scrutiny. Moreover, a vital aspect of this concern with 'ordering and enforcing' and with historical conflict involves language. Throughout sixteenth-century historical theatre, threats to social and political stability are presented as partly (sometimes even primarily) linguistic in nature. The spectres of seditious, treacherous or otherwise unregenerate speech haunt the divergent worlds of these plays and such forms of expression also become the subjects of some of their most daring political speculations.

Playwrights of the sixteenth century rarely viewed historical material in terms of fixed principles of composition; instead, the past offered them material and *topoi* for enquiry and development. This claim concerning the complex formal potential of drama has particular force in relation to language. Here it is important to extend to non-canonical theatre some of the most illuminating perceptions deriving from critical consideration of Shakespeare's works. Too often, powerful insights into the latter's plays have been used to draw a *cordon sanitaire* around their distinctiveness. Yet, the issue of form permits some of the limitations of this to become apparent. David Scott Kastan, for example, has made an important contribution to understanding the form of Shakespeare's historical drama by arguing that it gives expression to a unique historical vision. The implications of this perception can be enlarged, however, to make a broader claim about other kinds of history play. For Scott Kastan, Shakespeare's works in this genre present their action as entirely 'confined to the continuum of human time...with no supra-historical perspective to redeem the post-lapsarian experience they portray'.[8] As a result, their fundamental characteristic is 'open-endedness' whereby a 'seemingly complete action is embedded in a larger temporal context that the play is unable to enclose' (p. 271). The Shakespearean history play embodies, therefore, a specific form of historical conscious-ness: one that emphasizes the contingency of events and processes and the temporal nature of human agency. The events depicted are rendered as unfinished because time continues beyond the boundaries of the drama; their complexity also exceeds the shaping intentions of the protagonists. From a different perspective, Jonathan Hart agrees that Shakespeare's history plays are distinguished by their ironic conception. These works cultivate the recognition of human limitation; they create a sequence of temporal anxieties and dilemmas to which only 'tentative and necessarily incomplete solutions' can be found. This is especially evident, according to Hart, in the representation of language. The words the protagonists use, like their political identities and aspirations, are subject to 'temporality': they are the contingent and flawed products of human choices in particular historical circumstances.[9]

These arguments have relevance for all the plays under consideration here. To take one brief example, they provide an immediate purchase upon the form of Norton and Sackville's *Gorboduc*, discussed in Chapter 2. This play ends in a condition of catastrophe without closure. In act 5, the ruling house of Britain has been laid waste by Gorboduc's division of the kingdom. The king's younger son has murdered his older brother and the former is in turn slaughtered by his revengeful mother; Gorboduc and his queen are then consumed by a popular uprising. Yet, this unrelenting pattern of events continues without a foreseeable resolution and the play concludes with the leading counsellors of the realm despairing of the future. One of the British princes, Fergus, has begun an invasion (of indeterminate outcome) designed to ensure his succession by force; there are no other virtuous candidates for the empty throne. Human plans and projects appear under the aspect of irony in *Gorboduc*; the categories and concepts by which the king, his advisers and his family attempt to interpret events are fallible or powerless. Not the least significant consequence of this formal open-endedness is its effect upon language, specifically, the discourse of political counsel which predominates in the play but is ineffectual in forestalling, or even interpreting, its interrelated crises. *Gorboduc*, in brief, takes a complex view of the fate of language as it is enmeshed in historical conflict. An ability to discriminate evil counsel from good is placed under severe pressure and received ideas of beneficent and corrupt advice are superseded by events.

Shakespeare's perception of historical contingency, as it is embodied in the form of his plays and in his awareness of the mutable nature of political and linguistic categories, is not as distinctive as it appears. Indeed, such an understanding is a common feature of dramas that demarcated specific passages of time in part to explore the opposition between harmonious and 'disorderly' speech. The consequent representation of transgressive speech and its opposite was often far from consoling. Each chapter of this study focuses upon facets of language which were also topics of contention in early modern culture and it demonstrates how historical drama was profoundly involved in these debates. This analysis involves considering words that were either illicit in the strict sense (that is, subject to legal proscription: rumour, sedition, treason) or conceived of as dangerously immoral (intemperate or 'unreformed' speech). Where appropriate, social and political contexts will be examined, for example, in relation to those legal discourses that prohibited particular forms of speech, or broader cultural debates will be considered as they concerned language that was deemed to be destabilizing, unregenerate or debased. Throughout, the plays will be shown to enquire into the adequacy of these categories and definitions. It is this aspect of the genre that composed a significant part of its political fascination for both authors and audiences. To this end, this study will engage in the close reading of both canonical and non-canonical theatre in the spirit recommended by Patricia Parker: that it is 'unnecessary to short-circuit or foreclose the process of moving from literary text to social text', especially as one attempts to 'link the language of particular plays to the language of social ordering and political disposition'.[10]

Chapter 1 will demonstrate that the topic of sedition is central to the period's major inaugural instance of historical drama: John Bale's *King Johan*. This subject elicits a complex form of historical attention from its seemingly dogmatic author, shaping what is most original and innovative in his work. During its lengthy process of composition, the Vice of 'Sedicyon' develops in Bale's hands from simply embodying the church's sinful and sectarian nature to participating in its process of ideological exposure. This duality creates an unsettling proximity between the play's polemical intentions and the Vice's effect. The ambivalent potential of Sedition expresses Bale's insight into how his own godly principles could be (and had been) designated as a threat to the commonwealth. His understanding of sedition is complicated, therefore, by his awareness of historical change and the shifting (and unreliable) priorities of sixteenth-century authority.

In Chapter 3, Robert Greene's *The Scottish History of James the Fourth*, demonstrates how the presence of disruptive language persisted as a staple feature of historical drama in the Elizabethan public playhouses. In Greene's work this topic continues to provide a key stimulus and resource for critical reflection. This encompasses not only some crucial political issues within the play but also his sceptical response to the nascent Elizabethan genre of chronicle drama. In *James IV*, the relationship between national identity, monarchy and civil speech comes under critical scrutiny and the key *topoi* of the 'heroical' history play are ironized. In particular, Greene is questioning key elements of Marlowe's *Tamburlaine*, a work there is insufficient space to examine here. Although Greene's response to contemporary instances of heroic language and action in historical drama may be partial, his aim is to contest the ideological direction Marlowe – and, to some extent, Shakespeare – were giving to such work. The material of chronicle drama appears in *James IV* but in a wilfully fictional mode. The form of *James IV* is porous, playful, and it refuses closure; attempts to master the course of history within it result only in the destructive spectacle of intemperate speech and action. Here again, the form of the play insists on the contingent nature of history; Greene interrupts the action with meta-theatrical commentary to expose the motivations that inform homiletic or exemplary narratives. Furthermore, and in a further reversal of expectations, the play depicts the English and Scottish kings as sharing the same dangerous potential for monarchy to be the cause of, not the cure for, disruptive speech.

Shakespeare's plays inherit and develop these formal and topical concerns. Like his predecessors and contemporaries, the subject of inflammatory, injurious or divisive speech composed a central part of his historical interests. As with other dramatists, Shakespeare exploited the open-ended quality of historical drama so that the role of language in political conflicts became the basis for critical reflection. The adequacy of conceiving speech as illicit or degraded becomes a far-reaching subject for deliberation in Shakespeare's dramaturgy. This topic will be analysed here in relation to three plays that span his work throughout the 1590s: *King John*, *Richard II* and *Henry V*. The quizzical treatment of rumour, treason and 'unreformed' speech in these plays also helps to recover the radical dimensions of Shakespeare's historical interests. In contemporary criticism these works often appear as an essentially conservative body of writing: elitist, exclusionary and nationalistic.

Hence, Shakespeare's dramas are deemed to indulge unruly speakers only to silence them in the interests of elaborating an obsessive, if sometimes equivocal, fascination with monarchic power.[11] If we renew attention to the form of his historical dramas, as well as their relationship to other works, we can discover a Shakespeare of a very different temper: one intrigued by the capacities of popular speech and one full of sceptical insight into the prevailing ideological categories that sought to regulate language. Why this issue continued to be such a marked feature of historical theatre, including Shakespeare's works, will occupy the remainder of this introduction.

'Dangerous words': language and politics in the sixteenth-century history play

In his *O per se O. Or a new Cryer of Lanthorne and Candle-light* (1612), Thomas Dekker describes the fall of language. God dispenses his female messenger Confusion to confound the hubris displayed at Babel. Confusion has been bred in Chaos and is wild in appearance; in one hand she grips 'an heape of stormes' and in the other a whip to drive the three spirits that attend her:

> The *Spirits* names were *Treason*, *Sedition*, and *Warre*, who at every time when they went abroad, were ready to set *Kingdomes* in an uproare. She roade upon a Chariot of clowdes, which was alwayes furnished with *Thunder*, *Lightning*, *Windes*, *Raine*, *Haile-stones*, *Snow*, and all the other Artillerie belonging to the service of *Divine Vengeance*: and when she spake, her *voyce* sounded like the roaring of many *Torrents*, boysterously strugling together, for betweene her jawes did she carry 1000000 tongues.[12]

In this passage Dekker makes vivid the political turmoil that follows the ruination of human speech. The cacophony and storm released by Confusion's million tongues also releases a new and terrible potential for language to tear apart civilization. The malign spirits that are now able to possess speech allow it to sow terror, fury and division. Communication between human beings becomes hazardous, fraught with catastrophic possibilities for misunderstanding, deception and betrayal, the potential 'to set *Kingdomes* in an uproare'.

This capacity of speech to devastate human aspirations for political order constitutes the inverse of the beneficent power of eloquence that was so fulsomely celebrated by the rhetorical tradition. As has been thoroughly established, Renaissance culture inherited a rich and sophisticated body of classical discourse that exalted the expressive potential of the spoken word.[13] Speech was perceived as the catalyst for establishing well-ordered human communities when utilized in its highest function of persuading others to virtue; in this way, it helped to sustain just authority and civil fellowship. The rhetorical tradition emphasized that a society preserved its health and civility by encouraging open and honest discourse: 'the processes of teaching and learning, of communicating, discussing, and reasoning associate men together and unite them in a sort of natural fraternity'.[14] However, this mode of reflection was far from uniform or uncontested. As Neil Rhodes has suggested, even classical rhetorical writing recognized the concomitant power of words to wreak violence, fragmentation and destruction.[15] Furthermore, within the context of a Christian society, the fallen nature of humankind was deemed to have acute (and inimical) consequences for language. As a number of scholars of medieval culture and literature have elucidated, patristic teaching developed sophisticated modes of regulating the pervasive temptation to use language in sinful and discordant ways.[16]

One significant medium that absorbed these complex (and conflicting) traditions of reflection on the capacities and limitations of language was the early modern history play. Indeed, construing the past as a source of precedents and analogies for the concerns aroused by disorderly speech – as well as for the admiration pertinent to discourses that produce a satisfying order – has long been recognized as integral to Shakespeare's history plays; this can be extended usefully to other dramatic works.[17] Over twenty years ago, in separate studies, James L. Calderwood and Joseph A. Porter agreed that speech is not only the medium of the Shakespearean history play but its central subject matter.[18] It was through this topic that Shakespeare conducted his most searching evaluation of political life and endeavour. In this respect, they argued that these works, especially the 'second tetralogy', contained a deeply felt awareness of the post-lapsarian condition of language. In brief, language declines into a fallen, abject condition in *Richard II*; the king's deposition also involves the destruction of his 'univocal, unilingual, absolutist world of nomenclature' and, subsequently, Shakespeare 'plays out the consequences of linguistic debasement in England'.[19] These later works present a world where a bewildering variety of idioms can only claim relative grounds for trust, truth and legitimacy. Eventually, this crisis is resolved by the person and speech of Henry V. The latter matures, in Porter's phrase, into a 'responsible polyglot' who possesses an inexhaustible sense of linguistic decorum and who is able to order other idioms 'into a harmony that depends on translation and willingness to communicate and hear'.[20] It is fitting 'that a king who has acquired such a command of English should subject all other accents and languages to its strict dominion'.[21]

This model presumes, however, that Shakespeare's sense of historical destiny and of language has both a providential and a royalist character: speech falls with the deposed body of majesty and ascends when the legitimacy of kingship is renewed. As this study will demonstrate, this model is of little consequence for non-canonical drama, especially those plays (such as *Gorboduc* and *James IV*) where the king's word is the wellspring from which social dissolution flows. Such an interpretation has also been subjected to extensive critical scrutiny in relation to Shakespeare and it is no longer believed to account for the variety of political discourses in his plays or for the complexity of their represen-tation.[22] A more promising way of reconsidering the representation of speech – both in Shakespeare and in other forms of historical drama – is to examine it in relation to the social and political history of early modern language; such a course will be followed in this study. This directs us towards a less metaphysical understanding of the categories that defined and constrained destructive speech in the sixteenth century. Here, Peter Burke's formulation of the social dimension of language might be taken as a ruling premise for recent historical investigation: 'language is an active force in society, used by individuals and groups to control others or to defend themselves against being controlled, to change society or to prevent others from changing it... the social history of language cannot be divorced from questions of power'.[23] Analysis based upon this understanding reminds us of the 'active force' of language in early modern society and how significantly this interest marked the shaping of a complex debate within sixteenth-century historical drama.

As a number of studies have now demonstrated, the control of unruly speech was a significant concern of Tudor legislation.[24] In the post-Reformation period, as anxieties multiplied over key issues of political doctrine and loyalty, as well as religious conformity, the use of language to establish and enforce authority and to resist (as well as effect) change was of great moment. In the familiar idiom of the Tudor homilies, we find condemned 'the unprofitablenes and shamfull unhonesty of contencion, stryfe and debate...If we bee good and quiete Christian men, let it appere in our speache and tongues.'[25] Correspondingly, Tudor legislation both defined and prohibited forms of language that

promoted unseemly social speculation or that enacted political disobedience or religious dissent. In the chapters that follow, some key
forms of disorderly language will be examined in more depth as well as
those discourses that attempt to order and displace these 'dangerous
words'. For example, the speech of godly monarchy, in both *Kynge Johan*
and *Henry V*, or that of counsel in *Gorboduc*, are meditated attempts
to create a more harmonious and fulfilling social order; the quality
and integrity of these idioms is also subjected to forceful scrutiny.
Throughout, the analysis will assume that sixteenth-century drama
needs to be understood in the terms Cyndia Susan Clegg has proposed
for Shakespeare's works in the 1590s, that is, it will emphasize 'the
power late Elizabethan culture attributed to language...and the degree
to which speech acts occupied civic space'.[26]

In recent critical consideration, however, theatre has been conceived
of as a place where the threats posed by speech were rehearsed and
their regulation ratified. In this respect, the exercise of dominion over
language has, to a surprising extent, been at the centre of the new
historicist revaluation of Shakespeare's history plays. These new interpretations have emphasized how authority disciplines (and, at times,
appropriates) the key idioms of the speech community it aspires to
dominate.[27] The premises of this approach deserve some scrutiny if an
alternative to them is to be established. One major influence is Michel
Foucault's analysis of the gradual extension of disciplinary mechanisms
throughout early modern Europe.[28] This profound historical transformation witnessed the gradual evolution of a new regime of bureaucratic
state power based upon strategies of surveillance. The latter helped to
codify and to police more efficiently new moral and legal offences. Such
an account offers a powerful insight into the place of language in the
early modern polity. Like other forms of 'deviance', delinquent, alien or
truculent speech is exposed to more stringent regimentation. Moreover,
the endpoint of this process is not simply to dominate the body of the
unruly speaker through symbolic physical punishments – branding,
whipping, the nailing of the ear and tongue, abscission of the hand –
but to cultivate the internalization of guilt and shame with regard to
the idle, disloyal or recalcitrant word. The free-speaking citizen of the
classical rhetorical tradition is thus reconstituted as a docile subject:
'the individual subjected to habits, rules, orders, an authority that is
exercised continually around him and upon him, and which he must
allow to function automatically in him'.[29]

Such a view is cognate with, and extended by, Pierre Bourdieu's account
of the process of state formation. In his view, this process also witnesses

'the establishment of relations of linguistic domination'; these devalue and make shameful 'vulgar' idioms and popular modes of expression.[30] Thus, 'regional', dissenting and otherwise censurable speech finds itself in the grip of new and subtle forms of control. This interpretation is further underwritten by Althusser's influential account of interpellation and how we are constituted as subjects in (and to) ideology through language; this sanctions and enforces the normative quality of a dominated social position.[31] Hence, contemporary critical thought has inherited an extensive and sophisticated body of theory that postulates a gradual encroachment of state power into the sphere of language. The effect of this is to intensify processes of social subjection, to create new hierarchies of distinction between 'high' and 'low' forms of speech, and to constrain critical thought and expression.

Such ideas, implicitly or explicitly, have exercised a powerful sway on readings of the history play, construed as a medium where subaltern speakers find themselves subordinated or excluded from a newly stratified sphere of discourse. In these readings, historical drama endows the speech acts of Renaissance authority with value whilst rendering the language of a range of 'others' – catholics, traitors, rumour-mongers, the foreign, the uncivil – as dangerous or worthless.[32] Speech is no longer seen as metaphysically 'fallen', therefore, but it appears in this important medium to degrade or elevate subjects according to the desires and interests of early modern power.

This understanding of the complicity between language and power is questioned, however, in Judith Butler's recent critique of 'the fantasy of a sovereign action' in relation to speech; this helps to renew interest in the potential of language for agency.[33] Thus, 'there is a strong sense in which the body is alternately sustained and threatened through modes of address' (p. 15), but no guarantee of the efficacy of the speech acts which attempt this. Speech may well invoke and inscribe a structural relation of dominance, but it can also fail in this endeavour and produce, in turn, a critical response. For example, authority indulges freely in the same idioms of incitement and derogation that it condemns in the language of others, often in the very act of so reproving them. To grasp this paradox (as Chapter 4 will argue Shakespeare does in *King John*) is also to begin a process of deliberation upon the sufficiency of the controls exercised upon speech. Butler's approach helps to identify the variety of ways in which Shakespeare and other dramatists were alert to the presumptions of those who claim sovereign power over language. It was possible to recognize in the period how: 'by being called a name, one is also, paradoxically, given a certain possibility for social existence' (p. 2). In this way, even the most intrinsically injurious words can be appropriated and have their effect reversed. The crucial aspect of language here is what Butler terms 'the open temporality of the speech act' (p. 15). The most powerful codification of language cannot circumvent the ability of subjects over time to deprive words of their dominant definition. Speech involves a 'chain of resignifications whose origin and end remain unfixed and unfixable' (p. 14) and the solidarity they can evoke is not always of a conformist nature. Language needs to be conceived, in her account, as mutable, malleable and open to a constant process of adaptation and renewal; this allows for its most influential usages to be challenged. Hence, interpellation needs to be reconceived as 'not descriptive but inaugurative' (p. 33). As it seeks to construct a reality for the subject it also opens up the possibility of agency: 'for a counter-speech, a kind of talking back' (p. 15).

Butler's critique of a poststructuralist emphasis on language as interpellative and coercive opens up some exciting possibilities for re-examining the theatrical representation of forbidden or destructive language and of its relationship to those discourses of authority that so define it. This topic persists as a defining issue for early modern historical drama and it elicits some complex political interpretation. It allows, for example, the limitations of authority to be explored, especially in terms of its will to dispel perceived sources of linguistic instability. Here, the formal open-endedness of the genre is of great consequence as this permits the 'open temporality of the speech act' to become apparent. Defining the seditious, treacherous or intemperate subject is not straightforward in many of these plays and neither is the status of the godly or virtuous word: such designations are shown to be affected by changing historical circumstances. Furthermore, these categories themselves bear scrutiny; subjects 'talk back' to them in the history play questioning their efficacy and integrity. Alternatively, the language of virtue and authority is often implicated in, as opposed to being distinguished from, those forms of speech it seeks to prohibit. In all the plays examined here, received definitions of injurious or beneficent language are placed in complex historical contexts where their consequences and effects are not guaranteed. This demonstrates again the limits of an interpretation predicated on the homiletic tenor of such drama. In fact, historical theatre granted latitude to both dramatists and audiences to enter an 'arena of invention and meditation',[34] a place which encouraged an active process of political judgement. Here again, we can extend beyond Shakespeare the recent and welcome observation that his plays compose an 'argument with history' and that this arises 'in his reworking of both plot material and informing cultural beliefs in a critique which questions prevailing norms'.[35] Other dramatists share, therefore, the linguistic interests of the Shakespearean history play: works in this genre centre upon the nature of sovereign action as it attempts to contain hostile speech and reflection. The critical reactions this endeavour arouses are also explored, provoking further consideration of the adequacy of those categories that are used to regulate language. In Shakespeare's works, the issue of how language legitimizes and delegitimizes authority is the catalyst for some of his most forceful insights into the political composition of sixteenth-century society.

In this respect, Shakespeare examines how specific categories of speech emerge from, and are shaped by, historical events. In Chapter 5, *Richard II* is shown to conceive treason as a category whose implications change, especially as it is extended to apprehend language hostile to the crown. The play might be considered as a paradigmatic demonstration of 'the open temporality of the speech act'. At the outset, treason is defined by Richard in terms of actions directed against his person, authority and will. Yet, this conception of treachery is modified by those opposed to his rule. For Bolingbroke (and for John of Gaunt), this absolutist concept of treachery is perceived as a way of restraining the unwelcome insights that derive from free and customary speech. Yet, on becoming King Henry IV, Bolingbroke finds his own ascendancy threatened by treachery even as he attempts to brand the offence with his authority. Henry deems betrayal to be as serious in thought and utterance as it is in deed. It thus takes on a new and recognizably early modern complexion and the audience is given a suggestive insight into the rationale for this. The new king finds his authority to enforce this criticized by, among others, his old rival, the self-declared traitor to himself, Richard II. Here, the deposed king's language unravels the paradoxes and contradictions that attend the new definition of treason. In this manner, *Richard II* refuses to offer a unified definition of treachery: authority is claimed through it, especially as a linguistic offence, but the resistance this provokes (also in the sphere of language) illuminates its limitations. Betrayal appears not as an incontrovertible act (in speech, writing or deed) but as conditional in nature. It finds meaning, therefore, only in terms of the sovereignty that defines it.

It is important to recognize, in relation to this play and elsewhere, that the forms of Shakespeare's plays also compose an argument in relation to received categories of 'delinquent' language. Hence, the form of *Richard II* constitutes a complex dialectical investigation into the shaping of treason as a linguistic and political offence. This interest in dramatic form as a method of political argument, especially as it concerns the designations assigned to language, is also significant for Chapter 4. Here, this insight is applied to the dramatic techniques adopted in *King John*. This illuminates Shakespeare's scepticism towards the formidable early modern animus directed against rumour, construed as a vulgar and malicious misreading of history. In contrast to this, the play demonstrates that historical truth is not simply a prerogative of a sober or homiletic idiom; important insights can also be gleaned from seemingly 'exaggerated' or disaffected speech and perception. *King John* constantly deviates into fictional or heightened speculations about the true nature of events and, especially, the motivations of its protagonists. These help to disclose some uncomfortable realities and the participants involved are anxious to expunge these from the historical record. In this way, the play breaks down the boundary between 'high' and 'low' forms of language and insight. Again, Shakespeare engages in the critical scrutiny of a demonized speech-form and shows this to be dependent on the equivocal status of authority. His historical method is shown to be well-disposed towards 'unofficial' channels of information and sceptical of the distinction between these and more exalted truths.

Finally, in Chapter 6, *Henry V* is considered in terms of the humanist discourse that pursued the amendment and 'improvement' of speech. Here, the 'King's English' attempts to identify and correct the verbal deficiencies of his subordinates and his opponents. Again the form of the play complicates our understanding of this issue and exposes 'the fantasy of a sovereign action' in relation to speech; quite where the 'reformed' voice is to be heard is unclear. The impulse to correct the language of others appears in a number of guises in the play, not all of them creditable. Through a rich sequence of parallels, counterpoints and analogies, the endeavour to modify and to unify speech is shown to threaten, once again, the free expression of customary idioms. The latter are shown (as in *King John*) to possess substantial powers of critical insight. This interest intensifies in the critical nightscene before Agincourt when Henry's godly enterprise is made subject to an equally credible if opposing viewpoint, even if this inhabits a 'vulgar' idiom. The issue of who has a monopoly on historical perceptiveness remains an open one in the play and a range of subjects 'talk back' to the king's terms of definition. By comparing *Henry V* to the theory of language elaborated by the Elizabethan pedagogue, Richard Mulcaster, Shakespeare is shown to be in contact with a 'constitutionalist' thesis of language. This emphasized that language was the summation of its speakers' usages and was consequently hostile to any monopoly over its resources or its regulation into a single approved idiom.

The interpretation of *Henry V* and the other plays that is offered here has a bearing on recent critical interest in Shakespeare's connection to the 'new humanism' of the later sixteenth century and with 'constitutional' habits of thought.[36] This has served to emphasize Shakespeare's receptivity to important forms of civic consciousness, especially to 'the problem of corruption in political states'.[37] A full consideration of this issue is beyond the scope of this study, but it may suggest that one aspect of Shakespeare's political interests has particular significance for further research in this area: the necessity for 'full and open speech'.[38] As Paula Blank has argued, Shakespeare, in common with other historical dramatists, manifested a lively interest in the ethic of free speech and this provided him with a critical purchase on the means by which this might be obstructed.[39] In essence, the fullness of Shakespeare's habits of historical analysis and argumentation are in themselves testimony to his lack of regard for constraints upon expression. As the later chapters of this book propose, however, his history plays comprise a penetrating engagement with those early modern categories that sought to govern the tongue; the motivations and consequences of these provide a focus for one of Shakespeare's most intense involvements with the political process. Often, this discloses a radical set of sympathies with speech that was perceived as degraded and antagonistic.

There has been some illuminating analysis devoted to Tudor historical writing in recent years. This has brought to our attention its ideological complexity and its political range and perceptiveness; some equally important studies have appeared on Jacobean historical theatre.[40] Yet, the same latitude of critical interest has not been extended to Tudor historical drama. This book seeks to revalue this body of theatre and Shakespeare's relationship to it; it proposes new insights into this drama and into the connections between works whose complexities and continuities of perception have often been neglected.

1
The Paradox of Sedition in John Bale's *King Johan*

In John Bale's *King Johan* (c. 1538–63) we observe, according to Ivo Kamps, 'the slow and extraordinary birth of historiography in literature'.[1] This evaluation is generous, but not untypical of the critical attention the play has commanded. It is even more suggestive for this study, that Bale's resort to historical material is compelled by his interest in the threat of sedition. Yet, conceiving of the play as a foundational document – that is, as exemplifying how the national past could be made available for theatre – has also involved emphasizing its ideological inflexibility. Irving Ribner confirmed the play's status as a progenitor of later historical theatre by stressing three crucial features of its composition: first, Bale's drama is a formative expression of English national consciousness; second, it demonstrates how 'to reinterpret history in the light of doctrine'; and, finally, it exemplifies how historical events can be used to illuminate 'a political problem of the present'.[2] Hence, *King Johan* helps to elucidate the key motive that informs subsequent historical drama: the homiletic potential of the past.

In many respects, such a reading is entirely satisfying. Conveniently, *King Johan* contains an author-figure, 'The interpretour', who outlines the purpose of Bale's dramaturgy. This speaker, perhaps played by the author himself, concludes the play's first part by reiterating the admonitory lesson its first Tudor audience was to imbibe: catholic villainy destroyed King John's attempt to reform the church and disposed of his right to independent jurisdiction. For Ivo Kamps, such moments reveal Bale's blatantly didactic use of historical material: 'hence [he] strives to conceal the ideological strategies which affect to present the reader with "history" itself' (p. 65). It is only much later in the period – chiefly, for Kamps, in the more sceptical and sophisticated ambience of Stuart theatre – that dramatists can explore the

16

self-interested nature of historical assertions rather than simply endorsing propaganda.

Yet, *King Johan's* status as a foundational text needs both revision and expansion. Here, a fuller awareness of the play's protracted composition is illuminating, especially in terms of understanding how the passage of time exerted pressure upon the dramatist's reformation ideals. This experience engendered in Bale a complex form of historical awareness and this is expressed most fully through his concern with disorderly speech. Such insight derives from his religious principles but it is not, therefore, unreflective. In short, the figure of 'Sedicyon' becomes less easy to evaluate as *King Johan* progresses. The play embodies the dramatist's bitter understanding that the category of sedition can be used to incriminate godly speech. Consequently, the form of *King Johan* becomes more conflicted and less dogmatic in its theatrical effect. It is in this respect that Judith Butler's formulation of the 'open temporality' of the speech act illuminates the play's treatment of injurious language: the play is alert to the mutability that attends the status of such expression. Through the medium of historical drama, Bale begins to explore the alarming utility of sedition as an instrumental category for worldly power. Hence, the play's sensitivity to present as well as past historical experience involves it in a critical account of how categories of speech regulate political (as much as spiritual) life. It is in this sense, as well, that the play is foundational.

To question the dogmatism of *King Johan* appears absurd, however, in the light of its author's reputation for ferocious Reformation polemic: 'At times,' W. T. Davies remarks cruelly, 'John Bale seems to be not so much writing as barking in print.'[3] Yet, it is worth enquiring a little more carefully into what, precisely, is implied by Bale's presentation of 'history'. This issue is less straightforward than it seems. In one sense, Bale's mobilizing of the past in the interests of partisan argument and example has an obvious intention: *King Johan* seeks 'to remake the story of the past from the point of view of . . . proto-Protestants'.[4] Yet, current criticism conceives of historical interpretation in a double sense: a work's manifest understanding of the past and how this is conditioned by its own 'presentness' – the contemporary experiences and values that inform any act of historical comprehension.[5] In both these respects, Bale's historiography is indeed manifestly ideological. In *King Johan*, past events are illuminated to expose catholicism as 'a system of thought which propagates systematic falsehood in the selfish interest of the powerful and malign forces dominating a particular historical era'.[6] If the extraordinary longevity and scale of catholic power is based on fraud, evangelical history must 'reveal certain cultural and social patterns as both historically real and yet ultimately arbitrary in nature'; the past is recovered to insist that the false 'image be recognized as "historical" – made rather than given in nature'.[7] *King Johan* is thus a powerful instance of ideological critique that embodies the transformed historical understanding it hoped to produce. To this end, the play deciphers how the vested interests of the medieval church have obstructed a just estimation of the truth and it recovers persecuted voices that have attempted to promote a fuller vision of human community. Central to the perpetuation of social illusions and political deceits is the figure of 'Sedicyon' personified as the chief Vice of the play. His speech and actions are identified as the key means by which virtuous expression is constrained and as helping, therefore, to shape a pervasive false consciousness. This accords with a widespread anxiety in the period of *King Johan*'s performance in 1538 concerning the powerful opposition to the Reformation that seditious words both expressed and aroused.

At the centre of Bale's ideological exposure of catholicism, then, is a concern with delinquent language. The play adopts the traditional practice of late medieval plays such as *Mankind* (c. 1465–70), by inviting the audience to discriminate between, on the one hand, 'idle speech' and, on the other, words that are directed towards salvation. Bale's play diverges radically from this tradition in two crucial respects: by imputing the corrupting effect of sinful speech to the sacramental practices of the church that should correct and absolve them, and by representing the historical consequences of such verbal abuses as politically criminal. In *King Johan*, the catholic morality play is used to address historical events and to create a political psychomachia that registers language as malicious when it opposes national salvation. Thus the orders of the medieval church are identified as Sedition, Dissimulation, Private Wealth and Usurped Power, all of whom demonstrate great verbal and theatrical fluency, taking on the character of historical personages – respectively, Steven Langton, Cardinal Raymundus (and Simon of Swinsett), Cardinal Pandulphus and the Pope – and deploying an array of rhetorical, ritual and sacramental frauds to displace the loyalty of the king's three estates. Orchestrating this process, and embodying it most powerfully, is the alternately sinuous and bullying language of Sedition: depraved, irreverent and imaginatively fertile in thwarting the godly purposes of King John and the symbolically widowed England.[8] Eventually, England is intimidated into silence and John, cowed by the political threat Sedition directs against the nation, is forced to recant and is then assassinated. Finally, the play ameliorates this historical catastrophe with a coda that depicts Sedition's execution and the quelling of catholic power by Imperial Majesty, a figure of supreme monarchical resolution. This action renews the bonds of loyalty between the king's three estates – Clergy, Nobility and Civil Order – and restores justice and equity to the realm.

King Johan is an extraordinary creation. It subjects a dominant theatrical form to iconoclastic attack in the interests of establishing new, reformed habits of perception.[9] A schematic description of the play's symbolic action overlooks, however, the breadth of its political reflections. It is part of Bale's peculiar honesty as a writer that the 'presentness' of his work, especially his consciousness of immediate historical travails, is also dramatized and in ways that should inhibit a rapid classification of its ideological uniformity. The author's sermonizing instincts are expressed alongside an often-unflinching recognition of the struggles and reversals in the temporal world and this is especially evident in his paradoxical treatment of seditious speech. In relation to this, it is important to remember that the play's composition extended over decades. Briefly, the play consists of two sections of text written in two hands: an incomplete 'A-text' datable to the latter part of 1538 and a 'B-text', written entirely by the author, and ascribed normally to its revival in the period between 1558 and Bale's death in 1563. The latter makes substantial deletions, revisions and additions to the 'A-text' whilst incorporating and expanding it into a new version.[10] This complex process of composition has a particular bearing upon the representation of Sedition whose original role was expanded by Bale. Such an extensive period allowed the dramatist a critical insight into shifting government policy, and the changing fortunes of Reformation, that is often assumed to be solely the prerogative of his successors.

Bale's need to redraft the play also reflects what Christopher Haigh has characterized as the halting and uncertain nature of the Reformation itself: even 'the inexorable march of the Henrician first Reformation [is] an illusion concealing compromise and confusion'.[11] The troubled progress of reform was dramatized starkly in the malleability of sedition as an offence. During Bale's lifetime, both catholicism *and* his own evangelical beliefs were held to constitute precisely this kind of threat. In post-Reformation England, dissent and orthodoxy, treachery and loyalty, were prone to alarming changes in definition and any confessional commitment could be identified in the seditious terms that had once characterized one's opponents. Bale's attentiveness to this turbulence, as much as to the utility of history for propaganda, allows *King Johan* to register and explore these political pressures. This apparently doctrinaire play is acutely aware of the temporal 'open-endedness' that David Scott Kastan distinguishes as the hallmark of Shakespearean historical drama. For Bale, worldly experience was profoundly fallen and unstable; such a context impeded his aspirations for reform and, hence, for a satisfying end to history. Through the figure of 'Sedicyon', Bale's fullest understanding of history and of the political sphere emerges; this is evident in its divided, rather than uniform, representation of incendiary speech.

To explore these issues, the play will be seen initially as both absorbing and addressing a Reformation context dominated by the spectre of catholic sedition. Bale engages in an inventive, if sectarian, form of ideological critique that defines the church as devoted to exploiting fears and superstitions and ready to use violent means to preserve its worldly power. The play's conception, however, also needs to be perceived in relation to an unstable context where the godly could also be designated as seditious. In conclusion, Bale's awareness of this will be analysed in terms of, first, his recognition of the abiding power of the church and, second, *King Johan*'s contradictory portrayal of Sedition. Sedition colludes in exposing the church as a sinful and partisan body and such acts of self-disclosure create an unsettling proximity between Bale's polemical intentions and the Vice's effects. The duality of Sedition will be seen as expressive of Bale's profound unease over the ability of secular power to discriminate righteous expression from destructive words.

It is important to draw attention to this complicated aspect of *King Johan* to question why apparently dogmatic plays earn only a marginal place in the canon, especially when their often-searching responses to historical processes have been simplified. This may also fuel a more general consideration of the adequacy of current modes of historicizing early modern drama as either a direct or covert expression of ideology. As we shall see in the next two chapters, the political range and intricacy of pre- or non-Shakespearean theatre has been neglected by construing such plays as one-dimensional responses to immediate historical circumstances. Yet in their representation of disruptive language such plays contain more political deliberation and historical insight than is commensurate with theatrically animated propaganda. Bale's play is a striking example of this. Far from being ideologically resolute, *King Johan* acknowledges how any assault on authority, including its own, can be perceived as sharing the spirit of sedition and correspondences between the Vice and the play's own scurrilous language cut across and modify its structure of antagonisms. In this respect, Bale's play is evidence both for the contentious nature of legal, religious and political concepts in the sixteenth century and for the potentiality of historical theatre to reveal their partiality and contradictions.

1

Any account of the ideological intentions of *King Johan* must begin with its production at a time of evangelical reform. Bale's plays were composed for a troupe of actors, 'Bale and his ffelowes', who were patronized by Cromwell between 1538 and 1541.[12] At the end of 1538 Thomas Becket's shrine at Canterbury was dissolved during a campaign of government-sponsored iconoclasm, a month before the Christmas performance of *King Johan* at Cranmer's residence in the same diocese. Peter Clark emphasizes that Kent was notorious for its anticlerical resentment and was thus uniquely subject to organized evangelical activity in the interests of 'expanding the scope and effectiveness of royal authority'. A performance of *King Johan* fits coherently into this ethos as part of the 'remorseless destruction of the seigneurial power and jurisdiction of the Church which occurred in the mid and late 1530s'.[13]

Government anxieties concerning opposition to such policies were also a marked feature of this period and have been documented by Geoffrey Elton in relation to public criticism designated as inflammatory and divisive.[14] Integral to this process was sedition – 'inciting by words or writings disaffection towards the state or constituted authority' – a category of offence designed to control increased religious and political disputation.[15] Concern over the latter escalated after the Pilgrimage of Grace (1536–7). Writing in the wake of this uprising, Richard Morison defended the far-sightedness of Henry VIII in discerning that a 'remedy for sedition' was the central concern of good government:

> His grace...seeth his noble progenytours have ofte punished rebelles, and done no more, but cut awey the branches of sedition, for their tyme, his highnes intendeth to pull aweye the roote. He seeth, it is not possible to cure this sore, which in dede Plato calleth the greattest syckenes, that can come to a comune welthe, excepte he serche out, bothe where it ariseth, and what thing moste nourisheth it, and then do as phisicions are wont, whiche oft tymes laye not their medicines to the parte, that is diseased, but to that rather, from whens the disease first came, and is like to come stylle, onlesse it be there stopped.[16]

The theatrical design of *King Johan* reiterates this argument and this is consonant with the sensitivity of Cromwell's government to hostile expression.[17]

Ironically, Tudor proclamations first attempted to quell the 'sedition of Martin Luther': those 'who by perversion of Holy Scripture do induce erroneous opinions, soweth sedition among Christian people'.[18] Early uses of the term also construed it as a form of violent disorder and this sense is still preserved in such common formulations as 'to stir and incense them to sedition and disobedience', an effect being attributed here to the circulation of protestant texts and Bible translations. Yet, this same proclamation also describes how due to 'the evil and perverse *inclination* of seditious *disposition* of sundry persons, divers heresies and erroneous opinions have been late sown and spread'.[19] During the 1530s, the offence begins to accrue a set of connotations that imply its modern sense as language that incites rebellion and which therefore denotes a disloyal temperament. Again, this new emphasis on sedition as an idiom that promotes disaffection is central to Bale's conception of his Vice.

The verbal disparagement such legal innovation provoked was seized upon by Cromwell's government as a further example of recalcitrance. In April 1537, the sub-prior of Lenton Abbey in Nottinghamshire reported the monks' private 'railing at the King' and singled out one threatening exchange: ' "It is a marvellous world, for the King will hang a man for a word speaking now a days." "Yea," said Dan Ralph, "but the King of Heaven will not do so, and He is King of all kings; but he that hangs a man in this world for a word speaking he shall be hanged in another world his self." '[20] It is this lack of veneration for the king, as well as his policies, that defines seditious profanity. In the hundreds of depositions provided by Cromwellian informers and preserved in the Henrician state papers, the realm appears to be suffused with scandalous irreverence. Ralph Sadler, a government agent in the north after the Pilgrimage of Grace, confirmed to Cromwell that 'there are men who do nothing but go about to stir up sedition'.[21] A 'goggyll yed hoore' was how one Suffolk woman described Queen Anne; Sir Francis Bryan recommended to Cromwell that a Buckinghamshire man be drawn and quartered for saying: 'The King is but a knave and liveth in avowtry [adultery], and is an heretic and liveth not after the laws of God...I set not by the King's crown, and, if I had it here, I would play at football with it.'[22] As the character of Bale's Sedition also demonstrates, such comments bring the king's justice into disrepute by depicting royal policy as corrupt, self-interested or tyrannical. In an example of precisely the sentiments the Pilgrimage of Grace had arisen from, Dan Ralph

Swensune of Lenton Abbey, commented sardonically on the naiveté of the rebels in accepting the king's appeasement:

> it is alms to hang them up, for they may well know that he that will not keep no promise with God himself but pulls down His churches he will not keep promise with them; but if they had gone forth onward up and stricken off his head then had they done well, for I warrant them if he can overcome them he will do so by them.[23]

For Cromwell's regime, a seditious temperament was also betrayed by an emphasis upon the transience of political change. The refusal to accept reformation as permanent was often fused with nostalgia for the old order. Such an attitude is typified by the seemingly casual response made by William Gibson, an innkeeper of Leicester, to rumours of a new tax on beer: 'that the mayor and his brother should not set no assize on his pot, nor the king neither; and the said William said the world should mend: but a little while the king loved my lady Anne and should be in prosperity'.[24] 'Well, this fashion will not last always,' said Friar Richard Hopkins of the Grey Friars at Grantham in 1535; 'I trust we shall have the correction in our own religion again.'[25] One additional symptom of sedition, then, is a distorted understanding of the past as well as the present. When an evangelical parishioner challenged his priest to justify 'the mischievous and proud usurping of the bishop of Rome that so used king John', the latter replied 'the chronicles were false, and he was accused maliciously of malice and of false heretics'.[26] Such an unregenerate understanding of the English past could also lead to more threatening speculations. In 1535, a catholic priest prayed that Henry VIII's 'death I beseech God may be like to the death of the most wicked John, sometime King of this realm, or rather to be called a great tyrant'.[27]

Such statements, when read alongside Bale's play demonstrate that proponents of reform felt they were confronted with powerful, if often concealed, hostility. The realm was replete with those who 'wuld rather be toren with wyeld horsses then to assent or consent to the dyminis-shinge' of papal authority; those who believed that the king was 'A tyrant more cruel than Nero; for Nero destroyed but a part of Rome, but this tyrant destroyeth the whole realm.'[28] The policing of sedition sought to decipher a range of verbal slips and indiscretions which betrayed the malice of dissemblers, like Friar Forest, who instructed those in the confessional 'that he had denied the bishop of Rome by an oath given by his outward man, but not in th'inward man.'[29] In a range of official sources from the period of *King Johan*'s first performance a taxonomy of sedition appears. It is a language of insinuation, hostile to reform and disdainful of the sanctity of the king; it exploits or invents apparent symptoms of government hypocrisy and despotism. Above all, it is sympathetic to catholicism, to rebellion and, in tone, is precisely akin to Bale's Vice: mischievously creative, sardonic and derisive towards constituted authority.

The dominant ideological tenor of *King Johan* is profoundly connected to this key concern of the early Reformation. Sedition succeeds in creating a division between monarch and realm and in defeating godly purposes. In its lengthy first scene, the king is called upon to address England's complaint against the influence of Sedition who has devoured her 'cattell howse and land / my wodes and pasturs, with other commodyteys' (ll. 62–3)[30] and denied her spiritual needs through anti-Christian sermonizing and ceremonial. Sedition enters promptly to confirm this hostile description in his malicious observation of the growing reciprocity between king and country: 'what you ii alone? I wyll tell tales by Jesus / and saye that I see yow, fall here to bycherye' (ll. 43–4). This establishes not only the blasphemous indecorum of his interventions, but two crucial aspects of their broader significance that are of great moment for Bale and for the play's first audience. Sedition is, firstly, a discourse that interferes with healthy social cohesion, and, secondly, it disseminates lies that destroy reputation. Sedition's 'wordes are ungodlye,' (l. 45) addicted to the fabrication of slurs and innuendo at the expense of the monarch's integrity and that of 'Englande's ryght-full herytage' (l. 170). It is the 'gross capasyte' of the Vice to express a factional hostility to all rival claims of authority, confirming his identity with the sinister practices of the church: 'magry yowr harte / tushe, the pope ableth me, to subdewe bothe king and keyser' (ll. 98–9).

From its outset, the play presents the struggle of the responsible speech of John and England to be heard against a presumptuous register of derision and unseemly speculation:

Englande:	thes vyle popych swyne, hath clene exyled my hosband
King Johan:	who ys thy husbond, telme good gentyll yngland
Englande:	for soth god hym selfe, the spowse of every sort that seke hym in fayth, to ther sowlys helth and comfort
Sedicyon:	he ys scant honest, that so many wyfes wyll have

(ll. 107–11)

Moreover, Sedition soon turns from profane scorn to threats of action. When England condemns the ecclesiastical hierarchies as 'vyle swyne' who 'dylyght in mennys draffe, and covytus lucre all', his response is chilling: 'hold yowr peace ye whore, or ellys by masse I trowe / I shall cawse the pope, to curse the as blacke as a crowe' (ll. 85; 87–8).

This censoriousness demonstrates the intense hostility aroused by the language of godly conscience; the king's defiant capacity 'to rayle so withowt mesure' (l. 556) is scandalous to the Vices. For Sedition, the reverence and understanding that develops between king and nation is to be traduced as gibberish:

Englande:	god Reward yowr grace; I be seche hym hartely and send yow longe dayes, to governe this Realme in peace
King Johan:	gramercy yngland, and send the plentyus increse
Sedicyon:	of bablyng maters, I trow yt is tyme to cease
King Johan:	why dost thow call them, bablyng maters tell me?
Sedicyon:	for they are not worth, the shakyng of a pertre whan the peres are gon, they are but dyble dable I marvell ye can, abyd suche byble bable

(ll. 153–60)[31]

From this viewpoint it is the king's compassion which is both absurd and a grave danger to the church's sense of its liberties. The audience comes to perceive Sedition as the essence of catholicism: 'In every estate, of the clargye, I playe a part' (l. 196); it is the force that unites its proliferation of orders and which drives its impulse to overwhelm secular power (ll.196–212). Sedition achieves this ascendancy within the general context of a church that intends to fill up the public sphere 'with disordered, meaningless and corrupting words'.[32]

In rallying the church to quell John's dissent, Bale depicts not only Sedition's irreverence and his need to obscure the spiritual direction offered by scripture, but the bogus legitimacy this grants to political subversion. This is illuminated by the Vice's acknowledgement of his descent from 'prevy treason': 'whan prynces rebell, agenste hys [the pope's] autoryte / I make ther commons, agenst them for to be' (ll. 746–7). To this end, Sedition employs his familiar tactic of undermining established loyalties by slandering the personal reputation of the monarch.

In granting absolution to Nobility, Sedition persuades him to accept a distorted political image of his king as a tyrant to justify rebellion:

> ye know that king John, ys a very wycked man
> and to holy chyrch, a contynuall adversary
> the pope wyllyth yow, to do the best ye canne
> to his subduyng, for his cruell tyranny
> and for that purpose, this pryvylege gracyously
> of clene remyssyon, he hath sent yow this tyme
> clene to relesse yow, of all yowr synne and cryme

(ll. 1174–80)

Such depraved words are intended to embody the spiritual dereliction of the church's language and their logic is realized in the developing conspiracy to first subjugate and then assassinate King John. Again it is Sedition who is central to both of these pursuits, inventing stratagems to sap the faith of subjects in their king's virtue and organizing the external forces needed to vanquish him:

> Marry fatche in Lewes, kynge Phylyppes sonne of fraunce
> To fall upon hym, with hys menne and ordynaunce
> with wyldefyer, gunpouder, and suche lyke myrye tryckes
> To dryve hym to holde, and searche hym in the quyckes
> I wyll not leave hym, tyll I brynge hym to hys yende

(ll. 1953–7)

2

King Johan both capitalizes upon and helps foment a profound contemporary interest in inflammatory speech. It clarifies the injurious nature of sedition, sensitizes the audience to its consequences, and identifies (and stigmatizes) catholicism as responsible for it. In this respect, the complicity between the play's representation of language and the legal, spiritual and political goals of Cromwellian government is palpable. Another dimension of the play and its context is clarified, however, when it is recognized that even in the first heady phase of Reformation the identity established between catholicism and sedition was a tenuous one. Greg Walker's expert reconstruction of the late 1530s context of *King Johan* reminds us that proponents of reform had to proceed in a context of endemic insecurity.[33] As has been noted, proclamations during the immediate pre-Reformation period had defined the nascent protestant movement as seditious. Thomas More had avowed 'that Luthers bokes be sedycyouse, as I now say that Tyndales be to, and movynge people to theyr owne undoyng to be dysobedyent and rebellyouse to theyr soveryans'.[34] As Susan Brigden remarks, even the astonishing year of 1538 'saw the reformers at the height of their power – but most imminently threatened. In their triumph their downfall was prefigured.'[35] In November 1538, Henry VIII also presided over the trial and execution of the sacramentarian John Lambert. In the first edition of *Actes and Monuments* John Foxe lamented this in a compelling passage; this was excised from subsequent editions of the work:

> O kynge Henry (if that I maye a little talke with thee where so ever thou arte) if thou haddest ayded and holpen the poor litle sheape, beinge in so great pearils and daungers, requiringe thy aide and healpe againste so manye vultures and Libardes [leopards], and haddest graunted hym rather thy autoritye to use the same for his savegarde, rather then unto the other to abuse it unto slaughter.[36]

A royal proclamation the same month outlawed evangelical sermonizing as 'rash words of erroneous matters' that had inflamed 'seditious opinions'.[37] Foxe later summarized the disorientating effect of 1538 on the godly:

> To many whiche be yet alyve, and can testifie these thinges, it is not unknowen, how variably the state of Religion stode in these days: how hardly and with what difficultie it came forth: what chaunces and chaunges it suffered. Even as the kyng was ruled and gave eare sometime to one, sometimes to an other, so one whyle it went forward, at an other season as much backwarde agayne, and sometyme clean altered and chaunged for a season, accordyng as they could prevaile which were about the kyng.[38]

As Eamon Duffy has noted, Cranmer's impact upon the diocese of Kent – the location of *King Johan*'s performance in Christmas 1538/9 – exacerbated rather than quelled uncertainty and division. Here, 'the struggle between the old and new ways was more intense and existential than in most other parts of England'.[39] The cause of reform remained vulnerable to faction, foreign policy and shifting monarchical will and such variability, accompanied by the threat of reversal, became manifest in the growing reaction against Cromwell's policies. According to Philip Hughes, religious 'policy oscillated in an amazing way',[40] during the six months between late 1538 and the promulgation of the Six Articles in 1539. This latter measure crushed the hopes of reformers by implementing savage penalties against evangelical beliefs; after Cromwell's execution in July 1540 a conservative religious reaction continued until Edward's accession and then again under Mary. As time unfolded, then, it failed to provide any assurance for the godly; indeed, it was alarmingly open to alteration.

The significance of such instability for *King Johan* is increased when we remember the play's protracted composition during a period that threatened as much as it enabled its author's aspirations. Bale's political views certainly underwent stringent modification during this time, and this can be detected in the play's treatment of seditious language. As Paul Christianson has noted, disillusionment with worldly power can be perceived in *The Image of Both Churches*, the influential commentary on Apocalypse that Bale completed in exile between 1541 and 1547.[41] In the eternal drama of opposition this text postulates between the true church and that of antichrist, Bale laments that evil 'shall strongly delude the kings of the earth, and blind the governors of the universal world, making them drunken with the cup of all abominations'. Thus worldly justice remains under the thrall of papal corruption: 'And he that disobeyeth them shall not only be judged a felon and worthy to be hanged by their new forged laws, but also condemned for a traitor against his king, though he never in his life hindered but rather to his power hath furthered, the commonwealth.'[42] Such a transformation was lamented at the stake in 1540 by Bale's friend and fellow reformer Robert Barnes who questioned those around him: 'is there here any man ells that knoweth wherefore I dye, or that by my preaching hath taken any erroure?' Given their silence, he concluded it was due to the malice of his enemies: 'I have been reported a preacher of sedicion and disobedyence unto the kynge's majestye.'[43]

Bale's subsequent hostility to 'new forged laws' indicates the surprising proximity of his views with those that he once condemned for seeing earthly monarchy as corrupt and unreliable. In 1535 an embattled catholic curate had complained 'that these new preachers now-a-days that doth preach their iii sermons in a day have made and brought in such divisions and seditions among us as never was seen in this realm, for the devil reigneth over us now'.[44] Bale witnessed how this once seditious perception became accepted again as orthodox: his writings were banned in England 1542 and were ordered to be burned four years later.[45] Throughout his life, the power of seditious calumny was to pursue him. In one of his more sensational travails, Bale was abducted by pirates as he fled his Edwardian bishopric in Ireland upon the accession of Mary in 1553. One of his captors immediately slandered his godly work as the enterprise of a scheming Machiavel: he 'had made them beleve, that I was he, which not only had put downe the masse in Englande, but also I had caused Doctour Gardiner, the bishopp of Winchestre to be kepte so longe in the tower, and that also I had poysened (whome I loved & reverenced above all mortall men) the kinge with many other most prodigiouse lyes'.[46] Again seditious denigration confronts the godly with its prodigious ability to destroy reputation and warp beliefs, transforming the king's faithful servant into a regicide ('he that disobeyeth them shall...[be] condemned for a traitor against his king').

Bale's sensitivity to both the expression and restraint of injurious language also involves a perception of how *any* defiance of traditional authority can be recognized as seditious. This awareness of how language falls subject to time and to competing forms of appropriation and definition, complicates the reflection upon history within the play. As Sedition's own alacrity to quash antagonistic speech demonstrates, Bale is conscious of how righteous words provoke hostility; his own sermon, tracts and plays had often done so.[47] Of course, this was a familiar problem for the godly: 'Luther often preached that *scandalum* was unavoidable in this world because the Word of God stands in opposition to human actions.'[48] Bale interpreted the Pilgrimage of Grace as an example of how God's truth could be opposed: 'still they rise up against Christ and his word, and daily they counsel together to condemn his truth, that we should know him to be the sign of contradiction, the stumbling-stone, and the rock of reproach'.[49] Yet dissenting catholics could also represent their persecution under Cromwell as evidence that they possessed Christ's truth as 'the sign of contradiction'. Such conflicts and reversals are of significance for *King Johan*'s treatment of sedition insofar as it discloses its dubious adequacy in discriminating truth from falsehood. As Robert Barnes discovered, the very category used to stigmatize catholic opposition could be deployed against the godly. The play's theatrical effects are at their most interesting, and conflicted, when they acknowledge the permeability of the boundary between orthodox and heterodox expression. Bale perceives sedition as caught in a process of 'open temporality' in which its implications become confused or contradictory.

In this respect, *King Johan*'s polemical assurance is offset by Bale's insistent recognition of the power of catholicism. In the midst of his unsuccessful struggle to reform the church, King John finds himself accused by Private Wealth of 'heretycall langage', provoking the monarch's lament at this distortion of his reputation:

> the prystes report me, to be a wyckyd tyrant
> be cause I correct, ther actes and lyfe unplesaunt
> Of thy prince sayth god, thow shalt report no yll
> but thy selfe applye, his plesur to fulfyll
> the byrdes of the ayer, shall speke to ther gret shame
> as sayth ecclesyastes, that wyll a prince dyffame
> the powres are of god, I wot powle hath soch sentence
> he that resyst them, agenst god maketh resystence

> (ll. 1399–1406)

This passage gathers the judgements of scripture against the church's perversion of language: catholicism is deemed to perpetuate irreverence towards monarchy, to nourish contempt for nationhood, to cultivate ignorance of scripture, and to foster disobedience of divinely ordained law. Yet, as the king's concern for his wounded reputation shows, pathos is aroused when he is unable to convince others of his probity. Bale certainly synchronizes the king's language with that of evangelical reform, as in his complaint concerning Clergy and Nobility's ensnarement in superstition:

> lyke backes in the darke, ye alweys take yowr flyght
> flytteryng in fanseys, and ever abhorre the lyght
> I rew yt in hart that yow nobelyte,
> shuld thus bynd yowr selfe to the grett captyvyte
> of blody babulon, the grownd and mother of whordom
> the Romych churche I meane, more vyle than ever was sodom,
> and to say the trewth, a mete spowse for the fynd.

> (ll. 367–73)

As a testament, however, to the degraded condition of speech under the church's dominance, the king's word convinces no one within the text as it is harassed and defiled as heresy and sedition.

It is equally revealing that in his later additions to the original 'A-text' of *King Johan*, Bale lends greater emphasis to the strength of the church, and, especially, to the scope of Sedition's role. Among other additions, the Vice gains six extra lines of relics at ll. 1226–31 to help delude the faithful (including Adam's toenail and a 'fart of saynt fandigo'); the ferocity of his threats against the king are increased (ll. 1629–39), and he gains a lengthy passage of triumphant gloating – 'England is our owne' – at John's capitulation (ll. 1699–1711).[50] One symptom of catholicism's confidence in its persuasive power is displayed then in Sedition's theatrical dominance. In his early defiance of King John's repeated injunctions to remain with him onstage, Sedition exclaims: 'yea but fyrst of all, I must chaunge myn apparell / unto a bysshoppe, to maynetayene with my quarell / to a monke or pryst or to sum holy fryer' (ll. 297–9). It is through such ostentatious gestures of self-disclosure that we begin to approach the paradoxical qualities of the personification and these may remind us of the etymology of sedition: a going apart, a separation. The figure of Sedition works to set an audience apart from the play's action and to divide responses to it.

It is significant, therefore, that in one of Bale's later interpolations to the 'A-text', Sedition is criticized by the church itself. The Vice engages in a rapturous celebration of the wealth and power that will accrue to the church given King John's resignation of his crown to the papacy: 'Now shall we ruffle it, in velvattes, golde and sylke / with shaven crownes, syde gownes, and rochettes whyte as mylke' (ll. 1707–8). Noticeably, this provokes an angry rebuke from Pandalphus (Private Wealth): 'Holde thy peace whorson, I wene thu art accurst / Kepe a sadde countenaunce, a very vengeaunce take the' (ll. 1712–13). This is one of a number of occasions when Sedition is spoken to in a censorious fashion, provoking the crushing rejoinders usually meted out to John and England. Earlier in the play (ll. 799–1001), Sedition again continually threatens to betray catholicism itself. This is signalled partly by his own aggressive sense of superiority in insisting the other personifications bear him in aloft – 'I will beshyte yow all yf ye sett me not downe softe' (l. 800) – and, more fully, in the direction of his scorn against the church of which he is so energetic a disciple. For example, there is his shockingly explicit depiction of the four orders of the church as irredeemably corrupt (ll. 805–13). This culminates in his pithy depiction of Usurped Power's authority as 'neyther good ner trewe' (l. 812), provoking the Pope's response: 'under hevyn ys not, a mor knave in condycyon' (l. 814). Such tolerance soon evaporates as Sedition launches a battery of derisive comments at his own comrades. When Dissimulation seeks blessing and absolution from Usurped Power, Sedition peppers his obeisance with sardonic asides:

Dyssymulacyon:	for godes sake wytsave, to geve me yowr blyssyng here
	a pena et culpa, that I may stand this day clere
Sedicyon:	from makyng cuckoldes? mary that wer no mery chere
Dyssymulacyon:	a pena et culpa, I trow thow canst not here
Sedicyon:	yea, with a cuckoldes wyff ye have dronke dobyll bere
Dyssymulacyon:	I pray the sedycyon. my pacyens no more stere

(ll. 843–8)

At such moments the Vice's speech corresponds with the scurrilous language and attitudes of the play; Bale's play discloses that the political qualities of Sedition are also potential facets of his own doctrinal stance. This correspondence between the iconoclast and his target involves a revaluation of the implications of seditious discourse: the more Sedition is disparaged, the more his capacity for truth-telling is revealed. Such an insight derives from the persistent arraignment of godly language as seditious: it was the Marian regime, in *An Acte against sedityous Woordes and Rumours* (1 & 2 Philip and Mary, 1554, c. 3), that also proscribed the offence by statute to protect a catholic monarch 'of whom we are forbidden to thinck evill and muche more to speake evell'.

Sedition's fearless recognition of the absurdity of catholic ritual and hierarchy leads him even to abuse the Pope himself.

Sedicyon:	a man be the messe, can not know yow from a knave ye loke so lyke hym. as i wold god shuld me save
Privat Welth:	thow art very lewde, owr father so to deprave

(ll. 861–3)

The identity Sedition establishes between the pope's religious appearance and his criminal substance is precisely the kind of perception that *King Johan* strives to create in its audience. Private Wealth becomes especially exasperated at such license. His comments – 'thou dost mocke and scoffe' (l. 867); 'yowr parte ys not elles, but for to playe the knove' (l. 893) – are an index of Sedition's recklessness. Of course, the Vice is conventionally prone to the disclosure of its own iniquity as well as that of others.[51] In Bale's play, *A Comedy concernynge thre laws* (1548), the Vice, Infidelity, also indulges in some biting criticism of the church.[52] This is an isolated incident, however, that is rapidly quashed, whereas in *King Johan* Sedition has more equivocal implications: it is his systematic quality to demystify the ritual procedures of the church and to set an audience apart from its interests. Such an impulse is evident in his remarks to Private Wealth and Usurped Power as they prepare the indulgences and pardons that will ensure rebellion against the king: 'by the messe and that, is not worth a rottyn wardon' (l. 989). Similarly, the scabrous commentary that accompanies Dissimulation's obsequious submission to Usurped Power reveals the latter's true status: 'yet is he no lesse, than a false knave veryly / I wold thow haddyst kyst, his ars for that is holy' (ll. 889–90).

In the preparations Sedition makes with Dissimulation for the assassination of King John, the capacity of his language to dispossess the church of credibility grows stronger. For example, Dissimulation steels himself for administering the poison he will have to take with the king by ensuring he will avoid 'that whoreson purgatorye' with an eternity of requiem masses devoted to his soul (ll. 1985–93). Again the Vice's peculiar convergence with the spirit of the play is felt when Dissimulation suddenly considers his fate when the world has ended, to which Sedition replies: 'Than shyft for thy self, so wele as ever thu can' (l. 1999). Equally, his depiction of the pilgrims that will visit Dissimulation's shrine (addressed to the latter while he is dying), has a similarly outrageous effect: 'To the than wyll offer, both crypple, halte and blynde / Mad men and mesels, with suche as are woo behynde' (ll. 2088–9). In particular, Sedition proves difficult to contain; he demonstrates a striking ability to survive. Amid the concluding reform of church and society conducted by Verity and Imperial Majesty, the Vice reappears to remind us of the partiality of their success, a key aspect of the period's understanding of seditious reflection: 'The worlde is not yet, as some woulde it have' (l. 2415). This reinstates the capacity of seditious speech to make an apparently stable set of political circumstances appear relative and open to reversal. Even the lengthy divulgence of Seditions's continuing influence – 'we lyngar a tyme, and loke but for a daye / To sett upp the pope, if the Gospell woulde decaye' (ll. 2503–4) – produces a further disconcerting effect. The Vice reveals his activities only after having ensured he will receive a pardon from Imperial Majesty, a promise that is revoked in a manner that resembles the critical comments aroused by Henry VIII's manipulation of the rebels involved in the Pilgrimage of Grace.[53] Again it is Sedition that (potentially) divides an audience's reactions even to the spectacle of godly justice: 'whye, of late dayes ye sayde, I shoulde not so be martyred / where is the pardon, that ye ded promyse me?' (ll. 2533–4).

The unpredictability inherent in religious and political reform is expressed clearly in *King Johan* when Sedition recollects his past successes in inducing Nobility to perceive the godly as himself and, hence, to secure their persecution:

> *King Johan*: why, geveth he [Nobility] no credence, to cristes holy gospell?
>
> *Sedicyon*: no ser by the messe, but he callyth them herytyckes
> that preche the gospell, and sedycyows scysmatyckes
> he tache them, vex them, from preson to preson he turne them
> he Indygth them, juge them, and in conclusyon he burne them
>
> (ll. 280–4)

Such an acknowledgement makes it less surprising that Bale's play displays how its own views are perilously close to the sedition it helps define, and there are a range of examples of this. Even in its earliest exchanges it is possible to identify a correspondence between *King Johan*'s opposing forces: the play deploys the same inflammatory registers of insult, derision and scandalous allegation that it establishes simultaneously as the institutional identity of evil. Ultimately, it is King John who succumbs to the lure of political compromise and earns the hostile rebuke of Widow England that itself borders on sedition:

> Alack for pyte, that ever ye grantyd this
> for me pore ynglond, ye have done sore amys
> of a fre woman, ye have now mad a bonde mayd
> yowr selfe and heyres, ye have for ever decayd
> alas I had rether, be underneth the turke
> than under the wynges, of soch a thefe to lurke
>
> (ll. 1682–7)[54]

It is part of Bale's complexity as a historical dramatist that he responds with such sensitivity to the political pressures of his own period, as intently as he fashions an ideological version of the past. This alertness to the current fate of the godly, as much as their harrowing ordeals in an often misrepresented past, leads him to represent the fallibility of political categories that classify illicit language. In this respect, *King Johan* exemplifies Tom Betteridge's observation that sixteenth-century protestantism 'obsessively claimed an inherent exclusivity and integrity', yet, in the process of making this claim, it also revealed 'its fractured and culturally antagonistic basis'.[55] As much recent analysis of cultural identity reminds us, caricatures of a feared opponent also disclose defensiveness and anxiety; Bale's play may express a deeper paradox that informs all assertions of identity-in-difference.[56] Stuart Clark reminds us that 'contrariety is inherently ambivalent. It seems to promote order and coherence by fixing meanings in a clear-cut and economical relationship. But by defining contraries in relation to each other it entails a constant and ultimately unresolvable semantic exchange between them.'[57] Yet there are more specific, and equally revealing pressures, upon Bale's concept of sedition. If, as one recent account of Bale's *The Image of Both Churches* reminds us, 'a process of distinction is always one of resemblance',[58] it may be less difficult to accept sedition's mutability. Similarly, the appearance of its effects within the discourse which should define and master it is expressive of a period undergoing a radical fluctuation of categories in discriminating the orthodox from the heretical, the obedient from the rebellious. *King Johan* discerns both the growing utility of seditious expression to Tudor government, as well as its pliancy in relation to shifting political and confessional allegiances. It also demonstrates how the nascent genre of Tudor historical theatre could, in its representation of unruly speech, reflect critically upon the ruling categories and practices of political life.

2
The Language of Counsel in *Gorboduc*

1

Any relationship between Bale's *King Johan* and Norton and Sackville's *Gorboduc* (1561/2) appears to be one of disparity rather than resemblance. These two plays are distinct not only in matters of form and content, but also in the historical and political understanding they solicit from their audiences. If *King Johan* urges its auditors to act 'in the light of Christian virtue, expressed in the service of a theocratic society', Norton and Sackville encourage a more 'classically inspired, more distinctly secular virtue, expressed in the service of the national state'.[1] The latter's work also derives from the Elizabethan watershed whereby 'the humanists of the 1560s reshaped England's consciousness of historical processes' so enabling 'the recognition of a generational and philosophical change in the country's leadership'.[2] In his opening address to the Elizabethan parliament in January 1559, the Lord Keeper, Sir Nicholas Bacon, stressed the need to forgo divisive polemic and wished (optimistically) that a new spirit of concord be expressed through temperate speech:

> by councell provision would be made that all contentious, contumelious or opprobrious wordes, as 'heretike', 'schismatike', 'papist', and such like names and nurces of seditious faccions and sectes may be banished out of men's mouthes, as the causers, continuers and increasers of displeasure, hate and malice, and as utter enemyes to all concorde and unitie, the very marke that you are now to shoote at.[3]

For Bacon, those, like Bale, who indulge in inflammatory speech are guilty of fomenting the very sedition they purport to oppose.

36

Norton and Sackville's *Gorboduc*, first performed at the Inner Temple during the Christmas celebrations of 1561/2, returns to historical material in a very different spirit to *King Johan*. There is no overtly sermonizing approach to language and only an oblique address to political issues. This restraint must have been as noticeable as *Gorboduc*'s stylistic daring, with its: 'rigid decorum...its choruses, its long sententious speeches, its avoidance of all violence on the stage, its unity of action, and the blank verse now first used in the drama'.[4] These neoclassical qualities appear designed to cultivate a more dispassionate approach to the conflicts it depicts. In addition, the play's setting in a remote pre-Conquest Britain seems unlikely to spark anything approaching Bale's fevered interest in the contemporary repercussion of the past.

Despite these differences there are significant points of contact between the two plays. Indeed, if *King Johan* was revived for an Elizabethan production, both works may have been performed almost synchronously. Furthermore, as the previous chapter has demonstrated, the protracted composition of Bale's play also enriched his historical awareness and complicated his political insight. Indeed, these two works have been drawn together before as sharing the key ideological ingredient of historical theatre: political didacticism. For all their audacity with dramatic form, Norton and Sackville's political aims and historiographical methods have been understood as 'thoroughly conventional... [and] conforming to the tradition of the *speculum principis*'.[5] Irving Ribner acknowledges that *Gorboduc* may have been the 'first history play entirely free from morality abstractions', but beneath its surface 'we may still discover John Bale Senecanized'.[6] For Ribner, this confirms again how history appeared on the sixteenth-century stage primarily as material to be shaped for moralistic purposes. Conceiving of the Tudor history play as a didactic 'tradition', however, assumes that a consensus existed throughout pre-Stuart theatrical culture over the political utility of the past. This assumption can be questioned by analysing a topical interest these plays do possess in common: destructive political language. In their deliberation upon this topic, Norton and Sackville were as alert as Bale to the contingencies of time and to the limits of worldly power. The capacity of speech to destroy (and to order) society is a central aspect of their historical concerns, but again the capacity to distinguish between these forms of language and to extinguish (or sustain) their use is far from assured. The intricacy of this issue is explored in this play through the language of counsel.

One obvious manifestation of this interest is *Gorboduc*'s concern with evil counsel. When the king explains his desire to divide the kingdom it is welcomed by one counsellor as an opportunity to avert the most significant hazard for a new ruler: of being left 'An open prey to traitorous flattery, / The greatest pestilence of noble youth' (1.2.128–9).[7] The consequence of flattery is depicted in the play's second dumb show contrasting plain and golden glass. This demonstrates how 'a faithful counselor holdeth no treason, but is plain and open, ne yieldeth to any undiscreet affection, but giveth wholesome counsel, which the ill-advised prince refuseth' (*Dumb Show* 2. 14–17). Flattering words, conversely, 'beareth deadly poison, which destroyed the prince that receiveth it' (19–20). Such concerns were familiar axioms of Renaissance political thought. They drew upon the copious admonitions preserved in classical culture against flattering and self-interested speech and its capacity to 'make itself a stumbling-block and a pestilence in great houses and great affairs' which 'oftentimes overturns kingdoms and principalities'.[8] In his distinguished contribution to *The Mirror for Magistrates* (1563), Thomas Sackville described the plight of Richard III's doomed ally, the Duke of Buckingham, a counsellor who had failed signally in his obligation to restrain his master's tyranny.[9] *Gorboduc*, which largely consists of repeated scenes of deliberation, also invites us to recognize deficient counsel and the corresponding virtue of dispassionate advice. No subject was of more urgent interest to Tudor political society, especially when it is remembered that 'it was intrinsic to the tradition of the English monarchy that the supreme authority in the body politic was not the king alone, but *the king counselled*'.[10]

If counsel is a commanding interest of the play, Norton and Sackville explore it as a problem. Where *King Johan* embodies Bale's symptomatic recognition of the ambivalent potential of sedition, Norton and Sackville compose a more meditated account of the difficulties that attend the formulation of political analysis and advice. This aspect of the play is remote from any propagandistic intent and complicates any interpretation of its viewpoint. *Gorboduc* presents a range of speakers who evaluate its deepening historical crisis in very different terms, but these competing views provoke further controversy both on and off-stage. The credibility of each voice we hear, including the monarch's, is qualified by fast-changing historical circumstances. This makes it difficult to determine constructive speech from hasty, obtuse or malicious words. Again, the play's political intricacy lies in its sensitivity to the turbulence of history and how this affects preconceived notions of virtuous or vicious speech. In this respect, *Gorboduc* explores the difficulties and dilemmas active citizens, like those at the Inns of Court, confronted in public life, rather than proposing an ideal form of action. This awareness of the complexities that attend both the delivery and reception of counsel is expressed with great vividness in the play's opening act.

After its opening dumb show – a moralistic tableau of how internal divisions presage the destruction of the state – the play presents Videna, Gorboduc's queen, addressing her eldest son Ferrex in a vituperative temper. In the first of many hostile accounts the characters offer concerning the motivations of others, she condemns her husband's 'froward will' in wishing to divide the kingdom. Videna attributes this to Gorboduc's jealousy of the 'tender love' she bears for Ferrex and describes how the king has ignored her advice and intercessions (1.1.21–9; 45–50). Gorboduc's council would rather 'please the present fancy of the prince' (60) than defend right.

Videna's tirades appear designed to elicit some familiar cultural prejudices against the inordinate speech of women when it is directed against patriarchal authority: her words immediately evoke the spectre of evil counsel. Phyllis Rackin has argued that women are often presented as 'antihistorians' in early modern theatre, that is, as agents who obstruct and subvert national political progress (Rackin, pp. 146–200). Here, Videna also establishes the deliberative mode of the play in which characters attempt to persuade others of the future that awaits them and the action this demands. Yet, such conjectures are also intimated to be prejudicial; Videna concedes: '*if* things do so succeed, / As now my jealous mind misdeemeth sore' (38–9; emphasis added). In contrast, Ferrex emphasizes the impartiality of his father's justice, the integrity of his council and that any future threat from his brother's ambition 'shall hurt himself, not me' (44). Such a resolute response adds to the comprehension of Videna's words as a divisive attempt to enlist Ferrex in her suspicions.

Yet, the play immediately complicates the judgements aroused by this apparently flagrant abuse of language. In fact, Videna's words correspond closely with the 'official' morality presented in the first dumb show and its depiction of how individual sticks are easily broken when extracted from a bundle. This image of how a state 'being divided, is easily destroyed' (*Dumb Show* 1.12–13), confirms the queen's prediction that 'Murders, mischief, or civil sword' (62) will follow the violation of 'right succeeding line' (64). From this perspective, Ferrex's optimistic defence of his father's justice seems naive and his estimation of past experience hasty.

From the outset, therefore, *Gorboduc* throws contrary perspectives upon opposing uses of the past, as well as projections of the future, in the practice of counsel. This tactic is of further consequence when, in the following scene, the king and three of his council deliberate upon his proposal to resign the crown and divide the realm between Ferrex and Porrex. This scene presents *Gorboduc*'s most radical departure from its sources; the chronicles available to Norton and Sackville contain no account of land division.[11] Inevitably, this augments the significance of the advice we hear, as well as the threat of corrupt or flattering speech. Videna has prepared us to expect this and the speakers themselves repeatedly draw attention to the motivations that inform their language and to the danger of advice that is adulterated by sycophancy or malice. Gorboduc insists that his counsellors avoid 'poisonous craft to speak in pleasing wise' and, hence, the responsibility for 'ill-succeeding things' (1.2.30; 31). He invites them to weigh his words with care and to reflect whether they 'allow my whole device / And think it good for me, for them, for you, / And for our country, mother of us all' (69–71). *Contra* Videna, all the speakers share this dispassionate concern for the commonwealth and Gorboduc's collegial sense of kingship: 'the state / Whereof both I *and you* have charge and care' (25–6; emphasis added). For Gorboduc, the origins and continuing legitimacy of kingship derive from its preservation of the 'common peace': 'The cause that first began and still maintains / The lineal course of kings' inheritance' (23–4). The monarch pays tribute to the 'grave' and 'faithful' advice he has always received from his council (1–10). There is no hint of jealousy, partisan affection or self-interest in his thoughts (or theirs), only a concern to settle the succession so that 'Your wealth and peace may stand in quiet stay' (10). This intensifies both the natural interest of an Inner Temple audience in counsel as a key desideratum of the active life of citizenship, whilst making the evaluation of the competing advice we hear more demanding.

Gorboduc's court encourages frank speaking, the practice of *parrhesia* David Colclough has analysed as 'a guiding concept for the conduct of political life through negotiation and dialogue' in the sixteenth century.[12] Like his king, Arostus affirms that his words derive from 'rightful reason and of heedful care / Not for ourselves, but for the common state' (86–7). It is telling, in this respect, that in supporting Gorboduc's proposal Arostus's discourse is remote from flattery. He emphasizes bluntly his king's 'aged mind' and the cruel impact of the cares of office that 'waste man's life and hasten crooked age, / With furrowed face and with enfeebled limbs' (103–4). Arostus argues that Gorboduc's plan will rejuvenate the king, allowing him to be a 'longer stay' to his two sons and to circumvent the 'traitorous flattery' that threatens a youthful succession (90–147). Just as the words of his counsellors have shaped

Gorboduc, so his guidance will exercise its civilizing influence upon the commonwealth. The king will be able to 'bridle' and 'restrain' the 'green and bending wits' of his sons and curb their susceptibility to 'insolence': 'inured with virtues at the first, / Custom, O king, shall bring delight-fulness' (119–20). Arostus's speech, superficially the most vulnerable to the taint of credulity or of pandering to wilful power, is a meditated and responsible argument based on the need for virtuous and restrained authority.

Philander's response to this is equally tough-minded and direct. Although agreeing that the king's choice will best sustain the 'realm's behoof' (153) and advance the honour of the ruling family, he qualifies this in a striking way. Philander criticizes Gorboduc's decision to abdicate immediately as pre-empting the will of the gods and he opposes this, again bluntly, as 'not good for you, for them, nor us' (160). Where he does agree with Arostus is in the opportunities the division of the kingdom offers after the king's death. For Philander, this will allow greater proximity between monarch and people and, hence, the prompter exercise of justice. It will also foster a 'virtuous envy' (180) between the two brothers and circumvent the terrifying future, predicted in dense and convincing detail (186–99), consequent upon the exclusion of a younger son made susceptible to corrupt persuasions. In particular, Philander plots a dialectical relationship between obedience and rule. As with Arostus, he insists it is the king's responsibility to inculcate in his children an ethic of restraint: 'Whoso obeyeth not with humbleness / Will rule with outrage and with insolence' (229–30). Again he is careful to disavow, credibly, any 'envy or reproach' in his concern for the 'common weal' (211; 242).

As this interpretation demonstrates, a more patient attention to the detail of rhetorical debate in *Gorboduc* reveals it as being far from predictable in its political evaluations. Although we may 'know' from the play's official mouthpieces (the Dumb Shows and the chorus) that both these views are misguided, they are also genuinely persuasive. The audience is being asked to adjudicate a deliberative process.

Thus there are also strong hints, for the careful auditor, of the limit-ations of what we hear. Both advisers create a strange view of posterity where what is sundered will grow stronger and what might diminish love and trust will augment it; there are disconcerting moments where the credibility of the case is qualified by its expression. In a meandering rationalization, Arostus depicts the unified realm as gaining, mysteriously, a 'double weight' that requires a 'parted reign' (109; 106). Even more speciously, Philander recollects the past civil war that erupted between

Cordelia's two nephews when they divided the realm; this appears in an argument *for* Gorboduc's proposal (161–7). Similarly, his oxymoronic formulation of the 'virtuous envy' that will develop between the two brothers appears, suitably enough, to be debatable. Moreover, at the end of the scene, Eubulus disputes the recommendations of both counsellors with an alternative account of both past and future to prove his thesis: 'Divided reigns do make divided hearts' (260). Eubulus opposes the king's will entirely. He contests Philander's use of history by recalling the civil wars that followed Brute's division of the kingdom and argues that these will occur again if the same historical mistake is repeated (269–82). In another instance of argument *in umtramque partem*, Eubulus accepts that the 'desire of sovereignty' must be strictly repressed or else it will be easily stirred by 'Traitorous corrupters of their pliant youth' (266; 316); this now appears in a case against the partition of the realm.

The opening act of *Gorboduc* embodies Norton and Sackville's self-conscious reflection upon historical argumentation. The lesson of history is not presented as singular or straightforward, but as susceptible to competing appropriations and to debate. Eubulus's speech is often assumed to carry most weight with the authors and the audience and, given that his name denotes wise counsel, it may do so. Yet Norton and Sackville also make an audience experience the complexity of the issue at question as much as the solution to it. This is not the world of the morality play, but of a disputative drama that pressurizes received assumptions concerning duplicitous, obtuse or seditious counsel as a source of danger to the state. Political discourse at Gorboduc's court is conducted without any apparent dissimulation, malice or the artful cultivation of favour and yet it embraces entirely opposing viewpoints. As significant, and this point will be returned to, is the equalization this produces between the views of monarch and subject. Unlike *King Johan*, this pre-Christian monarch possesses no ordained authority nor is he located in a providential history. The king's word is just as partial, misguided or well-intentioned as that of his subjects. Interpretation of the play needs to recognize its specifically *imaginary* conditions as a tragic drama. This involves subjecting the language of counsel, construed as both a rhetorical method and as a political resource, to pressure that repeatedly tests its limits. In particular, the distinction between words intended to benefit the commonwealth and the language of flattery, seditious incitement, or treacherous speculation proves to be less than clear-cut. In this respect, the play evidences the complexity of Elizabethan thinking in relation to counsel both as an ideal and as a practice. As with Shakespeare's history plays, language in *Gorboduc* is also subject to temporality and the play's structural ironies underline the provisional status of the speech we hear. The prized idiom of counsel is shown to be a result of human evaluations and decisions and, consequently, it can find only partial solutions to historical dilemmas.

Before proceeding any further with this analysis, it must be acknowledged that it runs counter to a dominant understanding of both *Gorboduc* and its relationship to its context. A powerful body of criticism has argued that the play is an instance of counsel, rather than a critical meditation upon it. This tradition will be reviewed briefly here before arguing that an alternative context is available to explain its historical method: this lies in the practise of rhetorical controversy. Outlining these dominant readings will also provide an opportunity, as with *King Johan*, to ask further questions of current attempts to contextualize drama, especially those that engage in only a glancing way with its formal complexity.

The most familiar approach to *Gorboduc* perceives it as 'the first Elizabethan succession tract' composed to urge the new queen to designate a suitable heir.[13] Within this context, the play is seen as an admonitory lesson – drawn from, among other sources, Geoffrey of Monmouth's twelfth-century pseudo-history of ancient Britain[14] – concerning the chaos that follows from an uncertain or aberrant succession. More precisely, in the context of Elizabethan succession debates, *Gorboduc* has been understood as opposing the Stuart claim or that of any foreign prince.[15] *Gorboduc* can be adduced therefore as demonstrating how historical drama can make a principled intervention into an area of volatile public debate. As David Bevington suggests, the 'play's interest in rhetoric signifies the exploration of language as a useful public art', that is, as 'blunt advice'.[16] This interpretive tradition has been bolstered by the recent discovery of an eyewitness account of *Gorboduc*'s première at the Inner Temple.[17] In this intriguing document, an anonymous observer does indeed interpret the play as a succession tract intended to denigrate foreign competitors for Elizabeth's hand and to promote a native candidate, Robert, Lord Dudley (created Earl of Leicester in 1564).

This is a substantial and persuasive tradition of criticism, yet, as with John Bale's *King Johan*, such readings presuppose that theatre addresses relatively static circumstances in an undivided manner. Assuming that the response of a play to its context is governed by one purpose can delimit, strikingly, its range of political speculation. One issue is whether the eyewitness account, however valuable, should be elided with the audience's response and the authors' intentions, especially when 'there is no reference whatever to royal marriage or marriage *per se*' in the texts of *Gorboduc* that were printed in 1565 and 1570.[18] Given the terse accounts of Gorboduc's reign available in contemporary sources, this approach renders Norton and Sackville's considerable efforts of imaginative expansion and political deliberation as largely extraneous to its core meaning.

More significant is the consensus underpinning these interpretations concerning *Gorboduc*'s status as an act of political counsel. John Guy has identified counsel as the 'inspirational myth' that 'informed public discourse and shaped political institutions' throughout the Tudor and early Stuart polity and he begins his recent account of its significance with the play.[19] This was an issue of obvious interest to an audience at the Inns of Court who might aspire to, or have achieved, influence. The play is undoubtedly engaged with the responsibilities of public servants to promote virtuous policy, temper passion, correct misjudgement and protect the commonwealth. *Gorboduc* can be interpreted as a (perhaps self-advertising) demonstration by Norton and Sackville of how persuasive advice might be addressed to a politically informed, if sceptical, audience. This determines its overall argument with regard to the succession and the reception that it hoped to receive: 'the acceptance of good counsel was not just a moral or political duty for the governor, it was a public demonstration of his fitness to rule'.[20] It is this aspect of the play, Blair Worden argues, that commended it to Sir Philip Sidney in his *The Defence of Poesy* (1595), as well as influencing Sidney's own literary treatment of counsel: 'In the *Arcadia* and *Gorboduc* alike, plain, bold counsel is contrasted with the honeyed flattery of counsellors who tell princes what they want to hear.'[21]

Yet *Gorboduc* takes an inordinately pessimistic view of counsel. For example, in the play's third act, 'counsel' functions as a talismanic term, deployed by virtually all of its speakers to defuse the escalating rivalry between Ferrex and Porrex. Yet, at the outset, counsel has failed. The king receives a letter from a trusted adviser which describes how Ferrex has been 'misled / By traitorous fraud of young untempered wits' to prepare for war against his younger brother and he concedes: 'Ne can my counsel yet withdraw the heat / And furious pangs of his inflamed head' (3.1.32–3; 35–6). The solution to Gorboduc's despair at this news is presented by another adviser: the king should dispense more forceful counsel, so as to 'quickly knit again this broken peace' (50). This possibility is thwarted by another instance of failed advice as Philander confesses that he too has been unable to control Ferrex (69–91).

Gorboduc laments that neither 'father's awe' nor 'Our counsels could withdraw [them] from raging heat' (96; 97). Again the king's advisers urge that Gorboduc must dispatch some 'wise and noble personage... with good counsel' (147; 148) to each of his sons (although precisely this remedy has been seen to fail). As soon as this resolution has been stated it is again rendered futile: a messenger enters to relate that war has commenced between the king's sons, plunging their father into renewed despair. If, as F. W. Conrad has suggested, it was another key responsibility of counsellors to maintain 'their ruler's psychological well-being'[22], Gorboduc's advisers appear strikingly unsuccessful in this respect as well.

As a commentary on the efficacy of counsel, then, *Gorboduc* is drawn to moments where the persuasive word is outmatched by circumstances. This helps to question interpretations of the play that perceive it is a self-confident and uniform expression of 'counsel' addressed to the succession. Gorboduc's reign could certainly be cited in such a petitioning spirit[23], yet the play does not share the monologic form of such texts and this radically affects its meaning. *Gorboduc* is not a dramatized parliamentary petition, but a many-sided and self-qualifying work and the rhetorical conflicts it presents demand to be adjudicated carefully. Rather than being designed to provide a solution to the 'succession crisis', the play is an attempt to *embody* it, to rehearse the dilemmas, even the disorientation, characteristic of a time that presented grave and difficult choices. *Gorboduc* is exemplary, therefore, in its demonstration of how history elicits conflicting rather than unitary understanding. Norton and Sackville are sensitive to how difficult it can be, especially in pressured historical circumstances, to discriminate virtuous counsel from the 'dangerous words' of flawed or corrupt advice. Historical drama reflects again in a complex mode upon the nature of disruptive language. This issue is further complicated when, as in *Gorboduc* and *King Johan*, the experience of the sixteenth century had taught dramatists that events exceed attempts to predict or shape their direction.

2

One aspect of *Gorboduc's* originality and appeal lies, I am suggesting, in its practice of controversy. This method of argument had a deep resonance in the Inns of Court where the play was first performed and it had a particular importance in the early Elizabethan period. J. H. Baker and other scholars have explored how the system of learning exercises at the Inns were conducted through disputation, principally the examination of 'doubtful matter', that is, a legal question considered *pro* and *contra*.[24] By engaging in case-arguments, moots and readings, members of the Inns underwent an intensive and continuous rhetorical training in developing skills of argument:

> What was being taught was a method, and a cast of mind...the participants were less concerned to discover any right answer than to know whether a point was 'good and arguable' or 'mootable'... the procedure was not primarily designed to produce oracular pronouncements...Even the oracles of an inn could therefore, to provoke thought or controversy, argue against their own minds for the sake of argument.[25]

The vocabulary and protocols of legal debate are certainly pervasive in *Gorboduc*; indeed the abstracts of the plot provided in the two editions of the play printed in 1565 and 1570 are headed 'The argument of the Tragedie'.[26] Moreover, that the 'succession crisis' could be examined in a disputative mode, is demonstrated by a dialogue on the queen's marriage composed in April 1561 by Sir Thomas Smith, later author of the famous *De Republica Anglorum* (1583).[27] This text has never been used as an analogue for *Gorboduc*, but it demonstrates precisely how this issue, and the topic of counsel, could be subjected to a controversial process of reflection.

Smith explains his method in this work as that of rhetorical enquiry: 'a disputation much after the old sort of Plato's Dialogues and Tully's'.[28] Three interlocutors, their arguments defined by their names – Wedspite, Lovealien and Homefriend – dispute the issue of the queen's marriage and the succession *pro* and *contra*. Decorously, final judgement is suspended: 'I trust her Highness shortly will give sentence herself; and not with words, but with deeds, shew who took the better part to the contentation of us all' (p. 259). More interesting for our purposes than the detail of this controversy is the induction to it which presents a conversation between the author and Sir Francis Walsingham. The latter opposes hearing any debate on this crucial issue of policy. Only the 'wicked and foolish' could oppose the queen's marriage, and speculation upon it, by 'philosophers and rhetoricians' that 'care not what part you take', will only unsettle vulnerable minds: 'For if you list, you will never lack arguments; and would make some simple men, as I am that hear you, believe, that the cow is wood, and that the moon is made of a green cheese' (p. 62) Yet, Smith questions Walsingham's dogmatism, especially his disparagement of rhetorical flexibility. Modestly disclaiming to be learned, Smith indicates that he would continue to love the queen even if she does not marry, a possibility for which Elizabeth had a famous degree of sympathy and which Walsingham has just condemned as meriting public opprobrium.[29] The latter concedes hurriedly that 'duty compelleth us to love, honour, and obey her, and to take her part, whatsoever it shall please her Highness to do in that case'. Walsingham then commits a further solecism, however, by arguing that anyone who favours a foreign marriage must be 'some Italianated Englishman, or some mongrel, that hath good store of outlandish blood in him'. Smith, this time, is sharper in criticizing the latter's responses: 'Ye judge very fast, before ye either know the man, or have perused his reasons' (p. 62).

This dialogue illuminates the perils of 'fast' judgement as Walsingham's stock reactions are wrong-footed; this includes, interestingly, his opposition to a foreign marriage. Smith implies that, in a quick-changing political world, fixed responses can easily become heterodox; it is a deliberative temper that can best accommodate itself to change by being open to revision. Within the dialogue itself, Lovealien makes this point forcibly: 'if things of themselves may be honest and godly, and the contraries thereof may also so be, and the one and the other may be used; there the *circumstances* do alter the matter' (p. 208; emphasis added).[30]

It will be my argument here that Norton and Sackville share Smith's interest in fluctuating political circumstances and in the need to weigh events carefully and subject them to open (if not unlimited) debate.[31] It is a necessity for those in authority to decide upon a course of action; one dilemma of counsel intended to assist with this process is that it can be overwhelmed by events it can (sometimes) predict but not prevent. More compellingly, *Gorboduc* re-enacts the experience of the succession crisis, with its antagonistic claims, forceful, if contradictory, arguments, and the perils that attend both decision and delay. Rather than arriving at a one-sided solution to this, *Gorboduc* recognizes history as presenting problems of judgement, especially when good counsel cannot always be discriminated from evil. It is this controversial spirit that we see at work in the play's first act. As we listen to Gorboduc's counsellors deliberate, we are invited to respond as they do: testing arguments for disputable points, qualifying distinctions, and examining the quality of utility or principle intrinsic to a particular course of action.

The imaginative investment of the play in fostering controversy is manifested with particular clarity in its fourth act, which also has a strongly legal cast. The dumb show preceding this presents three furies 'clad in black garments sprinkled with blood and flames, their bodies girt with snakes' (*Dumb Show* 4. 3–5). These figures parade the kings and queens of antiquity who have committed unnatural murders and, hence, destroyed their own dynastic authority. At this point, the audience knows that the archaic Britain of the play is also descending into anarchy: the king's authority has collapsed, his sons are at war and Porrex has just slaughtered his elder brother, and rival monarch, Ferrex. Spectators familiar with the chronicles would know that Porrex is about to be butchered in turn by his own mother and that years of civil war were to follow destroying the founding dynasty of the kingdom, the legendary line of Brute.[32] The dumb show thus prepares an audience for the extreme consequences that attend Gorboduc's breach of primogeniture in dividing the kingdom. At the end of the act, the Chorus confirms this fatalistic interpretation: once 'greedy lust' and 'treason' have surfaced in public life, 'blood asketh blood' and the furies will pursue their cycle of revenge (4.2.267–94).

Both these visual and verbal statements seem to provide the only interpretation that each act of *Gorboduc* needs: this dramatized history provides its own continuous exegesis. Yet, are these 'authoritative' commentaries a trustworthy source of dramatic counsel? As Eric Rasmussen has suggested, the descriptions of the dumb shows are unlikely to have been provided by the authors and are, therefore, best understood as a form of commentary upon the play.[33] Similarly, as O. B Hardison indicates, one lesson Norton and Sackville may have absorbed from their interest in Senecan drama is that 'choruses sometimes behave like characters...the chorus in *Thyestes* is as deceived as Thyestes himself'.[34] In this way, the play establishes a critical dialogue between its turbulent historical circumstances and the commentaries pronounced upon these, although many critical responses blur this distinction.[35] The dramatic events of act four are intensely dynamic, demanding both modifications of judgement in the light of new evidence and great care in evaluating the credibility of argument.

Admittedly, the scene that follows the dumb show does much to confirm the expectations it arouses. Videna condemns Porrex as a 'Traitor to kin and kind, to sire and me, / To thine own flesh, and traitor to thyself' (4.1.31–2). The aim of her tirade is to place her younger son beyond the bounds of 'kind', as a 'monster of nature's work' (71) and to imbue him with the pathological instincts of the traitor. The consequence of Porrex's action is embodied promptly in his mother's disintegrating moral restraint.

The play then presents Porrex's arraignment before his father. The latter confirms it would not be against 'the law of kind' to kill him instantly, yet permits him 'leave to use thy speech at full' to defend his actions (4.2.22; 33). As soon as this entitlement is granted, simple moral and linguistic contrasts lose their clarity. In Judith Butler's terms, Porrex's response here demonstrates how 'the offensive call runs the risk of inaugurating a subject in speech who comes to use language to counter the offensive call'.[36] In a compelling display of rhetorical prowess, Porrex obliterates the inhuman image that has been ascribed to him. For the legal-minded audience at the Inns of Court, his speech is also a compendium of the techniques advisable for a forensic oration in one's own defence, combining proofs, logical argument, appeals to pathos and the verification of one's own integrity or ethos.[37] He begins by insisting that he is not seeking pardon, but he does attempt to transform an understanding of the circumstances surrounding his actions (35–51). Porrex pleads that if his true condition could be perceived it would move others to the same grief that overwhelms him and 'force even Wrath herself to pity me' (47). In arousing pathos, he moderates the anger that is distorting true judgement of him, not least his father's whose 'ireful mind with stirred thought / Cannot so perfectly discern my cause' (50–1). He reminds Gorboduc that it was 'from your highness' will alone' (83) that the realm was divided and that this aroused ambition and deceit in Ferrex. Although he sought to persuade him from this rancour these efforts failed to circumvent a conspiracy to poison Porrex, a plot confessed to by the servant that his brother suborned (104–15). It was only then that Porrex acted in a spirit of anguished self-preservation.

How are we to interpret this odd, self-qualifying episode with its competing versions of events and shifting perspectives? Porrex could, of course, be simply inventing excuses, but the prior evidence here is unclear.[38] The important point is that we are only granted rhetorical access to the truth of what has happened and we are uncertain who is being accused unfairly. Far from resolving this, such uncertainties are compounded. As the act closes, the servant Marcella recounts Porrex's subsequent destruction at the hands of his mother, how he 'cried to her for help' (208), but, once again, failed to move the 'cruel heart' of his kin (203–26). Contrary to the abject traitor described by Videna, Marcella then describes him in terms that rhetorical convention would define as epdeictic, praising him as an ideal type of chivalric nobility. So the act ends with precisely the opposite verdict upon Porrex with which it began.

Perhaps the play's specific interest in counsel makes its attitude less ambiguous than this account suggests. *Gorboduc's* depiction of the rival courts of Ferrex and Porrex narrates a simultaneous decline in the quality of counsel that includes explicit instances of insinuation, incitement and self-interest. One needs to proceed warily with this, however, and remember the play's reserve, in act four and elsewhere, in identifying apparently malign words or self-evidently treacherous speakers. In this respect, Norton and Sackville anticipate Shakespeare in *Richard II* by subjecting the category of treason to rhetorical scrutiny. The king's adviser, Dordan, certainly believes that we are in the presence of treason in the play's second act. He witnesses Hermon's attempt to convince Ferrex that he has suffered an unjustified wrong by the division of the kingdom, that he is under threat from his brother's ambitions, and that he must act pre-emptively to crush this (2.1.81–161). Dordan impugns the motivations behind this 'wicked' counsel as an attempt to 'travail by treason'; this will only achieve the destruction of both kings (68–80). As so often in the play, Dordan envisages the historical 'mischief' that will unfold from accepting Hermon's 'heinous tale'. In most respects, this is accurate: 'Your father's death, your brother's, and your own, / Your present murder, and eternal shame' (166–7).

Yet, it is important to remember that Ferrex accepts this counsel and *rejects* Hermon's advice. Dordan's fatalistic response to these 'youthful heads of these unskilful kings' (208) appears to ignore this moderate and statesmanlike decision. Generally, the older generation of the play is quick to impute rashness and immaturity to the younger, whilst exempting their own decisions from this scrutiny. Ferrex stresses the need to maintain the trust of his subjects by forgoing any assault upon the liberties of others (170–93); it may be more difficult than it appears to deduce whose response is rash here. For the careful auditor, Dordan's advice is also limited. In allaying Ferrex's suspicions, for example, he insists that his brother is a wise, just and impartial king (77–80); in the next scene, of course, we see this is far from the truth. Similarly, there is a discordant note of special pleading in his defence of Gorboduc's generosity in allotting him a segment of the realm that is worth 'double value of the part / That Porrex hath allotted to his reign' (43–4). Commentators have been quick to attribute 'parliamentary' sentiments in the play to the Calvinist-inclined Norton, but the range of Calvin's influence upon the play may be more extensive and less predictable than it might appear. Certainly, the fallibility of the older generation of royal advisers (and of the monarchy itself) may owe much to Calvin's dismissal of seniority in years as having any relation to wisdom.[39]

What is more difficult to resolve is whether Hermon's words are treasonous. They contain perhaps the most startling, if selective, statement
of Machiavellian doctrine yet heard upon the Tudor stage. Hermon
assumes a natural appetite for power and sovereignty exists, that it is up
to Ferrex to recognize this, and to become the master not the victim of
it. Any equanimity he displays will be construed as cowardice and such
inaction will weaken him. Hermon counsels Ferrex to seize this moment
to possess the realm and become its *de facto* ruler. His brother's death
will mean this is quickly accepted as inevitable and his father is unlikely
to have the will or capacity to resist this.

Yet, there are two aspects of this speech that make its delivery disconcerting. One is that there are no hints internal to it of any corrupt
motivation on Hermon's part. His speech seems remote from the appeals
to selfish emotion or irrational indulgence normally associated with the
flatterer who 'tries to divorce from the reasoning powers by contriving
for it divers low forms of pleasurable enjoyment'.[40] Hermon's *Realpolitik*
certainly manifests a complete disregard for the commonwealth; he
is concerned only with the amoral 'necessities' of statecraft.[41] Yet, this
is not derived from any identifiable strategy of self-advancement or
malicious will; his argument is curiously freestanding, a tough-minded
perspective to be reckoned with. In addition, this amoral case is also
searching in its political realism: circumstances alter cases. At the start,
Hermon emphasizes that if the gods had bestowed all their bounty
upon Porrex, even his elder brother would concede that 'birth should
yield to worthiness' (87). At the conclusion, he argues that conventional moral standards cannot be applied to the will and behaviour of
monarchs:

> Know ye, that lust of kingdoms hath no law.
> The gods do bear and well allow in kings,
> The things that they abhor in rascal routs.
> ...
> Murders and violent thefts in private men
> Are heinous crimes and full of foul reproach;
> Yet none offense, but decked with glorious name
> Of noble conquests in the hands of kings.
>
> (143–5; 152–5)

One might share C. O. McDonald's caution here at similar moments in
Euripidean and Senecan drama, where 'moral maxims are the last refuge

of the scoundrel...[they] indicate a deep-rooted perversion of values in the character using them which invites us to make a moral judgment of him and to assign to his arguments the more opprobrious values contained in the designation "sophistic"'.[42] It is clear that Hermon's advice *is* dangerous counsel, tempting Ferrex into defiance of his father's will and it is rejected as such. Yet the scene may be 'sophistic' in the deeper sense that McDonald argued Renaissance dramatists also inherited from Seneca, that is, it presents serious and convincing argumentation between opposed characters in a 'mature rhetorical dialectic' which demands careful adjudication.[43] It is difficult to dismiss Hermon's view entirely; any appraisal of the realities of power would have to acknowledge its force. He is applying reason of state to the chronically insecure conditions of political life, and opening an unsanctioned possibility as an equally intelligent response to this. The effect of this in a drama where apparently 'moralistic' responses can lead to disaster has its own compulsion.

3

It has become common to see Norton and Sackville as 'Protestant debaters', but perhaps the second term here needs as much emphasis as the first.[44] Either as individuals, or in the process of collaboration, the authors may have shared the common national experience, according to John Stow, of being 'wonderfully divided in opinions' over a political solution to the succession.[45] Hence, perhaps, *Gorboduc*'s interest in opposed arguments. In this respect, the experience of the 'succession crisis' needs to be recognized as affecting the composition of the play in complex ways. *Gorboduc* is as committed to investigating the effect of such a crisis on the practice of counsel as it is to proposing a solution to it. Both writers may also have been far-sighted enough to realize that, even if a royal marriage was contracted and an heir produced, the future was still full of hazard and this would necessitate continuous and careful deliberation.[46] The need for more dispassionate forms of political discourse demanded by Sir Nicholas Bacon did not mean that the status of language in *Gorboduc* became more reassuring. Indeed, the nonsectarian ethos of the play allowed both dramatists to explore how even the most deliberate use of speech can be affected by historical circumstances. In this respect the discourse of counsel, the antithesis of sedition, is also shown to have an uncertain relationship to virtue.[47] This occurs not only when counsel fails or becomes corrupt but it is intrinsic to those pressures exerted by the contingencies of history. It is this abiding temporal uncertainty and its consequences for speech that the form of the play aspires to recreate. As the later chapters of this study will demonstrate, Shakespeare's plays are also involved in a wide-ranging scrutiny of speech intended to order or disrupt the common-wealth. The scope of this also derives, in part, from their engagement with the fullness and complexity of historical circumstances.

This capacity for rhetorical enquiry needs more emphasis in our current understanding of Renaissance historiography. Recent interpret-ations of this have stressed its practical utility, an interpretation that has considerable sanction from the period's own commentary.[48] Thomas Norton described how 'a reader of histories digesteth every mater into his right place and to his right purpose, and thereof he layeth up the store of wisedome for himselfe, and counsell for other...he discerneth and judgeth rightly of thinges present, and foreseeth wisely of thinges to come'.[49] For Jacques Amyot, the translator of Plutarch used by Sir Thomas North in his influential English version of *The Lives of the Noble Grecians and Romanes* (1579), history 'teacheth us to judge of things present, and to foresee things to come'. Amyot emphasized that his-torical reading refined the power of prudential judgment and rendered more acute the discernment of constructive potential in any situation. It provided a source of honest counsel:

> So as it is not possible for any case to rise either in peace or warre, in publike or private affaires, but that the person which shall have diligently red, well conceived, and throughly remembred histories, shall find matter in them whereat to take light, and counsell whereby to resolve himselfe to take a part, or to geve advice unto others, how to choose in doutfull and daungerous cases that, which may be for their most proffit, and in time to find out to what poynt the matter will come if it be well handled.[50]

Lorna Hutson has suggested that the significance of reading skill and prudential judgement were connected to the experience of political crisis in the sixteenth century. They were 'related aspects of a notion of government predicated on the assumption that human affairs are always in a state of volatility, indeed of emergency'.[51]

It is worth pausing to consider whether this model of understanding applies as comprehensively to *dramatized* history, especially when it is cast in a tragic mode. However conscious Norton and Sackville were of an 'emergency', and, elsewhere, of the utility of history to evaluate it, *Gorboduc* does not perceive prudential activity 'as a method for the emplotment or reinterpretation of circumstances in the interests of a fortunate end'.[52] More daringly, the final act of the play might be adduced as a critical commentary on the idea of exemplary history.

Indeed, Eubulus laments explicitly the inefficacy of history. Nothing in the many admonitions against rebellion recorded in 'so many books, so many rolls / Of ancient time' (5.2.3–4) and inscribed upon the bodies of traitors succeeds in deterring popular anger (1–14). This is a curious, even self-cancelling, moment in the play and demonstrates the need for a more subtle approach to its didacticism. We discover also that the two beliefs attributed most frequently to the authors – opposition to 'foreign thraldom' and support for a parliamentary settlement of the succession – are both made by Arostus (115–22; 157–64). The authority of the latter is, of course, compromised by the disastrous consequences of his earlier counsel and neither of these points is reinforced by Eubulus. In his final oration, Eubulus dissents explicitly from his fellow counsellor's faith in parliament in the circumstances of ongoing revolt and uncertain legitimacy: 'though it be assembled by consent, / Yet is not likely with consent to end' (255–6).

The issue of uncertain authority continues to be expressed, rather than resolved, in the sophistic, self-qualifying dialogue of the play. In particular, historical evidence provides no certain means of arbitrating continuing disagreements over political solutions. As an historian, Eubulus's understanding is constrained by his own entanglement in events. His analysis of how the civil war arose is abrupt: 'Hereto it comes when kings will not consent / To grave advice, but follow wilful will' (234–5). As we have seen this evades a number of crucial questions, not only concerning Gorboduc's will, but also the quality of the 'grave advice' he received. Eubulus is thus implicated in the very failure to learn from history he attributes to others. Similarly, his deliberative address to the present crisis is seen to have limits; again events outrun their estimation. The solution he proposes to the popular revolt recommends a cunning piece of rhetorical manipulation (5.1.86–114), yet, it succeeds only in part; a third of the rebels remain intransigent (5.2.41–9). Moreover, Eubulus's violent hostility towards the popular uprising blinds him to the greater danger of aristocratic ambition presented by Albany. History continues in *Gorboduc* with no sign of resolution.

The relationship between counsel and history plotted by *Gorboduc* depicts it as both essential and fraught with difficulty. By meditating upon the limits of counsel the play presents history as threatening always to displace the most constructive as well as the most sectarian understanding of it. One conclusion might be, therefore, that the play's

controversial method reflects a largely sceptical attitude that emphasizes how historical contradictions are resistant to practical resolution.[53]
There is an alternative interpretation, however, of the play's formal
complexity that also enables a new appraisal of its political intentions.
A recent critic argues that Shakespeare's history plays intend to 'cast
their audiences in the roles of historians'; this means they must view
'events from a variety of perspectives' and struggle 'to make sense of
conflicting reports and evidence' (Rackin, p. 28). Such an analysis also
brings us closer to Norton and Sackville's dramatic intentions. Here too,
the audience is not presented with a single moral, but is shocked by the
difficulties it experiences, along with the protagonists, in diagnosing
and overcoming circumstances. Furthermore, there is a strong political
implication in this technique. Recent analyses of the Elizabethan polity
have emphasized a crucial division in attitude between the queen and
the broader political nation: 'She wanted to exercise imperial authority
in her own right, as her father had done. They wanted that authority
to be an attribute of the crown, or of the collective capacity of "her
majesty's supreme government".'[54] Elizabeth's reaction to the 'lycence'
she had granted in receiving the first parliamentary petition that sought
her marriage might be taken as typifying this conflict. The queen
welcomed that it:

> conteineth no limytacion of place or person. If it had bene otherwise,
> I muste nedes have myslyked it verie muche and thought it in yow
> a verie greate presumpton, being unfitting and altogether unmete for
> yow to require them that may commande...or suche to bynd and
> lymite whose duties are to obaye, or to take upon yow to drawe my
> love to your lykinges or frame my will to your fantasies.[55]

This strict sense of the limits to be placed upon political dialogue is
qualified by *Gorboduc's* presentation of the monarch's word. Royal
speech acts have no more percipience than those of subjects and, more
strikingly, catastrophic consequences unfold from decisions taken by
the crown.[56]

Yet, *Gorboduc's* interest in language, and in the political pressures
upon it, is more complex and self-critical than this: the play is difficult
to codify easily as an exemplary history. Peter Wentworth beseeched in
1576 that God 'endue her Majestie with his wisdome wherby she may
discerne faithfull advice from traytorous sugred speeches, and to send her
Majestie a melting yielding heart unto sound counsell'.[57] It is a demanding feature of *Gorboduc's* composition that making such discrimination

is made difficult for *all* concerned with the political well-being of the country. Again, it is useful to compare its historical method to more 'advanced' examples of the history play. Norton and Sackville, like Shakespeare, demonstrate a sophisticated awareness of 'the extent to which all use of the past in guiding public action is shaped by rhetoric'.[58] Circumstances change and history can be cited and addressed in a plurality of ways. This requires self-restraint and a willingness to accept qualification from both counsellors and those they counsel. It is in this sense that the play values outspokenness and the necessity for dialogue and debate. Paradoxically, it is by recognizing the fallibility of public, deliberative rhetoric that Norton and Sackville demonstrate the continuing necessity for it. Thomas Norton, often assumed to be the more dogmatic of the partnership, insisted, for example, on the need for disputation: 'where manie men be, there must be manie myndes, and in consultacions convenient it is to have contrary opinions, contrary reasoninges and contradiccions, thereby the rather to wrest out the best'.[59] As J. G. A. Pocock has argued, the necessity for a structure of shared power is often defined by demonstrating how individual instances of language can be modified, appropriated and be subjected to useful scrutiny and reply.[60] *Gorboduc* embodies both the necessity for this principle of dialogue and debate and the difficulties that attend it. The play is at its most challenging in showing how difficult it can be to evaluate 'contrary' speech.

In the next chapter, we will see how profound this interest in counsel was in Elizabethan historical theatre during the period of its most intense and extraordinary development in the public playhouses of the 1590s. The example, however, is a contentious one: Robert Greene's curious play, *The Scottish History of James IV*. Whether or not this work is a history play will be the first question explored and it will be argued that it was always intended to enjoy an equivocal relationship to the genre. Greene's critical response towards 'chronicle drama' is also the cue for his most searching political reflection and, as with Norton and Sackville, this is expressed most fully in relation to the issues of turbulent speech, self-restraint and counsel. Like *Gorboduc*, Greene suggests that the most substantial threats that arise from language originate with authority itself rather than challenges to it. In *James IV*, political disintegration follows swiftly once the free expression of counsel has been obstructed. Consequently, the play's engagement with the latitudes and limits of speech is at its most forceful when depicting the monarch's language and its resistance to dialogue and modification. This comprises one of the most significant concerns of the history play: the quality of the monarch's word as it seeks to unify the nation or as it provokes division and disorder. Both these aspects of monarchical discourse are the subject of extensive scrutiny in Shakespearean drama. In this respect, Greene is engaged with one of the great subjects of the history play and this and other ways in which his work should be seen as a contribution to the genre will now be discussed.

3
Language, Temperance and the Nation in Robert Greene's *The Scottish History of James the Fourth*

The most famous sentence Robert Greene never wrote continues to dominate and to cloud his reputation:

> for there is an upstart Crow, beautified with our feathers, that with his *Tygers hart wrapt in a Players hyde*, supposes he is as well able to bombast out a blanke verse as the best of you: and beeing an absolute *Johannes fac totum*, is in his owne conceit the onely Shake-scene in a countrey.[1]

Now this statement rebounds only to its author's discredit. It serves as a further ironic example, therefore, of a process that fascinated Norton and Sackville: how time and context outwit the intentions of language. Greene's rancour is normally attributed to artistic and social jealousy; he shares the snobbery of the 'University wit' towards the presumption of a common player. Such outbursts are also ascribed to a life that resembled one of his own prodigal fictions: hectic self-indulgence succeeded by an overwrought pursuit of repentance. Yet, as D. Allen Carroll has demonstrated, Greene is unlikely to have been the author of the posthumous *Groatsworth of Wit* (1592) which contains this notorious statement, although it may correspond to attitudes he was known to hold.[2] Even if these remarks do characterize Greene's antipathy towards Shakespeare, they now seem less simply vindictive. As Scott McMillin and Sally-Beth MacLean have argued in their study of *The Queen's Men and their Plays* (1998) – a company which performed many of Greene's plays including, most probably, *The Scottish History of James the Fourth* (c. 1590–1; printed 1598) – the feeling that Shakespeare had appropriated, even plagiarized, the work of others is not entirely groundless. In their account, it was the Queen's Men who pioneered the English history play as a popular dramatic form and it was Shakespeare who capitalized upon their efforts.[3] Greene's stance towards presumption as well as his attitude towards Shakespeare and the history play could bear more dispassionate scrutiny.

This chapter will argue that a deeper understanding of Greene's drama can be achieved by pursuing his interest in graceless or improper speech. In this respect, the dramatist's attention to the strengths and deficiencies of language and their impact upon public life is as pronounced and self-conscious as Norton and Sackville. This also illuminates some important features of historical drama, as well as Greene's relationship to the example of Marlowe and Shakespeare. Yet Greene's drama provides an idiosyncratic, even an indefensible, route into the historical theatre of the Elizabethan public playhouses. For many commentators, *James IV*'s relationship to serious-minded historical drama is, at best, negligible; at worst, non-existent. On this view, the play is composed in a deliberately unpredictable, even profligate, manner calculated only to appease an appetite for theatrical sensation. This idea of *James IV* as a free-floating and purely imaginative indulgence has a considerable pedigree. In a formative gesture, Sir George Buc – a keen collector and annotator of play texts throughout the 1590s and later both Master of the Revels and a distinguished historian[4] – traduced its status. Buc struck through half the title of the Quarto now held by the British Library, that is, its claim to present a history 'of James the fourth, slaine at Flodden', and amended this scornfully to read 'or rather fiction of English & Scotish matters comicall'.[5] Buc's judgement initiates a long tradition of disparagement towards such plays (and others) as containing 'hardly any thought about history at all'.[6] As has long been known, the narrative of *James IV* derives from a prose romance by Cinthio which he gleaned most probably from a French translation of *Hecatommithi* (1583/4); alternatively, it may imitate Cinthio's own adaptation of the same episode in his neo-classical play, *Arrenopia* (1583).[7] It is unlikely that this reading was supplemented by any consultation of historical sources and the author appears immune to embarrassment in this respect: James IV is presented to us in 1520, seven years after his death in battle at Flodden, and the Tudor dynasty (although not the 'English king') is ignored defiantly throughout. The play's lack of historical specificity – only the titles 'the English King', 'the Scottish King', are used for its royal protagonists – and its deployment of imaginary figures within a largely fictitious plot, may imply that its own title was purely quixotic or one sanctioned only by its publisher in 1598, eager to attract an established readership for historical drama.[8] *James IV*'s disengagement from issues of context extends to more topical matters as well: despite some industrious argument, the claim that it provides a subtle analogical commentary on the Scottish court of James VI remains unconvincing.[9]

This apparent lack of any serious-minded historical orientation has not added lustre to *James IV*'s reputation. In any respect, as Paul Dean has argued, 'pseudo' or 'romance' histories, plays 'which incorporate historical personages within a wholly imaginary, usually comic framework', have long been disparaged by comparison to 'true' or 'serious' examples of the genre.[10] Yet, as the same critic has demonstrated, romance motifs – supernaturalism, love-triangles, disguise – are pervasive within historical drama of all kinds, including Shakespeare's works. Moreover, such wholly imaginative theatrical modes offer an alternative means of both presenting and perceiving history to that offered by chronicle material.[11] Yet, despite this insight, romance histories remain neglected and the imaginative licence of the form has been seen as well-suited to the erratic and wilful temperament imputed to Greene.[12] This genre, it is assumed, allowed him to avoid the demands of historical research, to indulge extravagant forms of wish-fulfilment, and to pander to crass popular sentiment.

There is a way of reconceiving Greene's work, however, and of re-establishing its relationship to Elizabethan historical drama; this enriches critical understanding of the play and of the contested development of the genre. Again, this chapter will argue that the identity of the history play benefits from being perceived as complex, multifaceted and, in important respects for Greene, unresolved. In short, *James IV* contributes to a dialogue about the political direction of the genre. In her influential analysis of 'the king disguised' motif, Anne Barton suggests that 'Elizabethan drama seems to have developed to a large extent through a curious kind of dialogue among specific plays...the plays that have survived from this period are in a sense projections and records of these long vanished relationships and artistic controversies.' Barton nominates the history play as the subject of the most 'consequential dialogue' in Elizabethan theatrical culture and Shakespeare as its most commanding participant. It was Shakespeare who displaced the sentimental 'comical history' pioneered by the Queen's Men, in favour of the darker possibilities offered by 'tragical history': a 'serious and politically a somewhat incendiary examination into the nature of kingship'.[13] We might adopt Barton's idea of a shaping dialogue being at

work in Elizabethan historical drama, without sharing her disparagement of plays such as *James IV*, to re-examine the intentions of Greene's
drama.

The premise of this chapter is that Greene's indifference towards the
chronicles, and his emplotment of history as romance, constitutes his
response to, and critique of, the emergent theatrical genre of Elizabethan
'chronicle history'. This aspect of his work is manifested most clearly
in the treatment of language in *James IV*. In particular, his work is in
dialogue with Marlowe's *Tamburlaine* (1587/8), with its stress on heroic
self-assertion and imperial domination, and with Shakespeare's *The First
Part of the Contention* [*2 Henry VI*] (c. 1590/1), with its emphasis on
the distinctive experience of the English nation; to these issues I will
return.[14] This is not to argue that Greene's opposition to these works is
well-founded, he may well have remained obstinately inattentive to
their more complex and self-questioning elements, but that it stems
from a more coherent ethical position than is often assumed. In this
respect, it is notable that *James IV* does contain narrative features and
political concerns that are significant in both earlier and contemporary
instances of historical theatre. It depicts, for example, international and
dynastic conflict between England and Scotland leading to war and
political schism within the latter country. Greene is deeply concerned
with the increasing role of Elizabethan historical drama in presenting
narratives with a specifically national character. Furthermore, it also
contains aspects of language that, as we have seen, are of great import
in sixteenth-century dramatizations of the past: the role of counsel,
for example, that predominates in *Gorboduc* and, especially, the role
of monarchical speech in precipitating political crisis. The latter topic
serves again as the catalyst for *James IV*'s most concentrated attention
to those patterns of 'ordering and enforcing' that threaten or sustain
the life of the state. In the terms suggested by this study, we can also
identify in the complex form of *James IV*, Greene's quizzical interest in
how historical material is made to serve homiletic purposes, as well
as an acute sense of the mutability of circumstances. The dramatist's
hostility towards those theatrical *moderni* who have formed our conception of the history play does not involve relinquishing much of
the genre's staple material, but its reshaping. Similarly, the romance
form of *James IV* distinguishes the expression of its political interests
not their abandonment: the play refuses to allow chronicle material to
contain its utopian imagining or to dilute its critique of kingship or
myths of patriotic destiny. This can be made clear by considering its
treatment of three central and interrelated topics: impropriety of speech,

kingship and nationhood. All of these topics are presented in relation to the ideal of temperance and this affects markedly the play's distinctive approach to the subject-matter of the history play and its treatment of language and politics.

1

Uncivil monarchy

Greene was not devoid of historical curiosity. In his most famous play, *Friar Bacon and Friar Bungay* (1589–90; printed 1594), it has long been recognized that he read the extensive material concerning the reign of Henry III in Holinshed's *Chronicles* with great care, despite its obscure and somewhat uninspiring character.[15] In *James IV*, there is a remnant of this in the play's idiosyncratic, perhaps whimsical, recollections of real historical events and, as has been noted, its evocation of the broader interests of other historical drama. The play certainly resonates with the implications of Flodden, that is, it describes how Anglo-Scottish enmity results in invasion, war and Scottish defeat. Most tellingly, it recollects that other most noticeable feature of James IV's reign: his marriage to Margaret Tudor in 1503. *James IV* begins with the coronation of the English princess, Dorothea, as Queen of Scots and it continues to recount the (apparent) failure of this to surmount ancient hostilities. The Scottish king pursues his illicit passion for Ida under the corrupt tutelage of the 'Machiavellian' counsellor, Ateukin; together they plot the assassination of James's new queen. Elsewhere, the English lord, Eustace, offers us a more encouraging account of Anglo-Scots relations with the successful wooing of Ida. Oblivious to this frustration of his desires, James's reckless indulgence of his will results in the disintegration of his court: his counsellors desert him and Dorothea is forced to flee disguised as a boy (provoking an episode of erotic confusion). James's wife is attacked subsequently by an assassin commissioned by her husband and is assumed to be dead. Eventually, the English king is informed of his daughter's fate at James's hands and he pursues a bloody invasion of Scotland. In the end, romance conventions save the day and the apparently ordained course of history is rewritten: James's English wife reappears to redeem her husband and to foster a new and deeper unity between the two countries. (*James IV* also uses a frame structure: an induction and a sequence of choric interludes interleave with and comment upon these events; the significance of this will be discussed in the conclusion to this chapter).

The shape and content of this narrative indicate the nature of Greene's political interests. He is engaged primarily with what we might term the 'strong king' dilemma and this illuminates his response to Marlowe. Before returning to this issue, it is important to grasp the perspective from which Greene is presenting and evaluating his material: this lies in his interest in the virtue of temperance.[16] Temperance has endured some belittling from contemporary critics who have seen it as embodying the bad faith that pervades Renaissance ethical discourse. Its emphasis upon moderation, self-discipline and the regulation of appetite has been posited as helping fashion a versatile, pragmatic subject ready to repress unruly impulses in the self (and in others). Taking their cue from Foucault's history of inhibition, temperance has been perceived as both a product and a facilitator of the moral regime required by an increasingly colonial and mercantile society. Self-contained, socially adept, pragmatic, the temperate subject inculcates the skills required for success in a nascent market economy: good timing, plausibility and opportunism.[17] Yet, as the classical scholar Helen North has demonstrated, temperance was subject to a complex process of debate; this included its use as an ethical standard that held authority to account.[18] As Jennifer Richards has suggested, the virtue could also be used to criticize autocratic self-assertion and hubristic manliness.[19]

It is this more radical aspect of the virtue that engages Greene in *James IV*. Furthermore, this ideal afforded him a vantage-point from which to evaluate the responsibilities, aptitudes, and obligations of princes and governors throughout his dramatic works. Werner Senn has noted that *Friar Bacon and Friar Bungay* contains 'a political and moral note entirely absent from his source'. This describes Prince Edward's overcoming of his tyrannical lust and his acceptance of how inordinate personal desires must be regulated so that he can honour his public duties.[20] Similarly, Charles Hieatt has analysed the same play's humanistic conception of 'the good ruler's emotional integrity and self-control' embodied most clearly in 'the hero's crowning virtue of self-mastery, of conquering the love within himself'.[21] This concern with the constraint of autocratic will lends force to the use of romance form and the treatment of language in *James IV*. Greene's interest in issues of linguistic and moral decorum is central both to his political concerns and his engagement with the material of the history play. As with the discourse of counsel in *Gorboduc*, temperate speech and its opposite provide the occasion for *James IV*'s most forceful instances of critical reflection.

The political action of *James IV* begins with a masterfully orchestrated scene at the Scottish court.[22] It begins with the newly achieved alliance between England and Scotland, secured by the marriage between James and Dorothea, and adorned with the language of peace and neighbourhood, of hospitality bestowed and received:

> *King of Scots*: First, laws of friendship did confirm our peace,
> Now both the seal of faith and marriage bed,
> The name of father, and the style of friend

(1.1.5–7)

The gradually intensifying relationship between the two countries is confirmed by the coronation of Dorothea as Queen of Scots. At this juncture, she is immediately admonished by her father to guard against the damage caused by 'coy, detracting tongues' at court (43–56). Such precepts are offered in a spirit of both political and paternal care, although their anxiety towards the damage words can do seems remote from the prevailing atmosphere of joy and festivity. Yet, in a startling breach of decorum reminiscent of a play saturated by Greene's influence, *The Winter's Tale*, the Scottish king does indeed destroy this charmed mood with a drastic failure of decorum: his dismaying confession of 'the treason of my new-vowed love' for Ida (74–91). The corrupt quality of this longing is emphasized by its conception during the king's own matrimonial service (81–4) and it leads him to conceive of his marital (and political) union as an imprisonment. James conflates the satisfaction of his own will with the nation's well-being: 'wretched king, thy nuptial knot is death, / Thy bride the breeder of thy country's ill' (75–6). As the English king warned, the turbulent and competitive nature of life at court can distort the use of language and lead to the culpable misinterpretation of virtue. James describes his own desires as unspeakable; this requires the constraint of his speech and the pursuit of secrecy and silence:

> Yet fear and love hath tied thy ready tongue
> From blabbing forth the passions of thy mind,
> Lest fearful silence have in subtle looks
> Bewrayed the treason of my new-vowed love.

(85–8)

This desire is immediately pursued by the king, but Ida repels his discreet advances with a strongly worded critique of the erotic and moral peril intrinsic to the royal household: 'The farther from the court I were removed, / The more, I think, of heaven I were beloved' (109–10).

The play begins, therefore, with an archetypal example of intemperance centring upon the person and will of the monarch: this unfolds in his increasingly autocratic language and in his rash and selfish actions. The setting of this within the context of matrimonial rites and the coronation only increases the scale of its indecorum. As Tom McAlindon explains, ceremonial traditions in the Renaissance displayed 'solemn signs of good intent towards others or towards agreed values, codes and duties...ceremonies constitute that area of speech and action where propriety is most expected'.[23] 'Brother of Scotland', says the English king, 'love me in my child; / You greet me well, if so you will her good' (65–6). The solemnity of the new status and identity that has been bestowed upon both Dorothea and, indeed, James himself, is lost upon the Scottish king. Furthermore, the latter's absence of moral understanding leaves him vulnerable to the linguistic manipulation of others. It is at this juncture that the stage-Machiavel, Ateukin, one of those 'men of art, that rise by indirection' (1.2.49), and Greene's major addition to his source, seizes the advantage offered by the king's sudden mood of introspection.

Ateukin swiftly asserts himself within the king's affections by deciphering his deepest wants and, in a bravura display of dissimulation, by forswearing the motives that truly animate him (1.1.218–35). James's neurotic desire for self-communion after his marriage is related to his sudden fear of public scrutiny: 'Now am I free from sight of common eye, / Where to myself I may disclose the grief / That hath too great a part in mine affects' (155–7). His favourite releases the king from this linguistic solipsism and together they create an amoral world where any aspiration can be expressed. That James's desires have indeed spiralled out of control is made explicit: 'for fair Ida will I hazard life, / Venture my kingdom, country, and my crown: / Such fire hath love to burn a kingdom down' (170–2). Again the play stresses that a primary consequence of this is his immediate and demeaning vulnerability to poor counsel; his own act of self-deception leaves him ready to be deceived. James wishes to act 'and yet the world not see't' (180); Ateukin allows him to realize this possibility by entering a world of conspiracy that supersedes the demeaning demands made by 'common' concepts of morality and obligation. In this respect, Ateukin plays the archetypal role of the upstart favourite upon the Elizabethan stage: scheming, amoral, protean, swamping the monarch with artificial, insinuating language and drowning out channels of free and truthful advice.[24] This helps foster in James a dangerous sense of monarchical prerogative. In Ateukin's words: 'You have the sword and sceptre in your hand; / You are the king, the state depends on you; / Your will is law' (247–9). The favourite succeeds in securing a radical diminution in the efficacy of counsel; his ornate language of compliment corrodes the integrity of those who both bestow and receive it. Ateukin addresses the king in a copious register of flattery whose highlights include: 'Most gracious and imperial majesty', 'mighty potentate', 'I'll kiss your highness' feet', and the cheerfully unambiguous, 'my god on earth'.[25] Through this discourse, he claims to 'know the means / To work your grace's *freedom* and your love' (218–19; emphasis added). By the rehearsal of his own servility, Ateukin succeeds in subordinating the king to his own will. Such language also contaminates its object as it is echoed in the king's slavish admiration for his new servant: 'Thou talkest wonders...What god art thou, composed in human shape...to decide our doubts?' (211; 216–17). The king's determination to 'exalt' his servant as the sole means of achieving his freedom is given a fatal sense of consequence in Ateukin's insinuation concerning Dorothea's fate: 'if the lamb should let the lion's way, / By my advice the lamb should lose her life' (255–6).

The opening scene of *James IV* illustrates the drastic consequences, personal and political, of intemperance. This confirms that the play is a serious-minded contribution to a dialogue over the ideological direction of Elizabethan drama. In his splenetic outburst in *Perimedes the Blacke-Smith* (1588), Greene excoriates 'two Gentlemen poets' who had criticized him for his failure to write like Marlowe:

> for that I could not make my verses jet upon the stage in tragicall buskins, everie worde filling the mouth like the faburden of Bo-Bell, daring God out of heaven with that Atheist *Tamburlan*, or blaspheming with the mad preest of the sonne.[26]

Interestingly, in relation to Anne Barton's argument, Greene is explicit about his refusal to compose 'tragicall' drama. Most observers have sympathized, however, with the Gentleman poets; if only he could have written like his rival. Yet, there is a larger issue here than crude rivalry and one that features significantly in his dramaturgy: language and the propriety that should regulate it. If we follow Greene's thinking about Marlowe into the debatable territory of the *Groatsworth of Wit*, understood (conjecturally) as elaborating attitudes consistent with his views, we find not only the memorable confession of the atheism he once shared with Marlowe, but this comment on the latter's fondness for 'Machiavellian pollicy':

For if *Sic volo, sic iubeo* ['As I wish, so I command'], hold in those that are able to commaund: and if it be lawfull *Fas et nefas* to do any thing that is beneficiall; onely Tyrants should possesse the earth, and they striving to exceed in tyrannie, should each to other be a slaughter man; till the mightiest outliving all, one stroke were lefte for Death, that in one age mans life should end.[27]

Reading Greene as a writer who abhorred tyranny and the degraded consequences of power-worship can help to elicit a more interesting response to his work. If David Riggs is correct and the Elizabethan history play developed as 'a visual and rhetorical display of heroic deeds',[28] *James IV*'s dialogue with the genre becomes more consequential. The heroic tenor of Elizabethan historical drama marks a significant break with the earlier theatrical uses of the past examined here: these stressed the vulnerability of the human aspiration for order. This new emphasis appears to have disconcerted, even dismayed, Greene. In response, individual or national displays of martial fortitude, fearless aspiration, and rhetorical mastery find only critical representation in *James IV*; as does the exalted self-conception of worldly majesty. In contrast, the play establishes that kingship itself, rather than those forces opposed to it, is the most dangerous source of intemperate speech and action, reminding us of Clare McEachern's contention that 'the chief demon of Tudor political theory...was the threat of monarchic power'.[29] If Marlowe's *Tamburlaine* sought, in the words of one recent critical account, 'a dominated audience...impermeable to moral considerations',[30] his rival's aversion to this form of theatre may derive from a subtler viewpoint. In the person of the Scottish king, we see monarchy demeaned by lust and embracing forms of corrupt advice that produce a wilful and self-interested absolutism; this threatens his personal and political survival. Destructive speech is not perceived as a force opposed to authority, but as intrinsic to it. In this respect, *James IV* locates linguistic and behavioural disorder not in subjects who challenge the integrity of the crown – traitors, seditionists, rumour-mongers – but as a dangerous potential within kingship itself.[31]

Greene is adopting, therefore, one of the period's most significant bodies of language theory, the classical discourse of decorum, to arrive at his own evaluation of the heroic material of the history play. In *De Officiis*, one of the most influential of all classical treatises, Cicero advised that nature assigns to us all 'the roles of steadfastness, temperance, self-control, and considerateness of others';[32] the success of our social and political lives depends on our ability to act in accordance with this capacity. In this account, temperance is either sustained by virtuous speech that strengthens social bonds or it is obliterated by selfish uses of language; this places a particular responsibility upon those in authority. If a ruler loses respect for reciprocal obligations, as well as the power of self-restraint, this leads to more drastic consequences than a merely personal failure. In a forbidding quotation from a lost play Cicero emphasizes the dangers inherent to absolute power: 'There is no fellowship inviolate, / No faith is kept, when kingship is concerned' (I.viii.26). A key method of containing this potential lies in the systematic inculcation of decorum. This is understood as language and actions that are fitting and honourable: 'every action ought to be free from undue haste or carelessness; neither ought we to do anything for which we cannot assign a reasonable motive; for in these words we have practically a definition of duty' (I.xxix.101). We must, Cicero counsels, achieve a consistent propriety in our use of language and reflect critically upon our success (or otherwise): 'in this respect we should not let actors display more practical wisdom than we have' (I.xxxi.114). The constant practice of linguistic and personal self-control by those in authority will help to sustain a greater degree of social cohesion.

Connecting Greene's play to this complex system of ethical reflection upon language does much to illuminate its deepest concerns. *James IV* explores the growing threat of improper language and the failures of responsibility that produce and accompany this from the perspective offered by temperance. This value is found to be chronically wanting at the heart of authority and Ateukin's rhetorical diminishment of the ethical restraints that apply to monarchy is allowed to continue unabated. Again the play stresses the abuse of speech this involves. Ateukin's servant describes his master's command of language in ways that measure his remoteness from Cicero's ideal of eloquence by direct allusion to it:

> he that heareth my master's counsel is already possessed of happiness; nay, which is more miraculous, as the noble man in his infancy lay in his cradle, a swarm of bees laid honey on his lips in token of his eloquence, for *melle dulcior fluit oratoria*.
>
> (4.5.22–6)[33]

Ateukin demonstrates his own understanding of how this classical ideal nourishes civility by developing his thesis that 'it is no murder in a king / To end another's life to save his own' (35–6). To prove this case he uses Aristotle's doctrine of the mean in the most depraved sense: 'Of evil needs we must choose the least: / Then better were it that a woman died / Than all the help of Scotland should be blent' (42–4). Thus Aristotle's infinitely subtle and demanding concept of ethical awareness and practice – 'an ever-moving, elusive point of natural perfection situated between extremes of excess and deficiency'[34] – is used to rationalize homicide. In this manner, the claustrophobic relationship between king and favourite culminates in their most drastic breach of obligation: their plan to assassinate Dorothea. This is accompanied by Ateukin's most fulsome statement of his political credo:

> Why, prince...
> For you are not as common people be,
> Who die and perish with a few men's tears;
> But if you fail, the state doth whole default,
> The realm is rent in twain in such a loss.
>
> (35–40)

The king concurs with this, arguing that the guilt that restrains his violent desire has succeeded in lodging a 'tyrant' in his breast; again, both the country and he will benefit from his liberation. This possibility is conceived by him in rapturous terms as an ecstatic (and here defiling) moment of Marlovian consummation: 'I, in touching of her milk-white mould, / Will think me deified in such a grace' (61–2). His transfiguring sexual union with Ida will allow him to transcend moral restraints and he instructs his servants to curb any public criticism:

> ...bring me tidings if thou canst perceive
> The least intent of muttering in my train;
> For either those that wrong thy lord or thee
> Shall suffer death.
>
> (66–9)

To prevent the dangerous potential of a single, overbearing will, Cicero favours, of course, a republican model of government whose active citizenry will protect the best interests of the commonwealth. Such a possibility appears entirely foreign to the monarchical dominion that prevails throughout *James IV*. Yet Jonathan Scott's recent observation concerning the 'intellectual pre-history of English republicanism' illuminates an important element of the play's political potential when we understand that the former hinged 'not upon external constitutional structures, but upon a partially internalised moral philosophy of self-government'.[35] The language of the commonwealth is certainly pervasive in *James IV* and it is used to present important episodes of rhetorical and practical resistance to the king. Furthermore, there is a strong gender bias to this presentation as both Ida and Dorothea exercise the 'manly' virtue of continence in comparison to the monarchic incivility they encounter. In this respect, they have achieved the rational regulation of appetite that distinguishes the temperate man, who in Thomas Elyot's words: 'desireth the thynge whiche he aught to desire, and as he aught to desyre, and whanne he aught to desire'.[36] Perhaps the most eloquent of these voices is that of Ida of Arran, the object of the king's illicit desires. She dismisses Ateukin's discourse of courtly compliment as a typical product of the unreal world of majesty: a 'means to draw the mind / From perfect good, and make true judgment blind' (2.1.5–6). Her response reminds the monarch of his duties and of his accountability to the commonwealth. In contrast to Ateukin's inflated address, 'fair countess', 'comely nymph' and so on, Ida's grasp upon practical and moral realties remains unshakable: 'Is he not married, sir, unto our queen?' (128). What matters in this scene is Ida's refusal to allow court language to distort her sense of proportion or value: in this respect, her keyword is 'virtue' (16; 42). This is used in contrast to the king's belief that he acts beyond the power of judgement: 'The world may shame to him account, / To be a king of men and worldly pelf, / Yet hath no power to rule and guide himself' (147–9). In this respect, Ida refuses to comply even 'in secret' or 'in private' (114; 134) with the king's will. It is the courtier's responsibility, she reminds him, to use language that will return him to moral sobriety: 'So counsel him, but soothe thou not his sin' (153). In common with a number of other characters, Ida asserts that there are limits to allegiance and the king cannot expect obedience to demands that are not virtuous. She formulates her belief in this principle, by reminding Ateukin that 'in duty I am his', but in relation to the lawless or unseemly 'good I will not deem him' (195–6).

This scene merges with the long lament of James's counsellors concerning the public repercussions of his private iniquity: 'the wrack of commonweal' (2.2.1). Unlike Gorboduc, James abandons even the pretence of consultation. Central to the social disarray this produces is the denial of free and truthful speech, as the counsellors lament to each other: 'cast rein upon thy tongue / ... reproof will breed a scar', 'fear shuts our mouths: we dare not speak' (20–1; 24). Here the term 'commonweal' runs like a binding thread throughout their deliberations; the obligation it demands reveals James's drastic abuse of office. The Bishop of St Andrews describes how the sole rationale for 'high estate' is the advantage it provides to 'discern the common harm' (35; 38). The

Scottish king has deserted these responsibilities, damaging himself and
his kingdom and creating the grounds for his own imminent 'over-
throw' due to his 'abject care of counsel':

> ...we cannot draw
> His eye or judgment to discern his faults,
> Since we have spake and counsel is not heard,
> I, for my part (let others as they list),
> Will leave the court and leave him to his will
>
>   (50–4)

As soon as the Bishop expresses to the king the 'certain signs of thine
incontinence' (129), James's fury demonstrates his absolute revulsion
from counsel as 'stays and lets to pleasure' that 'plague my thoughts'
(146); hence, he dismisses the last voices that speak of the 'commonweal' from his court. Indeed, the latter term itself passes into a degraded
state as it is uttered in flattery by Ateukin's servant – 'this commonweal
should have a great loss of so good a member as you are' (3.2.69–70) –
and by the favourite himself as he cultivates Dorothea's assassin (103).

James IV contains a subtle and sustained meditation on the virtue of
temperance and the rhetorical, moral and political consequences that
transpire when it fails to regulate the life of the state. The play locates
responsibility for this squarely with monarchy. Yet, Greene's interest in
this virtue, as well as his dialogue with other Elizabethan historical
drama, is more expansive than this. In particular, the threat from monarchic intemperance in *James IV* does not observe national boundaries
and it is depicted, in different ways, in the monarchies of both England
and Scotland. In the person of the English monarch, we witness the
workings of anger upon one who has both the most extensive authority
and means to prosecute it. The English invasion that consumes Scotland
in the final act is divested of any patriotic appeal; again Greene's detes-
tation of violence and domination is prominent.[37] This allows him to
offer an equally sceptical account, as we shall see, of national feeling
and its typical embodiment in the history play.

2

James IV and the romance of the union

Contemporary criticism has made us familiar with the escalation of
nationalist sentiment in the sixteenth century and especially with the

role of historiography and the Shakespearean history play in fostering and shaping this.[38] In an influential account, Richard Helgerson argues that for 'men born in the 1550s and 1560s, things English came to matter with a special intensity' and that 'Chronicle was the Ur-genre of national self-representation. More than any other discursive form, chronicle gave Tudor Englishmen a sense of their national identity.'[39] Such interpretations have emphasized that the audience's enlistment into the 'imagined community' of England also demanded the symbolic disciplining of foreign and uncivil speech.[40] In this respect, Tudor historical writing can certainly be mined for a rich seam of xenophobia in relation to Scotland understood as England's barbarous and untrustworthy neighbour.[41]

It is striking, however, how remote Greene (born 1558) is from conceiving of opposing kingdoms as civil and uncivil, or from any emphasis upon English superiority. *James IV* is thus also uncongenial to the current critical narrative surrounding the history play which stresses its rhetoric of national endeavour and the empathy this induces both for a heroic conception of English identity and kingship. As Anthony Esler observes of Greene's (post-Armada) prose work *The Spanish Masquerado* (1589): '[he] has no notion of a British imperial destiny in which his heroes are playing a role...He has no conception of the sacredness of the British [*sic*] way of life, of Anglo-Saxon blood, or the precious soil of England.'[42] His indifference to chronicle material is also connected to his doubts concerning theatre's role in stirring the 'national-popular' imagination. Some Tudor drama is undoubtedly in harmony with Thomas Elyot's assertion that reading the history of Roman conquests 'maye be taken [as] necessary instructions concernynge the warres, agayne Irisshemen or Scottes: who be of the same rudenes and wilde disposition, that the Suisses [Swiss] and Britons were in the time of Cesar'.[43] *James IV* refuses such distinctions. Shakespeare's *The First Part of the Contention* may well have appeared to Greene (perhaps unfairly) as promoting the English nation as the central object of historical attention given that its most intense episodes of pathos are provoked by the spectacle of national division. *James IV* perceives discord strictly in terms of monarchical self-assertion and this is combined with a marked inattention towards the specific institutions, temperaments or experiences of either England or Scotland. These emphases can be interpreted as expressing scepticism towards the disposition of other plays, rather than negligence. We might grasp his critical response to the place of national feeling in the history play through Bakhtin's idea of 'hidden polemic', a way of criticizing a given discourse by 'naming it, portraying, expressing, and only indirectly striking a blow...clashing with it, as it were, within the object itself'.[44] *James IV*'s lack of interest in nationality is determined by the dramatist's broader ethical awareness that civility, and its opposite, are not categories commensurate with opposing national identities, but potentialities which can imperil or ennoble any national community.

Greene's interest in temperance and self-conquest also governs his response to the related issue of nationhood; in this case he emphasizes the need for authority to be limited by a process of union. *James IV*'s vision of the relationship between England and Scotland as achieved, endangered and renewed turns upon a movement from intemperate speech and behaviour to more civil modes of expression and conduct. For both monarchs, this transition is predicated upon the relinquishing of ambitions and the forsaking of an appetite for dominance. The play, therefore, can be considered as a romance of the union, and of the civil potential of union, in both explicit and, as I shall illustrate, in more subtle and self-questioning ways. To begin to grasp the significance of this in *James IV*, it is important to note that the temperate or intemperate language of monarchy is charted throughout in terms of its responses to various kinds of union. The most deliberated aspect of the play's structure lies in its interlocking sequence of marital, familial and political unions and the pressure they are subjected to by the play's romance form. These relationships are endangered by an inadequate or distorted understanding of their potential and renewed by clarification of their significance. Central to these, and determining the fate of the others, is the King of Scots' perception of his marital union with the English princess, Dorothea. This relationship changes from being, at the outset, the medium by which a dynastic alliance is secured, to becoming, at its conclusion, a means of securing the submission of the male protagonist. Furthermore, it is the many-sidedness with which the play explores both the civil potential of union, as well as its limitations, that also distinguishes the political seriousness of its interest in history.

Thus, the play's second major instance of ungoverned monarchical will concerns the furious progress of the English invasion. This is prosecuted at its conclusion by the English king in revenge for his daughter's (assumed) death at James's hands. The play, however, cultivates no patriotic empathy from the audience; indeed, the spectacle of conquest arouses only distaste at another unfeeling exercise of autocratic will. Hence, we hear the language of the English king pitched in an extravagant register of feudal violence that is impelled solely by revenge:

> The plough shall furrow where the palace stood
> And fury shall enjoy so high a power
> That mercy shall be banished from our swords.
>
> (5.3.7–9)

Conquest appears in the play as injustice. We hear of 'Seven thousand Scottish lads [slain] not far from Tweed' (5.5.5) and the English king's avowal 'to heap thy land with carcasses' (5.6.68), 'kill, forage, spoil' (5.3.44). Such peremptory displays of will are subject to some of the play's most powerful strictures; the 'commonwealth' discourse of the play appears in this context as well. One of its most powerful expressions is present in the appeal of Douglas for the survival of the city of Dunbar: 'For what offence? For what default of ours?' (5.3.15). Douglas continues to provide a scathing critical account of the experience of victims caught up in the heedless pursuit of vengeance:

> What though the lion, king of brutish race,
> Through outrage sin, shall lambs be therefore slain?
> Or is it lawful that the humble die
> Because the mighty do gainsay the right?
>
> (5.3.19–22)

Dorothea's role is equally significant here as she becomes the subject of another display of masculine (and royal) will that is unwanted because of its repercussions upon the commonwealth. Here, the play stresses how her concept of marital union has obliterated any sense of patriotic heritage. Dorothea conceives any assault upon Scotland, or its king, as an assault upon her, an enlargement of perception that is beyond her husband or her father: 'As if they kill not me, who with him fight.../ One soul, one essence doth our weal contain. / What then can conquer him that kills not me?' (3.3.82; 86–7).

   This unillusioned depiction of English violence helps to reveal one of the play's most subtly treated themes: its interest in anger and its power to dispossess those subject to it of reason and civility. Anger afflicts a number of characters in the play, but its consequences are registered as most serious and degrading in those, like the English king, who have the most power, in Douglas's words, 'To prey on those that never did offend' (5.3.18). Again, we can compare Greene's evaluation of this issue with some crucial elements of classical ethical discourse. The play's treatment of anger and violence is cognate with the period's major classical treatise on this subject, Seneca's *De Ira*. This text emphasizes how a truly civil society is bound together by an ethic of mutuality, kindness and accommodation: 'Man is born for mutual help; anger for mutual destruction. The one desires union, the other disunion... For human life is founded on kindness and concord, and is bound into an alliance for common help, not by terror but by mutual love.'[45] In particular, Greene's drama shares with Seneca the perception that rage exists as an ethical threat beyond nationality: 'there lives no race that does not feel the goad of anger, which masters alike both Greeks and barbarians, and is no less ruinous to those who respect the law than to those who make might the only measure of their right'. This poses a significant threat, in Seneca and Greene alike, to the self-control of those in authority who must learn that 'no man is able to rule unless he can also submit to be ruled'.[46]

   It is through insights such as these that we can understand the significance of Greene's romance of union at the end of the play, conceived as a means of restraining the royal wilfulness depicted by it. Further warfare is only averted by the reappearance of Dorothea at the play's climax, restoring her marriage, the fellowship between the two kings and inspiring her own hopes for an enlarged and strengthened union between the two countries: 'These nations, if they join, / What monarch with his liegemen in this world / Dare but encounter you in open field?' (5.6.180–2). For both the English and the Scots king, the wonder generated by Dorothea's restoration involves confronting their mutual errors of will and a need to submit to correction. As James is reunited with the wife he had presumed assassinated, he now prays that his obedience will be sufficient: 'Or did I think submission were enough.../ You heavens can tell how glad I would submit' (154; 157). Greene envisions union as achieved through a principle of mutuality not incorporation and this requires a constant willingness to surrender the demands of the self for the benefit of another. It is this impulse for self-abnegation that directs the English king's closing attitude towards his daughter: 'I will embrace him for to favour thee; / I call him friend and take him for my son' (176–7). Far from concluding on a reassertion of vassalage through conquest, the union achieved in *James IV* presents animosities being surrendered on both sides; this recognition of both independence and relationship is of mutual benefit. The superficial dynastic alliance between the two countries is reconceived as a deeper form of political relationship, without a union of crowns, institutions or the suggestion of a greater British state. Instead, Greene conceives of union in a utopian, romance mode: a form of mutual recognition that does not obscure or subordinate the independence of either party. In *James IV*, this process is predicated on new forms of humane awareness and new modes of temperate address, especially on the part of its royal protagonists. This is consummated by the hard-won triumph of good will and renewed integrity over competitive and selfish desires; it is only then that the enduring cycle of national suspicion, betrayal and the resort to violence is broken and that distorted relationships between the two countries can be revised. Furthermore, Greene also implies that the development of a civil, rather than a political, union, will also benefit subjects, as it helps to tutor both rulers in a more humane form of kingship. In this way, Greene creates a counter-theatre to that of Marlowe's by grounding his history upon the importance of personal and linguistic self-abnegation. This also allows him to question, simultaneously, the priority given to patriotic feeling in the nascent genre of the history play, including Shakespeare's work. Yet, the reconciliation and renewal achieved at the play's conclusion has a dream-like quality. This derives principally from the return at the conclusion to the framework that comments upon (and distances) the entire action and it is with the significance of this device in Greene's dramaturgy that this chapter will conclude.

3

Arguments with history: the frame structure

Any comprehensive analysis of *James IV* must also recognize how the utopian quality of the play's conclusion is modified by its mode of presentation. Greene's complex, and self-conscious, method of *presenting* events indicates that his apparently blithe unconcern with historical sources is also bound up with a deeper scepticism on his part towards Renaissance historiography. The play invites reflection not only on the artificial emplotment of the events we witness, but also upon how easily the historical process can exceed the desires projected upon it. In respect of this motif, the play is, again, as self-conscious and complex in its awareness as *Gorboduc*. It is important to note that the narrative of *James IV* is in one sense not the work of Robert Greene at all. The events we see are presented as a play-within-a-play, controlled (and disputed) by figures that remain onstage throughout. In fact, the play is invented by Bohan, the 'stoical' Scot, or, more revealingly, the 'angry Scot' (Induction, 7), a disillusioned aristocrat who recounts this history as an argument that will justify his rejection of the world: 'I will show thee whay I hate the world by demonstration' (Induction, 105–6). Bohan's narrative originates as a response to the supernatural figure of Oberon who questions his separation from the world and who appears to exercise an alternative influence upon the narrative. The 'angry Scot' rejects Oberon's fellowship and maintains his stance of opposition to the world by recounting his personal experience of disillusionment. Hence, 'fair words and large promises' destroyed his career at court; the 'craft of swains' and 'wives' tongues worse than the knavery of courtiers' ruined his retreat to the country; and, finally, his 'wife's gossips' and 'kindred' plagued his city-life and betrayed him (50; 57; 59; 65; 66). Everywhere, Bohan finds language to be untrustworthy, an instrument of duplicity, coercion and betrayal and this is infused with a strain of misogyny. It is to prove this case that he begins to invent the narrative we see unfolding as 'the Scottish history of James the Fourth': 'In the year 1520 was in Scotland a king, overruled with parasites, misled by lust...' (106–7).

In *James IV*, Bohan mediates everything we see. It is not that Greene has confused the categories of fiction and history, but that the history we see is a kind of fiction motivated by a strong authorial intention. Yet, as with other areas of the play, the will to dominate events and to fashion a persuasive language comes unstuck. Bohan may intend to produce a satirical or a tragic history, but the play, as we have seen, is eventually configured as a romance. Perhaps Oberon's influence wins out, or Bohan is an unreliable narrator; his intentions certainly appear to fluctuate as the play progresses. The supernatural presence of Oberon also raises the question of which level of the play is the more fictional. To add to the game-like intricacy of its composition, some characters in the main plot show an awareness of those in its frame, and at crucial moments the boundary between the two is crossed.[47] Who is in control of this narrative is not altogether clear and neither is its interpretation. In the exchanges at the end of the second act, Bohan is delighted with his unfolding creation. What he sees fits neatly with his sense of the corruption of the world and how this is manifested through language. Bohan comments on the depravity of the Scottish king and the inge- nuity of his favourite's eloquence: 'Sweeting his thoughts of luckless lust / With vile persuasions and alluring words' (Chorus 2, 5–6). Yet, what Oberon sees, or rather hears, is very different: the nobility of Ida's resistance which he commends by reiterating her keyword: he has never 'seen more virtue in a country maid' (9). We might remember Bohan's misogyny and how poorly this fits the rhetorical pattern of the history we witness.

Clearly, Greene is recapitulating in this framing device the motifs and interests of his main narrative. Here too, we find the resistance to union undermined and fixed prejudices losing cohesion; the distorting power of anger is dissolved, boundaries are crossed, and affinities emerge from opposition. Significantly, Bohan is a 'Redesdale man' (Induction, 0.4), that is, from the borders and living, from a metropolitan viewpoint, in the no-man's-land between rival suzerainties. Prejudices concerning the uncivil speech and habits of such people ran deeply in Tudor culture. Archbishop Cranmer, for example, described the inhabitants of the Scottish border as 'devastators':

> a certain sort of barbarous and savage people, who were ignorant of and turned away from farming and the good arts of peace, and who were so utterly unacquainted with knowledge of sacred matters, that they could not bear to hear anything of culture and more gentle civilisation.[48]

George Puttenham too used the language of the 'Northern-men' as an antithesis against which to measure the pleasing and civil discourse associated with the 'speach of the Court'.[49] Yet, as so often in this play, such linguistic and ethical prejudices are discommoded. The Bohan we see, for all his limitations, is an artful and accomplished speaker, the maker of a sophisticated historical narrative. The categories by which we distinguish civil from uncivil speech are questioned, especially if it is believed that the former reaches its apotheosis in court discourse and declines into coarse vulgarity at the social and geographical margins.

James IV contains, therefore, another area of scepticism towards authority: the authority of history itself. The audience is allowed to see how historical material is shaped for homiletic purpose and to identify the limits of this. Throughout, the process of history is kept 'open-ended'; its purposes can be altered and contested. The most commanding voices have their intentions defeated and voices at the periphery are able to influence the sequence of events. Greene thus displaces some of the most significant habits of mind and political satisfactions associated with the composing and reading of history. The history play has often been seen as means of ordering the civility of the Elizabethan subject, that is, as tutoring an audience in the distinctiveness and continuity of English experience and as ratifying the hierarchically structured community that will realize its exalted future potential. Greene's work alerts us to the strains in this project by creating a drama that reflects on the ideological shaping of history.

Phyllis Rackin argues that one of the most complex areas of Shakespeare's dramatic technique lies in his tendency to 'disrupt, parody, and interrupt the historical action to undermine the authority of historical representation'. This encourages the audience to 'meditate on the process of historical representation rather than attempting to beguile them into an uncritical acceptance of the represented action as a true mimesis of past events'.[50] We can see in Greene's play precisely such an enquiring and self-reflexive method of composition and one directed to similar ends. Greene suggests that expecting closure or finality from any historical narrative, or, indeed, from the prospect of union, is premature: past events become subject to dispute and debate. There are similar dangers in creating a 'closed' sense of theatrical history when this is derived from the vantage-point of its most enduring successes: 'a balanced view of the past might better come from tilting the other way, toward the forgotten agents, the losers, the discarded'.[51] In 1590–1, no one knew what the history play would become or who would be its most influential exponent. As this chapter has demonstrated, what the history play did become, or was becoming, in the judgement of Robert Greene at least, was far from inevitable or desirable.

Greene's critical evaluation of the work of his contemporaries provides a key to unlocking some of the riches of his own achievement; the adequacy of his response deserves serious scrutiny. In fact, as the next three chapters will argue in relation to Shakespeare's plays, if Greene did perceive his rival solely as a careerist and one eager to pander to dominant cultural norms he is misleading. In contrast, the audacious and radical nature of Shakespeare's treatment of disorderly language, as well as issues of authority and resistance, will now be explored in three of his plays. Shakespeare's dramas are sometimes treated as if commensurate with the category of the history play, that is, as defining it. As this study has argued, however, the uses of the past in sixteenth-century drama are better seen as both variegated and subject to debate. Yet the intensity of Shakespeare's interest in the apprehension of illicit speech reminds us of how significant this issue was and how deeply it affected the form of historical attention we find in his drama as well as its content. This perception will now be explored in relation to *King John*.

4
Misreading History: Rumour in *King John*

King John demonstrates the pervasiveness as well as the radical nature of Shakespeare's interest in illicit language. The status of monarchical speech – as well as those forms of language that question or oppose this – provides the source, as with Greene's *James IV*, of the dramatist's most forceful political insights. Furthermore, disruptive speech is not simply a topic of *King John*, but a key ingredient in its formal composition: in brief, the play views historical events from the vantage-point offered by the discourse of rumour. As with counsel in *Gorboduc*, Shakespeare's play both explores and enacts a specific form of speech; both plays also comprehend how historical pressures complicate understanding of seemingly disorderly discourses and their opposites. This is a large and unfamiliar claim for *King John* and it will need careful elaboration.

As John Bale's work demonstrates, the reputation of King John was central to the formation of protestant historiography in England during the sixteenth century.[1] Subsequently, John's reign was a natural choice for historical drama in the 1590s, both for Shakespeare and for the anonymous author(s) of *The Troublesome Raigne of King John* (c. 1591).[2] Yet, Shakespeare's *King John* (c. 1595/6), a play whose remote setting detaches it from the two 'tetralogies', has often been perceived as isolated, anomalous or transitional; an experiment indulged in 'between tetralogies'.[3] This chapter will argue, however, that according a new critical priority to *King John* provides some fresh insights into Shakespeare's practice as a historical dramatist as well as his political attitudes. In particular, the play is characterized by an audacious use of dramatic form; this establishes an important understanding of the historical process. This emphasis also permits a new consideration of Shakespeare's attitude towards popular speech, especially in terms of its association with rumour and vulgar historical misinterpretation. In later chapters, a similar degree of historical curiosity will be analysed in relation to the representation of treasonous speech in *Richard II* and the 'unreformed' or unregenerate voice in *Henry V*.

King John's scepticism with regard to social (and religious) shibboleths is made manifest in its general treatment of King John. Here, the heroic and martyr-like aspects of the king's identity, so cherished by John Bale, are radically diminished. In stark contrast to this, Shakespeare's monarch is well versed in the arts of secular political machination; this is a king who governs and is governed by pure 'commodity' or instrumental self-interest. A. R. Braunmuller perceives this critical disposition of the play as being far-reaching in its implications: '*King John* dramatizes – and thus both demystifies *and* makes unfamiliar – some of the most intensely serious cultural assumptions in late Tudor England.'[4] This conception of the play as demystifying can be extended to its treatment of linguistic as well as social and religious issues (although these categories are interrelated) and, especially, to its evaluation of the popular voice. In one respect, the task of identifying popular speech in *King John* appears futile as this is a work where the populace is largely spoken for. Yet a more flexible approach can be taken to an issue that is often posed in terms of representation. In relation to the history play, critics have attempted to ascertain the degraded or favourable estimation of the common people as manifested by their characteristics, of thought, expression and perception, as well as their involvement in actions such as riot and rebellion.[5] Yet this subject can also be conceived in relation to dramatic form and, in particular, to the implications of a theatrical composition adopting an idiom associated, rightly or wrongly, with popular culture. This chapter will argue that Shakespeare's exposition of his historical material in *King John* is shaped by his interest in and evaluation of rumour; this has, in turn, important implications for the dramatist's habits of historical and political reflection. This approach is contentious given the identity ascribed to rumour in early modern culture as an abuse of speech that inspired criminal disaffection and threatened social harmony by the deliberate distortion of the truth.

It will be argued here that *King John* surmounts this widespread denigration of rumour by employing its own calculated deviations from the dominant narrative of John's reign. Chronicle histories often asserted their authority by superseding and subordinating 'mere' rumour as a culpable habit of misreading.[6] *King John* confounds this hierarchy not only by weaving around the agreed pattern of the past an entirely imagined set of events – a common enough exercise of imaginative licence in the Elizabethan theatre – but by allowing this to expose the limits of how history is comprehended both as it occurs and in its sub-sequent interpretation. Shakespeare maintains this inquisitive stance, in part, by upholding a markedly unprejudiced view of rumour; the latter has a turbulent effect, but only insofar as it invites consideration of how the 'truth' of history is constituted. Like Robert Greene in *James IV*, Shakespeare is alert to the way in which the past is constituted and the motives that inform this. In *King John*, however, this spirit of enquiry involves a direct correspondence between the play's dramatic form and the disorderly speech that is normally deemed to distort historical perception. *King John* does not simply represent rumour; its dramatic form adopts some of its most important characteristics: scurrile invention, the deflation of authority, and an impulse to expose the disparity between public and private realities. In this way, Shakespeare demonstrates that historical truth can also be grasped in a spirit of imaginative licence, as much as homiletic sobriety. *King John* demonstrates that to perceive rumour as a correlative of a debased popular voice is, in itself, a misreading.

1

One obvious source for Shakespeare's interest in the reliability of historical interpretation in *King John* derives from the unresolved debate surrounding the king's reputation. As Phyllis Rackin has suggested, Shakespeare composed his history plays when 'historical fact was now open to question, and historical truth was now debatable'.[7] The radical fluctuations King John's reputation underwent in the sixteenth century demonstrate this.[8] Godly admirers of the monarch, such as John Bale, saw him as a victim of catholic slander. John Foxe traced this blighted reputation not simply to the jaundiced work of posterity, but to the misguided popular hostility the king endured during his lifetime. Foxe describes how the catholic clergy sponsored the false prophet, Peter Wakefield 'an idell gadder about, and pratling merchaunt...rumouring his prophecies abrode, to bring the king out of al credit with his people'. This misinformation spread and it accumulated credibility: 'Continually from thence, as the rude maner of people is, old gossyps tales went abroade, newe tales were invented, fables were added to fables, and lyes grewe upon lyes. So that every daye newe slaunders were layed on the king, and not one of them true.' The consequences of this were drastic for John's reputation: 'rumours arose, blasphemies were spread, the enemies rejoyced, and treasons by the priestes were mainteined'.[9] King John's emancipation from these libels was eventually secured by his inclusion in that bulwark of Tudor orthodoxy, the Elizabethan *Homelie against Disobedience and Wylfull Rebellion* (1570). Here John appeared as the victim both of illicit papal ambitions and of his subjects' rebellion in a period of abject political and spiritual ignorance.[10]

Yet this sustained attempt to promote a godly and patriotic King John was never wholly successful. Reservations had crept into Reformation thought by the mid-century concerning the integrity of John's motivations given his 'covetousnes' and 'frowarde minde'.[11] Richard Grafton, pledged to rescue John 'from slanderous reportes of foreyene writers',[12] but the Elizabethan period saw the renewal of some homegrown doubts concerning the monarch's integrity and these contested the pieties of orthodox historical interpretation. Foxe remained outraged at John's eventual submission to the papacy and the king's reputation for cruelty and despotism remained inexpugnable.[13] Shakespeare's play has been seen to acknowledge this legacy of competing readings, rather than presenting a fixed interpretation of John's moral character.[14] At the very least then, *King John* confronts complex political realities and this, by implication, questions 'official' attempts to promote the monarch's status.[15]

There are more surprising twists, however, to Shakespeare's political comprehension of John's reign than wariness towards single-minded responses to it. *King John* also brings to bear an unusual and unsettling variety of perspectives upon its historical material; these demand a constant modification of response. The play acknowledges not only that John's reputation was subject to competing evaluations, but that historical judgement always depends upon the wants and expectations we bring to it. We witness throughout, for example, how the protagonists misread events and have their integrity compromised by moments of scandalous disclosure. This chapter aims to provide a new context for this ironic mode of composition and to further understanding of its implications. This approach helps to identify an important element in the dramatist's practice as a historian: an attentiveness to unconventional, even dissident, sources of political speculation. Further examination of the early modern historical context within which rumour was defined helps demonstrate that Shakespeare's interest in such a widely stigmatized form of speech is both deliberated and politically assertive.

The power of rumour was intense, of course, 'in a society in which communications were slow and information difficult to verify and stories to substantiate'.[16] On 3 June 1487, the new and vulnerable Tudor regime, confronting Lambert Simnel's rebellion, initiated a long, proscriptive campaign against false news:

For as much as many of the King our sovereign lord's subjects be disposed daily to hear feigned, contrived, and forged tidings and tales; and the same tidings and tales, neither dreading God nor his highness, utter and tell again as though they were true, to the great hurt of divers of his subjects and to his grievous displeasure.[17]

As Kenneth Gross comments: 'such texts speak as if "false reports" and "seditious libels" about the actions or policies of sovereigns...had the power to bring the whole structure of authority into jeopardy'.[18] Bearers of such stories were sentenced to the pillory. The proclamation declares rumour to be a forgery of the truth, making it difficult to be detected, that demeans subjects by confusing their sense of reality. Similar measures were promulgated throughout the sixteenth century regardless of the varying confessional and political dispositions of successive governments. All of these emphasized that contrived and distorted news, uttered without dread of either divine or monarchical displeasure, was a threat to order. Regrettably, 'many of the King our sovereign lord's subjects' were willing both to hear and transmit such irresponsible information and this required

strict laws of sedition and censorship which made it a criminal offence to speak or write ill of the government, its personnel or anyone in authority...underpinning these policies was a belief in the fundamental fickleness, irrationality, and instability of popular opinion.[19]

From a government perspective, therefore, rumour falsified history, or, more accurately, it rivalled the regime's presentation of events so as to induce mistrust and panic. Stories of Henry VIII's adulterous appetites, for example, provided an alternative historical account of the Reformation that identified its origins in monarchical cupidity.[20] Rumour-mongers were acknowledged as having powers of invention and plausibility as well as an acute sense of timing and context: 'divulging to the people such kind of news as they think may most readily move them to uproars and tumults' (*TRP*, I: 337). Rumours of the monarch's death, for example, were a constant source of concern. Edward Lyttlelworke was set in the pillory 'in the myddest of the market day' at Wallingford in 1537: 'His yaers fast nayled, and after to be cut of by the hard hed, and then he to be tyed to a cartysayrse, and to be strypped naked to the wast of his body, and so to be whypped round aboute the towne.' This punishment was 'for spreading the rumour [of the king's death] and not producing his authority'.[21] Many proclamations stressed the importance of extirpating a rumour by discovering its author – 'to search forth and get out the first author and beginner of the said tales' (*TRP*, I: 281) – but this was a difficult task. As Lyttlelworke discovered, those who failed to report a rumour were taken as the author of it. Stories of the monarch's death recurred throughout the sixteenth century and were construed as having an equally sinister intent.[22]

Whatever the practical difficulties involved in detecting the author of a rumour, Tudor government drew upon a richly pejorative lexicon when it speculated about their identity. 'Devilish and slanderous persons', 'lewd and vagrant persons', 'malicious, vain, and seditious lie-tellers and sowers abroad of false and lying rumors', 'poisoned evil people', 'unruly vagabonds', 'light and seditious persons', and, by 1580, 'traitors abroad' and 'their secret complices and favorers' at home.[23] Rootless, disloyal, animated only by destructive impulses, rumour-mongers are 'desperate persons' who promote division, having 'neither place to inhabit in' or employment: 'having been either condemned of felonies and prison-breakers run from the wars, and sea-rovers departed from the King's garrisons, and loiterers' (*TRP*, I: 337). Such opponents of the regime were distinguished, however, by their verbal fluency and feverish activity: 'running and prating from place to place, county to county, town to town, by day to day, to stir up rumors, raise up tales, imagine news' (*ibid.*). It is important to remember the popular character attributed to this form of speech. Stephen Gosson deplored the credulity of the theatre audience in these terms: 'the meaner sorte tottre, they are caried away with every rumor, and so easily corrupted, that in the Theaters they generally take up a wonderfull laughter, and shout altogether with one voyce'.[24] Such words were often deemed not only to circulate freely among the people, but to originate with them. 'Divers lewd and light tales', lamented an Edwardian proclamation, are 'told, whispered, and secretly spread abroad by uncertain authors, in markets, fairs, and alehouses, in divers and sundry places of this realm' (*TRP*, I: 281). These tales multiplied in popular spaces, perversely covering their own traces the more effectively they spread; the judicious needed to resist the seductive appeal of such stories by exercising careful discrimination. 'Me Semes it Were no Wisdom to creadit every light tale', George Cavendish counselled in his *Life of Cardinal Wolsey* (c. 1554–8; printed, 1641), 'blazed by the blasphemous mowthes of rude commonalty, for…they spred abrode innumerable lyes'.[25] Here, rumour is perceived as embodying the coarseness of popular life. For Cavendish, the 'wyse sorte' ignore the 'false Rumors & fonde opinions of the fantasticall comonaltye, who delytith notheng more then to here strainge thinges, *And to see new alterations of authorites'* (p. 3; emphasis added). This attributes both an appetite for the sensational and for insubordination to the common taste for rumours. Such speech was inflammatory and manifested, at best, popular gullibility, at worst, hostility.

The principal threat presented by rumours lay in their claim to expose the hidden and often squalid realities behind the world of imposing public appearances. Elizabeth, like her father, was also the subject of disgraceful stories concerning her sexual improprieties and, here, 'hostility intertwined with attitudes about a woman in power'.[26] 'We shall never have a merye world', said a Kent labourer, 'so longe as we have a woman govener and as the quene lyved.'[27] In Sussex, Robert Fowler believed 'that the Earle of Essex was the sonne of the Queene of England', but, much more common were tales of the Queen's long, illicit affair with the Earl of Leicester: 'my Lord Robert hath had fyve children by the Queene, and she never goethe in progress but to be delivered'.[28] Alice Austen, of Southwark, disagreed only about the number of illegitimate children, saying, in 1585, that 'the Queene is no mayd and she hath had thre sunnes by the Earle of Leicester, and that they shold have bene made Earles'.[29] Five years later, Dionisa Deryck recounted the macabre conclusion to this shameful history, saying the queen

> hath had alredye as many childerne as I, and that too of them were yet alyve, thone beinge a man childe and thother a mayden childe. And furder that the other were burned...by my Lord of Leycester who was father to them and wrapped them upp in the embers in the chymney which was in the chamber wher they were borne.[30]

The Queen lamented 'Howe redy vulgare peple...ar disposed to dispearse sedycyous rumors thereby to procure trobles and mocons.'[31] Elizabeth had confided in the Spanish ambassador as early as 1564 that, despite the blameless and well-attested conduct of her public life, her reputation was being damaged by these testimonies concerning her private misdemeanours:

> They charge me with a good many things in my own country and elsewhere, and, amongst others, that I show more favour to Robert [Dudley] than is fitting; speaking of me as they might speak of an immodest woman...but God knows how great a slander it is, and a time will come when the world will know it. My life is in the open,

and I have so many witnesses that I cannot understand how so bad a judgment can have been formed of me.[32]

If rumours compromised seemly perceptions of authority, this could produce more truculent forms of hostility; the crown understood that 'people whose reputations have really gone will find it hard to dominate'.[33] Edward Fraunces, of Melbury Osmond, Dorset sought to justify his own wanton behaviour by commenting the queen 'had three bastards by noblemen of the Court, two sons and a daughter, and was herself base born'. He concluded: 'the land had been happy if Her Majesty had been cut off 20 years since, so that some noble prince might have reigned in her stead'.[34] As with its equally malicious twin, sedition, the disaffection sponsored by rumour was deemed to foment revolt, as it worked

> not only to alienate the true and loyal heart of our people from that their natural love and affection which they ought to bear unto us, their sovereign lord and King, but also to procure and stir up division, strife, commotion, contention, and sedition among our people. (*TRP*, I: 168)

Given that this discourse is perpetually untraceable, it legitimizes the continual surveillance and restraint of speech.[35]

Modern scholarship has done much to illuminate the significance of rumour. As the strain of misogyny in Elizabethan examples demonstrates, it is important to remember that such language had the potential to be loosed upon less powerful subjects. The populace was not immune from the social prejudices that stigmatized women as witches and Jews as arsonists and poisoners. Rumour's capacity for transgression and symbolic inversion can also involve the 'displaced abjection' Peter Stallybrass and Allon White have discerned in other popular discourses.[36] Similarly, we need to heed Ethan H. Shagan's warning that rumours should not be taken as typical or interpreted in terms of 'a closed system whose significance can be unambiguously reconstructed from their content alone'.[37] That so many rumours were recorded in the process of their prosecution indicates that their reception was often hostile. Yet, as Shagan's own analysis demonstrates so richly, the circulation of rumour reveals the vitality of political commentary and debate throughout sixteenth-century society; it was the disruptive capability of this that preoccupied Tudor government. It is this potential that informs Henry VIII's furious letter to Justices of the Peace concerning 'tale-tellers...and spreaders of rumours and false inventors of news' whose profanity extends to the deliberate misreading of the religious Injunctions of 1538: 'so confusely, hemming and hacking the word of God'.[38] In retrospect, it is this aspect of rumour that Adam Fox perceives as expressing 'not merely intemperate invective' but 'thoughtful opposition', identifying breaches of customary norms and directing ridicule towards the excesses of power.[39] Such an analysis is reinforced by James C. Scott's influential distinction between the 'public' and 'hidden' transcripts of social life. Scott defines rumour as expressing values that have been excluded from public life and urges us to take its fantastic, 'untruthful' qualities seriously as an expression of protest.[40] During the Pilgrimage of Grace (1536–7), for example, Henrician proclamations excoriated the 'slanderous, false, and detestable rumours' that were inflaming popular opinion.[41] Yet, as R.W. Hoyle notes, these stories, however exaggerated, did capture the bewilderment at 'a world gone mad' in the 1530s.[42] Here, rumour offers 'not only an opportunity for anonymous, protected communication', it serves 'as a vehicle for anxieties and aspirations that may not be openly acknowledged by its propagators'.[43] In other words, it transcribes (or encodes) popular suspicions about the 'real story' behind the public presentation of events. As Simon Walker has suggested, it is an important ingredient of the sphere of 'infrapolitics', that 'broad area of discussion, complaint and dissent that fell somewhere between wholehearted consent and open rebellion'.[44] In this respect, the widespread insistence in early modern discourse upon propriety in speech functioned, in effect, to conceal the squalid motivations, bad faith and double standards of authority.

It is important to remember that critical reflection upon the phobic definition of rumour was possible even in a period so exercised about its dangerous effects; we shall see some striking evidence of this in *King John*. Even the most cursory understanding could grasp that the social identity of rumour was more complex than its rhetorically loaded depiction in contemporary legislation. Indeed, more meditated reflection could hardly avoid noticing that elite political life was a principal source of the traffic in 'exaggerated' stories. George Cavendish emphasized how Cardinal Wolsey's enemies used 'Imagyned tales made of his procedynges & doynges'.[45] His work aimed to dispel these allegations, but Cavendish also acknowledged how Tudor government sustained this pernicious libel and an enduring historical conception is revealed to be dependent upon, rather than divorced from, rumour. In Cavendish's account, therefore, authority does not simply appear as a victim of popular libel but as an agent in its invention and dissemination; rumours slipped over social boundaries with ease and they had a pervasive role in shaping historical perceptions. Thus, Elizabeth's complaint to the Spanish ambassador that her life was beset with corrupt speculation may have been heartfelt, but she was addressing (perhaps knowingly) a source of rumour. The ambassador's predecessor had conveyed to Philip I the 'common opinion, confirmed by certain physicians' that 'this woman is unhealthy, and it is believed certain that she will not have children, although there is no lack of people who say that she has already had some'.[46] Yet, some weeks later, this same diplomat could express his outrage to Dudley that 'common rumour' was implicating him in catholic conspiracies. Innocent words of his 'by passing from mouth to mouth may have changed their sense' and, thus: 'I am to be considered as a conspirator against the Queen' (122).

Common rumour had a surprising tendency, therefore, to appear, or even to originate, in much more exalted forms of social discourse.[47] Stories of Henry VIII's sexual licence were disseminated in catholic polemic to shocking effect. Nicholas Sander's *The Rise and Growth of the Anglican Schism* (1585) related the most scandalous speculation of all concerning the origins of the Reformation:

> Henry was told in no doubtful way that Anne Boleyn was his own child, and yet he married her, he who was afraid to keep his wife because she was the widow of his brother...This was rashness not to be believed, hypocrisy unheard of, and lewdness not to be borne; but it was the hypocrisy and the rashness and lewdness of one man.[48]

It was not only outspoken opponents of the regime, however, who sullied themselves by circulating rumours. Sophisticated politicians took measures to orchestrate favourable publicity both by circumventing negative reports that originated with their opponents and by generating their own counter-rumours. In the miasma of claims and counter-claims concerning the seizure of Cadiz in June 1596, for example, the Earl of Essex and his secretary, Henry Cuffe, composed their own immediate account of events. The earl's secretary stressed the need to keep their authorship secret. For Cuffe, anonymity, a key means by which rumour was imputed to falsify history, would, in their case, increase the credibility of their apparently dispassionate version of events: 'His lordship's purpose is, that it should with the soonest be set in print, both to stop all vagrant rumours, and to inform those, that are well affected, of the truth of the whole.'[49] Cuffe was percipient: Essex's enemies were indeed

circulating rival reports and calumnies concerning his role at Cadiz.[50]
As this example demonstrates, it can be misleading to speak of 'Tudor
government' as a self-consistent regime. This overlooks not only significant internal tensions and rivalries, where the boundary between
fact and rumour was contested, but also changes in, and disputes over,
legitimacy.

There were many opportunities, therefore to consider the social
identity of rumour in a more complex way and to regard its opposition
to historical fact as less assured. Who held the monopoly of truth in
relation to King John? Those Reformation polemicists who stigmatized
all evidence of his wrongdoing as papist slander, or those popular libels,
still recorded in Foxe and Holinshed that documented the king's cruelty
and self-interest? Defining events as 'mere' rumour depended upon
one's affiliations, a point observed in Quintilian's widely read *Institutio
Oratoria*:

> Rumour and common talk are called 'the verdict of society' and 'the
> testimony of the public' by one party; to the other, they are 'vague,
> unauthenticated talk started by malice and developed by credulity,
> something that can happen to the most innocent of men through
> the fraud of enemies who spread false tales.' There will be no lack of
> examples on either side.[51]

This critical awareness that the truth-status of rumour was contingent
was also current in the period. The notorious catholic tract commonly
known as *Leicester's Commonwealth* (1584) offers a particularly rich
example. This attacked Leicester by circulating the most vitriolic reports
concerning his behaviour. It also included a sophisticated account of
how this powerful aristocrat attempted to stifle scandalous comment
with 'a law...against talkers', so that:

> under that general restraint [Leicester] might lie the more quietly in
> harbrough from the tempest of men's tongues, which tattled busily
> at that time of divers his Lordship's actions and affairs which perhaps
> himself would have wished to pass with more sercrecy.[52]

Rumours, in this account, disclosed important historical truths; their
restraint was an attempt to demean opposition and control public
debate. This is a far cry from perceiving such exchanges of news as
a symptom of the degraded nature of popular life. The meaning of such
speech was debatable, therefore, its definition provoked reflection upon

whose version of events was ratified and whose was excluded. In this way, it offered a powerful insight into the contingencies of history and how particular understandings of the past were enforced and contested. Shakespeare's play is an especially forceful example of a work that 'talks back' to this category of demonized speech by recreating its effect; this calls into question the motives that inform the phobic definition of rumour and whose interests this serves. As we have seen in relation to sedition, evil counsel and intemperate speech, such apparently straightforward discourses could take on a challenging presence in historical drama. In complex historical circumstances, recognizing these forms of speech also involved awareness of how limited their prevailing definition could be, a feature that is especially prominent in the treatment of rumour in *King John*.

2

King John has a pervasive interest in how the truth of events is discerned and how boundaries are imposed so as to exclude some historical viewpoints as worthless. One of the play's characters, for example, distinguishes truth from mere rumour. The Messenger who enters in act four bears forbidding news to King John: the Dauphin and his forces have invaded England and Queen Eleanor, the king's mother, on the 'first of April died'.[53] In conveying these events the Messenger discriminates nicely between different sources of information. He reports that Lady Constance, John and Eleanor's great dynastic rival, may have predeceased the queen: 'but this from rumour's tongue / I idly heard – if true or false, I know not' (4.2.123–4). True or false, Constance's fate is never confirmed; as with many issues in the play the facts prove difficult to ascertain. Significantly, this means that the credibility of rumour is not seriously compromised. The Messenger concedes the low status often attributed to such language; whether Shakespeare's play perceives rumour as equally devoid of historical insight is less easily determined.

  King John's commitment to a speculative consideration of historical material is embodied most fully in its inclusion of the Bastard as an actor within and commentator upon it. The Bastard also deploys and eventually abandons a language of scandalous speculation, but this relinquishment is as ambivalent as his earlier relish for insubordinate speech. His concluding embrace of more orthodox forms of thought and reflection also precludes his access to those scathing political insights that required imaginative licence. The Bastard's role, however, is only one strand of the play's interest in a discourse of scandal and rumour and it is placed in a critical perspective by the broader range of the play's theatrical effects.

It is significant in this respect that the opening of *King John* turns swiftly towards imagined events. Like *The Troublesome Raigne*, Shakespeare's play also offers an extraordinarily compressed treatment of the 'high' political action, that is, the challenge issuing from France, in the name of John's nephew Arthur, concerning the latter's prior claim to the English crown. This, and the subsequent declaration of war between England and France, is bustled offstage in under fifty lines in favour of the lengthy sequence concerning the Falconbridge brothers and their quarrel over who succeeds to their father's estate. The play deserts the arena of dynastic and national conflict recorded so substantially in Holinshed as easily as Philip Falconbridge relinquishes his newly secured estate and embraces his bastardy. Indeed, the Bastard appears to distill much of the play's unconventional disposition as 'serious' responses are undermined continually by his displays of sardonic, glancing wit. Even within the opening flourish of diplomatic business, we are invited to take a disenchanted view of court life. Queen Eleanor, the king's mother, rebukes John as a poor interpreter of the threats to his throne and, in a notorious flash of *realpolitik*, clarifies the grounds of his sovereignty:

King John: Our strong possession and our right for us.

Eleanor: Your strong possession much more than your right,
    Or else it must go wrong with you and me;
    So much my conscience whispers in your ear,
    Which none but heaven and you and I shall hear.

(1.1.39–43)

The bulk of the act confirms Lily B. Campbell's insight that *King John* indulges in 'extreme departures from historical fact',[54] although it is equally important to note the character of these departures. The dispute between the Falconbridge brothers over their late father's estate rapidly diminishes both the reputation of past authority – Richard the Lionheart is exposed swiftly as the seducer of Lady Falconbridge – and its present successors. King John settles the issue by insisting on the sacrosanct nature of primogeniture, a principle that, if applied consistently, would concede the throne to his rival Arthur.[55] None of the protagonists is discomfited by moral scruple or by the need to preserve the reputation of others. Both the country gentry and their royal superiors share a rivalrous appetite for land and status: if Eleanor reminds John (privately) of his 'strong possession', Robert Falconbridge is prepared to uncover (publicly) his mother's adulterous liaison with the previous king. By introducing this speculative plot the audience becomes accustomed to scandalous inferences regarding the improvised character of Plantagenet legitimacy.

This aspect of the play is strikingly akin to the critical form and disposition of rumour as it was conceived in sixteenth-century society. Far from prohibiting such reflections, *King John* is everywhere receptive towards unconventional information and the Bastard is a primary exponent of this. This impluse appears with particular force in his soliloquy on 'worshipful society' that accompanies his sudden rise in fortunes – here he imagines the new kinds of social dialogue that are now available to him:

> Now your traveller,
> He and his toothpick at my worship's mess,
> And when my knightly stomach is sufficed,
> Why then I suck my teeth and catechise
> My pickèd man of countries: 'My dear sir',
> Thus leaning on mine elbow I begin,
> 'I shall beseech you' – that is Question now,
> And then comes Answer like an Absey book:
> 'O sir', says Answer, 'at your best command,
> At your employment, at your service, sir.'
> 'No sir,' says Question, 'I, sweet sir, at yours.'
> And so e'er Answer knows what Question would,
> Saving in dialogue of compliment,
> And talking of the Alps and Apennines,
> The Pyrenean and the River Po,
> It draws toward supper in conclusion so.

(1.1.189–204)

Here we perceive how the artful management of 'compliment' inculcates social deference. Such linguistic performances utilize what Frank Whigham terms 'the sheerly formal, learnable, vendible skills of persuasion',[56] eliciting, in effect, a widespread form of misreading. Interestingly, the Bastard sees himself as implicated in such deceptions and he vows to refine his powers of observation so as to aid 'the footsteps of my rising' (216). As the play continues, however, the

Bastard does not simply personify its dramatic spirit, he is also observed critically by it.

This process complicates our response to the broadening of the action in the second act. Here a choric figure would do much to stabilize its turbulent effect and to correct habits of 'misreading' that seem endemic to this historical world as John and his forces arrive at the walls of Angiers. Here, John defends his sovereignty from the claim made upon it by Arthur and his French allies and the scene seems set to orient sympathies towards the English king: Arthur embraces the Duke of Austria, the killer of Richard the Lionheart, and the former makes a chilling vow to assault the 'white-faced shore' of England in 'a just and charitable war' that will bring a French proxy to the English crown. By the time Chatillion, the French ambassador, relates his stirring evocation of John and his 'fiery voluntaries' moving with heroic speed from England, a normative response to this scene appears secure. We anticipate the English king's devastating entrance along with 'the mother-queen, / An Ate stirring him to blood and strife' (2.1.62–3). Yet this allusion to Eleanor also associates her with rumour as well as discord and revenge. Ate is evoked memorably in the *Faerie Queene*, for example, as the venomous, double-tongued companion of Duessa: 'Fild with false rumours and seditious trouble, / Bred in assemblies of the vulgar sort, / That still are led with every light report.'[57] Again, Shakespeare maintains a discreetly equivocal viewpoint upon the royal protagonists, as well as confounding the distinction between 'high' and 'low' responses to (and interpretations of) history.

To provide some bearings on the complex scene that follows, we might recall that part of the unhallowed effect attributed to rumour concerned its irreverence. Rumours circulated without regard for decorum, deference or national vulnerabilities; they intruded across the boundary between public and private and dragged shameful material to light. In *King John*, patriotic feeling is also waylaid by doubts, reservations and counter-information. After all, Arthur is *there*, rather than being an invention of slanderous report and he is a physical reminder that John is, to some eyes, an illegitimate usurper. Similarly, the elevated language of principle soon degenerates into that of an unseemly verbal brawl. Eleanor's association with contention is soon confirmed in her quarrel with Constance, Arthur's mother. Both women trade insults and imputations over their sons' legitimacy in as discreditable a manner as any popular libel (2.1.121–33; 159–94). The willingness of the royal and aristocratic elite to dredge up rumour in their own interest is made shamefully apparent. As Phyllis Rackin remarks, in *King John* 'history-making is impossible;'[58] the play is attentive both to the temporal nature of human agency and the limitations upon interpretative power. It is impossible, for example, to adjudicate who wins the consequent military struggle: misreading events is a constant hazard when equally compelling (or contingent) versions of truth and legitimacy are being promulgated.

It is at this juncture that the Citizen of Angiers becomes significant, a role it is important not to conflate with that of Hubert, John's follower.[59] Like the Citizen of Angiers, the audience cannot fairly achieve a loyal response in a divided situation:

> A greater pow'r than we denies all this,
> And till it be undoubted, we do lock
> Our former scruple in our strong-barred gates,
> Kinged of our fears, until our fears resolved
> Be by some certain king, purged and deposed.
>
> (2.1.368–72)

As Robert Lane has suggested, the effect of the Citizen's prudential attempt to resolve this crisis and to protect Angiers, reveals the short-sighted militarism of the two kings, as they avow 'the destruction of the very substance of the kingdom that [the] crown represents – its subjects'.[60] The survival of the city is threatened by royal intemperance and only the common voice succeeds in modifying this and, in the process, discloses the limitations of both monarchs' insistence that they possess legitimacy. Moreover, this identification between the viewpoints of the Citizen and the audience is rendered most intensely by the Bastard's outrage at the defiance shown by these 'scroyles of Angiers' who 'stand securely', 'As in a theatre, whence they gape and point / At your industrious scenes and acts of death' (2.1.373–4; 375–6). He then proposes the kings unite to lay waste the city: 'I'd play incessantly upon these jades, / Even till unfencèd desolation / Leave them as naked as the vulgar air' (385–7).

The use of a theatrical metaphor serves as a reminder to consider a range of voices and perspectives in the play. In particular, this speech reveals that the Bastard's earthy idiom of speech is not necessarily commensurate with a popular perspective. There are a number of occasions in *King John* where those in authority attempt to dismiss or silence unwelcome criticism and the Bastard's intervention is one of the most shocking of these. It is directed squarely at the popular voice and its successful assuagement of force; this is read as a presumptuous intrusion into affairs of state. Thus the Bastard's brilliant soliloquy on the reigning principle of 'commodity' – a speech often read as expressing the viewpoint of the play – is not quite sufficient to the complexity of events. 'Commodity' does not do justice to the Citizen's painstaking and resourceful attempt to defend his own community and the dismissal of this is a notable misreading on the Bastard's part. This, along with his desire to embrace what he abhors, endorses Christopher Hobson's observation that the rhetorical contortion of the soliloquy embodies 'the apparently logical but distorted reasoning of those who serve commodity' as much as it presents a critique of it.[61]

What is also intriguing about the events at Angiers is that they are also subject to an immediate process of interpretation within the play. For the royal party, the events need to be consecrated in the public memory as a feast-day commemorating their triumphant statesmanship. But other dissonant voices interpret Angiers in a very different manner. For Constance, this idea is as gross a travesty of history as the two kings are of kingship – they are a 'counterfeit / Resembling majesty' (3.1.99–100) – and this scandalous perception has considerable validity. It is equally ironic that at this point in the play, King John asserts most fully that moral stature attributed to him by John Bale in his defiance of the papal legate Pandulph (162–71); the latter's excommunication of John destroys the new-made alliance. Yet, however locally compelling this moment is in reminding us of the 'official' version of King John, the consequent renewal of hostilities between England and France ushers in the darkest moment of the play and also its watershed: the king's commissioning of Hubert to execute John's nephew, and rival, Arthur.[62] With this act, the play confirms one of the most shocking of all the historical rumours concerning the reign. Holinshed is careful to phrase this possibility in the most conditional manner and in the (possible) source play, *The Troublesome Raigne*, these events appear 'in such drastically curtailed form that...an audience could easily fail to realize what has happened'.[63] It is also with regard to the events surrounding Arthur's destruction that the play manifests its most sympathetic attention to the voice of rumour.

In Shakespeare's text, unlike *The Troublesome Reign*, the brutality of the king's intention is augmented by the pathos of Arthur's childish (and successful) attempts to arouse Hubert's compassion. Significantly, both victim and assailant display their courage and resourcefulness in circumventing a corrupt royal will and the remainder of the play unfolds the drastic consequences of John's attempt to destroy his nephew.[64]

Arthur does eventually die in an escape attempt and this calamity (mis-interpreted as a successful assassination) lends legitimacy both to the French invasion of England and to the defection of John's magnates. Interestingly, most of this action is conveyed by the exchange of news and through acts of interpretation, lending these scenes a decidedly 'textual' aspect. The act emphasizes the suppositions, inferences and deductions that inform historical understanding as well as attempts to control that process. It also stresses the dubious role of social status in determining the meaning of events.

At the apex of the social hierarchy, the king is attempting to govern responses to his own authority in the most blatant way: by staging a second coronation to celebrate his earlier triumph over French and Papal foes. In fact, John's nobles immediately decipher this laboured spectacle as betraying the very anxieties it would conceal: 'an ancient tale new told, / And, in the last repeating, troublesome' (4.2.18–19). Salisbury depicts this repeated coronation as confusing the boundary between truth and suspicion:

> In this the antique and well-noted face
> Of plain old form is much disfigurèd,
> And like a shifted wind unto a sail,
> It makes the course of thoughts to fetch about,
> Startles and frights consideration,
> Makes sound opinion sick and truth suspected
> For putting on so new a fashioned robe.

> (4.2.21–7)

This description of royal agency is strikingly reminiscent, as we have seen, of phobic responses to rumour as startling, disorientating and leading to disaffection. Moreover, this contrasts with the stability of popular perceptions. Pembroke, for example, defends 'the murmuring lips of discontent' and their 'dangerous argument' (4.2.53–4) that John's legitimacy is visibly contradicted by his need to immure Arthur. Pembroke, however, has his own disaffection to defend here and offers a mediated account of popular attitudes. It also becomes clear that the nobles' own perceptions are far from unclouded. Simply on seeing the suspected Hubert, they (mis)interpret his physical presence as criminal testimony: 'The image of a wicked heinous fault / Lives in his eye' (4.2.71–2). The magnates are now convinced that Arthur has been killed and they desert their king. More 'ill news' floods into court of the

French invasion and Queen Eleanor's death and the Bastard returns to report the people are 'Possessed with rumours, full of idle dreams, / Not knowing what they fear, but full of fear' (4.2.145–6). These anxieties have been stirred up by the prophecies of Peter of Pomfret, condemned as an 'idle dreamer' and imprisoned under sentence of death for predicting the king's imminent resignation of his crown.

Yet, the accuracy of this swirl of prophecy and rumour is confirmed by Hubert's extensive description of how rumour is being transmitted through the kingdom:

> Young Arthur's death is common in their mouths,
> And when they talk of him, they shake their heads,
> And whisper one another in the ear.
> And he that speaks doth gripe the hearer's wrist,
> Whilst he that hears make fearful action
> With wrinkled brows, with nods, with rolling eyes.
> I saw a smith stand with his hammer, thus,
> The whilst his iron did on the anvil cool,
> With open mouth swallowing a tailor's news,
> Who, with his shears and measure in his hand,
> Standing on slippers, which his nimble haste
> Had falsely thrust upon contrary feet,
> Told of many thousand warlike French
> That were embattailèd and ranked in Kent.
> Another lean, unwashed artificer
> Cuts off his tale and talks of Arthur's death.

> (4.2.187–202)

We may remember here Hubert's intention to spread false reports concerning Arthur's death (4.1.127–31); this may be another of the play's wholly instrumental displays of rhetoric. Popular opinion, however, appears to have exceeded Hubert's attempt to speak for it. In these images of arrested work and action we see the power of rumour as it disgorges its burden of demoralizing news: 'Young Arthur's death is common in their mouths.' And we know, in the strict sense, that this is false; Hubert has spared Arthur. Yet, as the next scene demonstrates, common rumour speaks more truly than it (or Hubert) knows, as Arthur does indeed leap to his death. Similarly, the tailor's slippers may be 'falsely thrust upon contrary feet', but his information is not confused – an invasion is in progress and the word of a 'lean, unwashed artificer' rivals that of his betters. In this way, attention is drawn again to the truths that inhere within scandalized speech. As so often in the history play, events outmatch the ability of protagonists to interpret or control them and, here, this works to equalize the status of unofficial and official versions of events. By sharing its suspicions, the populace uncovers what authority would conceal, just as the prophecy of Peter of Pomfret that John will yield up his crown on Ascension Day is vindicated in act five when the king submits to papal authority. Moreover, Hubert's evocation of rumour's social agency, interrupting and disrupting the quotidian flow of daily life, is also congruent with theatrical effect. Emrys Jones has commented upon *King John*'s 'deviously ironical construction' as if it was 'designed to produce an effect of frustration'.[65] Yet it is the king's word that is most heavily frustrated. John's attempts to take command and to escape the consequences of his actions are everywhere deflected and undermined. 'Hadst not thou been by', the king remarks to Hubert as he receives from him the false news of Arthur's death: 'A fellow by the hand of nature marked, / Quoted, and signed to do a deed of shame, / This murder had not come into my mind' (4.2.220–3). Yet John's drastic misinterpretation of the recent past – attempting to blame Hubert's physical being as a textual incitement to assassination – is only the most absurd instance of his desperate attempt to maintain authority. Through its use of jolting news and sudden interruptions, the scene's formal construction reveals the depleted nature of John's integrity. In this manner, the play discloses the arresting, embarrassing details that disconcert the political plans and projects of both royal and noble power.

Earlier in *King John*, when the king insinuates to Hubert his desire for Arthur's death, he wishes to communicate outside language:

> ...if that thou couldst see me without eyes,
> Hear me without thine ears, and make reply
> Without a tongue, using conceit alone,
> Without eyes, ears, and harmful sound of words;
> Then, in despite of broad-eyed watchful day,
> I would into thy bosom pour my thoughts.

> (3.2.48–53)

John desires an untraceable, inaudible discourse with which to pour out his intimate desires without the scrutiny and debate provoked by the 'harmful sound of words'. Yet evasions such as these are forestalled by the play. The king resorts to hint and euphemism in his dialogue with Hubert, but his criminal intentions and shameful secrets are disclosed. The monarch is not alone in having his motives and actions exposed to an attention as unwelcome as that devoted to his legitimacy: Hubert's corrupt ambition is also unmasked. The play continues to comment sardonically on the interpretive capacities and political choices of its protagonists as they are superseded by events.[66] The magnates' discovery of Arthur's body, for example, facilitates a forgivable, if misguided process of attribution that bolsters their rebellion but it is based on error: 'It is the shameful work of Hubert's hand' (4.3.62). Hubert's own attempt to defend himself is dismissed as the desperate words of a social and moral inferior – 'Out, dunghill! Dar'st thou brave a nobleman!' (87) – and yet, as he reminds them, he is more of an equal than they think: 'By heaven, I think my sword's as sharp as yours' (82). The nobles eventually contract a dishonourable and badly misconceived alliance with the Dauphin; King John declines into an exhausted muddle of error and indecision.

It is not easy to determine, therefore, where sympathies coalesce in relation to this action: with those who rebel against an immoral, illegitimate king for the wrong reasons or with those who remain loyal, like Hubert and the Bastard. Arthur's earlier embrace of England's opponents has compromised even his increasingly desolate presence. Even the Bastard appears to acknowledge that with Arthur's death, the rightful heir to the throne has been annihilated and, hence, 'The life, the right, and truth of all this realm / Is fled to heaven' (144–5).[67] Act four of *King John* thus encourages scepticism with regard to the integrity of both the royal and baronial parties as well as their powers of historical comprehension. In comparison to this, those outside the circle of political power and influence are possessed with a clearer degree of insight; rumour is one means of articulating this.

It is perhaps more accurate to observe that *King John* peters out rather than concludes as if to reflect a pervasive diminution of authority and agency. The invasion and conspiracies against John are gradually overturned by serpentine twists of circumstance and yet the king is, as the chronicles record, poisoned by a monk. The reasons for this regicide are never clarified and appear insignificant. In these final scenes, all of the protagonists' plans and aspirations are foiled and their expectations reversed; oaths are made and unmade according to the disposition of events. Every scene revolves around the exchange of news – 'foul shrewd news!' 'news fitting to the night, / Black, fearful, comfortless, and horrible', 'dead news' (5.5.14; 5.6.19–20; 5.7.65) – that intrudes to unravel settled resolutions and to alter understanding of events. This reveals ever more sharply the limits of the leading characters and, crucially, of their historical perceptiveness. Suasive rhetoric becomes an ever more blatant medium for political deception. The Bastard's defiance of the rebels evokes a majestic king who will smite those who threaten him (5.2.148–78); this is wildly divergent from the defeated, harassed figure we have seen in private. Here, the Bastard acts as a disciple of rumour in the service of his king, falsifying the facts as easily as the imputed enemies of lawful authority. As we might expect, the play concludes with a moment of troubling 'open-endedness'. The Bastard's final act of 'true subjection' towards the new child-king (presumably played by the same actor as the vanquished Arthur) offers only a conjectural hope – '*If* England to itself do rest but true' (5.7.118; emphasis added) – directed towards an unpredictable future and, for the audience, an unfamiliar past. This new spirit of obedience, accompanied by a new decorum of speech, would also appear to be self-blinding. It will deny the Bastard access to his more irreverent, if equally insightful, discourse. This also marks an abandonment of a perspective that allowed him to comprehend a fractious, unstable historical process.

This chapter has suggested that the interpretation of Shakespeare's history plays can be enriched by considering the form of his historical attention. As with the other works examined earlier in this study, attending to the formal qualities of these plays can disclose unexpected degrees of critical engagement with key political questions. In *King John*, this is especially evident in relation to Shakespeare's response to dominant conceptions of 'illicit' language and the popular voice, as well as their relationship to historical truth. Stephen Greenblatt has drawn attention to the way in which Shakespearean drama appropriates (as much as it represents), significant forms of early modern discourse; this could include recreating the effect of dissonant (and dissident) cultural idioms.[68] *King John* enacts many of the functions associated with rumour in that it evokes alarm, critical insight and, at times, disaffection. As a historian, therefore, Shakespeare in this play does not evince any hostility towards 'storytelling, the myths and legends of the collective memory, and the meanderings of the oral tradition' that Michel de Certeau detects as integral to the development of a modern scientific historiography.[69] This does not imply, however, that Shakespeare did not perceive his plays as serious exercises in historical reconstruction. This has been emphasized in Pauline Kiernan's recent account of *Shakespeare's Theory of Drama* (1996). She argues that Shakespeare's history plays sought to supersede their predecessors by displaying their own triumphant (and self-authorizing) fictionality. Hence, the plays are replete with invented material, hearsay, belated report and a fondness for the 'unhistorical moment'; this allows Shakespeare 'to make a truly historical enquiry into history writing's claim to truth'.[70] Yet it is not simply Shakespeare's appropriation of the literary authority commanded by rival playwrights, or the cultural capital accruing to other forms of historiography, that determines the political implications of *King John*. This diminishes the play's searching account of how multiple forms of social, political and religious authority are claimed and contested. *King John's* engagement with heterodox and often disparaged habits of expression suggests that Shakespearean historical drama is unhampered by reverence in its mode of social and political reflection. This derives, in part, from his attentiveness to those disenchanted voices around him, and their forerunners, especially as they are preserved, often disapprovingly, in the historical record. Furthermore, it is in relation to the categories that would demean and regulate specific forms of language that the radicalism of Shakespeare's historiography is made manifest: this will now be explored in relation to *Richard II* and *Henry V*.

5
The Language of Treason in *Richard II*

There was no more devastating instance of injurious speech in early modern English than to be condemned as a 'traitor' and no clearer demonstration of the relationship between language and power than the ability to ascribe this term successfully. Treason represents an especially acute example of the claims made by sovereign action over speech: to define treason and to assign it effectively is a fundamental sign of political authority. Yet an effective ascription of treason was not necessarily commensurate with legitimacy. The condemnation of the traitor often exposed authority to detailed (and public) scrutiny of its motives for so doing. Shakespeare's *Richard II* rehearses precisely this kind of public questioning of treason as a medium through which sovereignty is expressed. As with rumour in *King John*, this offence has a contested status in the play and crucial issues of historical truth and political legitimacy depend upon its arbitration. Treason is also construed in linguistic terms: it is an offence that can be committed in language and it is subject to competing definition by opposing political discourses. In *Richard II*, treason is located within a world of mutable historical circumstances; these affect its characterization, as well as, from the spectator's viewpoint, enriching and complicating an understanding of its nature.

That *Richard II* is engaged with the consequences of historical and political change has often been observed and, equally often, the language of the play has been identified as expressing this. One significant view of this issue emphasizes Shakespeare's interest in a transition from a medieval political ethos to early modern conditions. In depicting the violent extinction of Plantagenet monarchy, *Richard II* also distinguishes the ascendancy of Lancastrian pragmatism, setting a 'divinely sanctioned monarch against Machiavellian "new man" whose power resides exclusively in his own will'.[1] It depicts the collapse of a world which assumes political values are divinely ordained, and the emergence of one dominated by the functional pursuit and maintenance of power. In terms of language, this is embodied in the *topos* of the 'fall of speech': the play portrays 'the secularization of politics...paralleled by the commercialization of the word'.[2]

However, increasingly telling questions have been raised concerning the adequacy of this interpretation of the play and the kinds of political recognition it advances. Joseph A. Porter reminds us that there are a variety of political idioms in *Richard II*, which qualify any reception of, and identification with, the monarch's: 'What falls after all, is only *Richard's* speech – his conception of language – not..."Speech" itself.'[3] More recent criticism has been similarly attentive to the range and ambivalence of *Richard II*, as well as its sympathy for the language and values of those who challenge the integrity of Richard's 'sacramental' speech and bring about his deposition. The play's notable utility for the Essex rebels has inflected historicist readings of its theatricality as demystifying, subverting dominant conceptions of political obedience.[4] From this perspective, *Richard II* is held to envision the 'medieval past not as a lost world of symbolic unity but as the scene of a continual struggle between aristocratic and constitutional liberties and a monarchy that kept trying to appropriate public resources for its private interests'.[5] The stress on parliament as the context for the deposition scene, as well as the latter's striking absence from the three Elizabethan quartos of the play, has been interpreted by Cyndia Susan Clegg, as endorsing 'an authority over the monarch far more consonant with resistance theory than with the government's understanding of parliamentary authority'.[6]

Such distinct critical emphases are expressive of the ambivalence created by the play's opposing political perspectives, and these can be analysed in terms of their shared concern with defining treason. Any political reading of *Richard II* involves an evaluation of treachery, emphasizing either Richard's or Bolingbroke's betrayal of fundamental obligations; the play foregrounds this issue. In *Richard II*, 'treason' and cognate words appear with greater frequency than in any other Shakespeare play, and its principal conflict might well be characterized as a struggle over the authority to define the offence.[7] In a play peculiarly devoid of realized action, its language is dominated either by the attribution or evasion of the stigma of treachery; virtually every significant dramatic episode is constructed around purported breaches of trust, and most characters are depicted as implicated in or, at the very least, reacting to such violations. Specifically, formal accusations of treason provide an induction into the distinct regimes presided over by Richard and Bolingbroke, and the adjudication of these helps decipher their respective strategies of governance as well as the forms of opposition they arouse. The drama culminates, of course, with the defining actions of high treason: the deposition and assassination of a monarch.

What is distinctive to *Richard II* is not simply the centrality of treachery to its political exchanges, but the inquisitiveness with which competing formulations of the offence are considered. Again, the form of the play is as crucial here in asking important political questions as its content. This emphasis allows for further scrutiny of whether the play represents a fundamental transition between two distinct regimes. However vehemently treason is ascribed within the play, evidence is rarely constituted in a definitive way. Thus, Bolingbroke and Mowbray charge each other with treachery without the audience being able to judge who is telling the truth. Later, Richard's adherent, Aumerle, is, in turn, accused of treason against Bolingbroke in a manner that is equally difficult to appraise. Moreover, such ambiguities over identifying the figure of the traitor are accompanied by uncertainties in defining treason. Political betrayal can thus be depicted as the violation of honour and fealty (as Bolingbroke forcibly asserts in the play's opening) or, primarily, an offence against the king's person and will (as King Richard and, later, the Bishop of Carlisle believe). It can be apprehended as a violent action or as a form of corrupt speech (as Mowbray argues in his defence against Bolingbroke, a view adopted by his opponent as he assumes the crown). The play's structure is reflexive, rather than being organized in a sequence or in terms of a definitive historical transition; it is through the shifting configuration of treason thus generated that some of *Richard II*'s most daring political speculations can be discerned.

Rather than expressing a singular or an antithetical conception of treason, *Richard II* is characterized by a relational or, more accurately, dialectical approach, in which treason is viewed as dependent on modulations in authority, finding meaning only in relation to the sovereignty it would help establish or undermine. If opposition to King Richard is 'gross rebellion and detested treason' (2.3.109) – and Richard, of course, will see himself in his resignation of the crown as 'a traitor with the rest' (4.1.248) – once Bolingbroke is crowned, opposition to his rule is, in turn, no less treasonous: Aumerle is, even to his father, guilty of 'foul treason' (5.2.72).[8] Betrayal appears not as an incontrovertible act which distinguishes the faithful subject from those doomed by their corrupt ambition, but as a far more conditional offence. By locating its attributions of treason within mutating historical circumstances, the play elucidates the political conflicts intrinsic to such allegations. Repeatedly, treachery is defined in the struggle to constitute or diminish authority, and by the language used to substantiate this; as such, it can be modified, contested and redefined in relation to varying claims of political legitimacy. One can conceive of the play's 'ambivalence' then, in the terms suggested by a recent analysis of the dialectical method of Machiavelli's writing: as engaged in an 'internal critique and negation of positive claims to authority'.[9] In this respect, the play presents a counter-statement addressed to any attempt to reify the nature of treason; instead, the offence is shown to take shape in, and to be challenged by, competing forms of political discourse. The language of treason does not 'fall' in *Richard II*, it is shown to be subject everywhere to temporality; contingent claims are made upon it at every juncture of the unfolding historical conflict. As with the depiction of rumour in *King John*, disorderly or criminal language is also granted access to important political insights.

One obvious influence upon, and context for, these fluctuations in the play's representation of treason lies with its principal source: the 1587 edition of Holinshed's *Chronicles*. In reinterpreting the inclusiveness of Holinshed, as well as the work's organizing commitments to constitutional government and an ethic of civic prudence, Annabel Patterson argues that a form of 'early modern relativism' emerges in its account of the historical formation of treason, an attitude symptomatic of its 'critical perspective on "Law" as a set of socially and politically constructed rules, rules that particularly at this stage in history were subject to sudden and continuous change'.[10] This helps in both identifying and interpreting one of the most noticeable features of Holinshed's treatment of the turbulent reign of Richard II: how treason is made to accommodate changes in the disposition of power, rather than embody a consistent concept of justice.

In its detailed narration of the struggle between royal and baronial parties, the attribution of treason and the resistance it provokes helps structure Holinshed's account: it is the instrumental means by which factional ascendancy is secured and (temporarily, at least) maintained. The text, however, is notably reluctant to denote any stable conception of treachery; it is, consistently, a matter of perspective. This is expressed in Holinshed's recurrent citation of treason accusations with an accompanying phrasal qualification: 'whom they called traitor', 'those whom they reputed to be traitors', 'whom he tooke to be plaine traitors',

'traitors (as they tearmed them)'.[11] Here, treason is situated rhetorically, located in conflicting and partisan attempts to validate authority.

An economical example of Holinshed's pragmatic view of treachery is demonstrable in the account given of the events that lead to Richard's attack on two pivotal figures in the baronial opposition: the abduction and covert assassination of the Duke of Gloucester, which so substantially informs the action of Shakespeare's play, and, simultaneously, the trial and execution of the Earl of Arundel. In 1388, the king dissolves a statutory council of state, which maintained an 'oversight under the king of the whole government of the realme' (2:776), imposed on him by his magnates. Richard and his advisers exert extraordinary pressure on a council of judges to have those responsible for this body deemed treasonable and to agree on an elaborate defence of the king's prerogative: 'it was demanded of them how they ought to be punished that interrupted the king so, that he might not exercise those things that apperteined to his regalitie and prerogative. Whereunto answer was made, that they ought to be punished as traitors' (2:782). In response, the baronial party 'gathered their power togither, determining to talke with the king with their armour upon their backes' (2:784). They demand, by issuing a feudal challenge, the expulsion of those advisers who are responsible for such a treacherous abuse of legal process, insisting Richard 'take awaie from him such traitors as remained continuallie about him...And to proove their accusations true, they threw downe their gloves, protesting by their oths to prosecute it by battell' (2:787). Despite his initial acquiescence, the king continues to conspire against the lords and succeeds in having Gloucester forcibly removed from the realm and assassinated (2:836–7). He then secures a trial, in parliament, of the Earl of Arundel for treasonably taking up arms against his authority. When the king's favorite, Bushy, articulates the 'demand' of the Commons that Arundel's guilt be punished, his mordant reply provokes the same theatrical display of outraged feudal honour deployed earlier against the king's favorites:

> The earle turning his head aside, quietlie said to him; 'Not the kings faithfull commons require this, but thou, and what thou art I know'. Then the eight appelants standing on the other side, cast their gloves to him, and in prosecuting their appeale (which alreadie had beene read) offered to fight with him man to man to justifie the same. (2:841)

What is noticeable in this treatment of treason is its reversibility; the same ritualistic means of proving the offence can be used either for or

against royal power. Arundel (as well as Gloucester) can appear as agents
in the definition of treason and as traitors. For Holinshed, betrayal can
be both a corruption of the law that should protect subjects or an
encroachment upon the royal prerogative; any consensus over what is
unpardonably illicit is not secured. Treachery is a medium in which
antagonistic political interests are expressed. Furthermore, it also provides a language in which claims of authority are made and contested.
As Arundel's case demonstrates, the discursive status of the offence
means it can be exposed as partial and contingent. Holinshed's text is
alert to the interests that inform public speech, political displays and
legal procedure. None of the latter is free of political mediation, a feature
which is registered most powerfully in that both the object and the
nature of treason can be redefined in the enforcement or modification
of sovereignty. Significantly, this is equally true at all stages of the
political process he represents; there is no palpable sense of a transition
between distinct modes of authority. For Holinshed, treason is given
a static form according to the needs of specific circumstances. It is this
conception of the offence that has significant consequences for the
dialectical construction of *Richard II*. The relationship between the
language of treason and the struggle to legitimize authority is equally
integral to Shakespeare's play; its implications merit detailed scrutiny.

2

At the opening of *Richard II*, an explicitly feudal political discourse is
established in the attempted trial by combat between Bolingbroke and
Mowbray who perceive treason in terms of the obligations, and rights,
of subjects in relation to the code of honour. It is this that Richard
abrogates by correlating treachery with his own person and will. This
monarchical conception of treason is revised by those opposed to his
rule; moreover, an audience learns quickly of the cynical pragmatism
with which Richard exploits the judicial and other prerogatives of his
office (1.4). This modified evaluation of the sovereignty of the king's
speech is rendered distinctively through the play's treatment of betrayal,
especially in relation to Bolingbroke who, on his illicit return to the
realm, deploys a tactical language in which the distinctions between
treasonous and loyal sentiments are no longer clear. Bolingbroke's
flexibility of speech proves his political versatility, yet the rhetorical
manoeuvring it demands is also subjected to critical examination and
not only as a dilution of his earlier commitment to honour. In its later
phase, the play demonstrates that his usurpation fosters the subsequent

prosecution of treason committed in words, an offence with which he had earlier been charged, as much as through deeds: this definition finds new significance in the light of Bolingbroke's own actions. Rather than arrange its conflicting registers of speech in a hierarchy, *Richard II* stages these as mutually qualifying. Each figure who claims political credibility and, ultimately, authority, derives this from the ascription of treachery; however, the rhetorical status of such claims is disclosed simultaneously by an alternative conception of betrayal. The play's treatment of this topic is proximate in spirit to *Gorboduc's* inquisitive approach to counsel. Both plays elicit a complex engagement with historical events by refusing to define a controlling viewpoint in relation to these distinct discourses.

From the outset, *Richard II* depicts a rivalry between its protagonists over the power to define treason and an argument is rehearsed over the political ideas it validates and therefore the priority of social allegiances.[12] Significantly, in the conflict between Bolingbroke and Mowbray, any affiliation with a controlling viewpoint, including that of the crown, is obstructed, in that the appellants are opposed on broadly equal terms. Moreover, informing this irresolution in discerning the traitor is a far more profound inability to identify the nature of political treachery. The dissension of the appellant knights is based on an expressed commitment to chivalric honour, which the king perceives as superseded by his own person; their competitive behavior embodies the 'moral autonomy' of the honour code Mervyn James has made familiar in leaving 'little room for the concepts of sovereignty, or of uncondi-tional obedience'.[13]

We can see this schism in the definition of treason emerging in the king's opening query to Gaunt, regarding Bolingbroke's motivations:

Richard: Tell me, moreover, hast thou sounded him
If he appeal the Duke on ancient malice,
Or worthily, as a good subject should,
On some known ground of treachery in him?

Gaunt: As near as I could sift him on that argument,
On some apparent danger seen in him
Aimed at your highness; no inveterate malice.

(1.1.8–14)

The king is already sensitive to Bolingbroke's sense of principle: the phrase 'ancient malice' is dismissive both of an enduring feud with

Mowbray and of its archaic expression. For Richard, the worth of 'a good subject' is determined by his attitude towards treachery, and Gaunt, intriguingly, is unsure of his son's status. Here, as in the following scene, Gaunt expresses a conception of social relations familiar to Tudor sensibilities in that betrayal is conceived of primarily as an intended assault on the monarch. This emphasis on the monarch's person as the supreme object of treason had long been ascendant in legislation; yet, in *Richard II*, the language of betrayal is not concentrated wholly upon the king.[14]

The chivalric intensity with which Bolingbroke expresses his sense of profaned honour signifies his sense of treachery; any defilement of the privileges intrinsic to nobility is treason; even the mute element of blood speaks, or cries, with the force of scriptural injunction to avenge the injustice and dishonour committed by the murder of Gloucester. Mowbray:

> ...like a traitor coward,
> Sluiced out his innocent soul through streams of blood –
> Which blood, like sacrificing Abel's, cries
> Even from the tongueless caverns of the earth
> To me for justice and rough chastisement.
> And by the glorious worth of my descent,
> This arm shall do it, or this life be spent!

> (102–8)

There are unchivalrous connotations, of course, in the offences attributed to his enemy: Mowbray has misused the public purse, embezzling for 'lewd employments' money intended for military pay and, in a wild accusation, has engineered all the political conspiracies 'for these eighteen years / Complotted and contrived in this land' (95–6). However, aside from such self-interest, cowardice and lack of knightly largesse, the core act of treason is Mowbray's desecration of blood for which the right of redress is claimed.

Bolingbroke does present his indictment of Mowbray as 'a traitor and a miscreant' (39) as an act of protective loyalty toward his king. The monarch and the realm must be protected from such a dangerous subject; this care issues from 'the devotion of a subject's love, / Tend'ring the precious safety of my prince' (31–2). Yet the rhetorical opportunity this affords him for a charismatic assertion of his own dynastic authority diminishes this as a central motive; Bolingbroke acts under the sacred obligations entailed 'by the glorious worth of my descent' (107). His words are spoken under the hearing of God, rather than the king, and their truth will be testified to in a providential verdict elicited by his own will:

> ...for what I speak
> My body shall make good upon this earth,
> Or my divine soul answer it in heaven.
> ...
> With a foul traitor's name stuff I thy throat,
> And wish – so please my sovereign – ere I move,
> What my tongue speaks my right-drawn sword may prove.

(36–8; 44–6)

The fact that Richard's desires are mentioned here only in passing is consistent with Bolingbroke's acting as both the bearer of proof and the instrument of retribution. There is political audacity in the correspondence drawn between the words he uses and their validation in the justice his body will enact.

Mowbray also addresses treason as a violation of honour; for him, it is Bolingbroke's speech that enacts this violation. In insisting that the allegations are made by a 'slanderous coward' (61), Mowbray indicts his opponent's words as issuing 'from the rancour of a villain, / A recreant and most degenerate traitor' (143–4). Again the physicality of the language is striking, as well as the forcible manner in which aristocratic honour is to be vindicated independently through the trial by combat. Mowbray will 'prove myself a loyal gentleman / Even in the best blood chambered in his bosom' (148–9), a demand that outweighs the king's command: 'My life thou shalt command, but not my shame' (166):

> I am disgraced, impeached and baffled here,
> Pierced to the soul with Slander's venomed spear,
> The which no balm can cure but his heart-blood
> Which breathed this poison.

(170–3)

Here, Mowbray further intensifies the personal dimension of betrayal in his sense of the spiritual peril consequent upon obliterated knighthood. Similarly, Bolingbroke insists that he cannot obey Richard's command to forgo resorting to arms against Mowbray; this would be a 'deep sin', an injustice done to honour which he is obliged to rectify regardless of the king's will (187–95).[15]

Clearly, Richard is alert to the political implications of this shared language which transcends his own entitlement to obedience. This is apparent in his implied admonition to Bolingbroke as 'our subject' (115–23) and in his countermanding of the trial by combat. The king is determined to subsume the role of providence and resolve the issue of treason within his own judicial prerogative. Moreover, he offers a scathing commentary on chivalric justice and the equivalence it draws between honour and treachery. For the king, the 'rites of knighthood' (75) are merely an imposture, animated by a mixture of 'eagle-winged pride / Of sky-aspiring and ambitious thoughts, / With rival-hating envy' (1.3.129–31). Richard perceives their martial display as a regressive and sectarian indulgence which threatens:

> To wake our peace, which in our country's cradle
> Draws the sweet infant breath of gentle sleep,
> Which so roused up with boist'rous untuned drums,
> With harsh-resounding trumpets' dreadful bray
> And grating shock of wrathful iron arms,
> Might from our quiet confines fright fair peace,
> And make us wade even in our kindred's blood:
> Therefore, we banish you our territories.
>
> (132–9)

Richard insists on his possession of the kingdom – 'our fields'; 'our fair dominions' (140; 141)[16] – construing its welfare as that of an infant threatened by the clangour of feudal violence. The peace of the realm is individuated physically, and it is this which can be made subject to assault and betrayal. Richard's identity is symbiotic with that of his kingdom as the object of treason, and the king rebukes the knights as subjects whose primary duty is to obey his will.[17] The obsolescence of their conception of treachery is forcibly demonstrated, both in the peremptory sentences of banishment and in the arbitrary revision of Bolingbroke's exile, eliciting his stunned recognition of the power of words issuing from 'the breath of kings' (213–15). Richard, then, initiates a process of great significance for the play: by displacing the authority that the appellant knights claim through treason, he establishes a critical perspective on the interests with which it is informed.

It is integral to the play's 'internal critique' of authority, however, that the legitimacy of Richard's appropriation of treason is, in turn, qualified by those who dissent from it. The king's ability to make effectual his injurious speech becomes subject to qualifications that seek to deprive it of force. Opposition to the monarch is not conflated with treachery; indeed, *Richard II* extends considerable latitude to those who perceive the king's actions as a destructive repeal of custom. The ethos whereby fealty and honour are primary forms of social obligation allows assumptions regarding political obedience to be revised when it is the king who is responsible for their violation.[18] In the exchange between Gaunt and the bereaved Duchess of Gloucester that precedes the planned trial by combat, Gaunt's insistence on the compliance owed 'God's substitute' (1.2.37–41) must withstand powerful criticism. For the Duchess, Gaunt's noble blood should reveal that his 'patience' is equivalent to 'pale cold cowardice', excusing Richard's involvement in her husband's assassination and inviting future annihilation (25–36). In another compelling metaphor of personification, the Duchess envisages Edward III's dynastic tree being 'hacked down', its destruction that of a living identity: 'Yet art thou slain in him' (18–25).

Finally, Gaunt himself testifies to this understanding of Richard as betraying the values from which his royal authority is drawn. From Gaunt's historical perspective of an England governed by 'true chivalry' (2.1.54), it is the king who appears dishonourable and alien, enslaved to Italianate fashions, the flattery of favorites, and his own corrupt will. In the growing intensity of this condemnation, Richard's 'England' is depicted as engaged in the conquest of itself, a paradox whose dreadful implications demands opposition (57–68). The culminating moment in Gaunt's verbal assault on Richard's status comes in his direct challenge to his continuing legitimacy: the heroic spirit of Edward III is invoked as desiring the king's deposition even before his accession to the throne (104–8).[19] In a crushing formulation, he asserts that Richard has now effectively deposed himself – 'Landlord of England art thou now, not king. / Thy state of law is bondslave to the law' (113–14) – a statement whose treasonous implications the king immediately recognizes (115–23).[20] Gaunt continues to subject the king's actions to corrosive rhetorical scrutiny, climaxing with the monstrous image of his pelican-like consumption of the slaughtered Gloucester's blood, 'tapped out and drunkenly caroused' (126–7) After Gaunt's death, York continues this critique of Richard's entitlement to the throne, given his betrayal of 'customary rights' (196) embodied in Richard's confiscation of his brother's estate, and the discord this will arouse among 'well-disposed hearts / And prick my tender patience to those thoughts / Which honour and allegiance cannot think' (206–8).

York's desperation at reaching the limits of his fealty, at being brought
to the brink of treason, brings us to a key episode in the play's developing
concern with the effect of political crisis on existing social duties. The
insecurity *Richard II* cultivates over a reliable definition of treachery is
augmented when those opposed to the king's will further complicate
attitudes to the offence by a subtle process of verbal arbitration: it is this
that allows for the dissent repressed by York's sense of 'honour' and
'allegiance'. In contrast to the often stark and declarative language that
accompanies the play's earlier antipathies, Bolingbroke and his allies
develop an equivocal mode of speech which can be adjusted tactically.
Again, emphasizing the influence exerted by treason on the play's formal
presentation of political conflict is useful in identifying how much
verbal expedience is required to evade its ascription. Rather than establish
feudal disenchantment as the principal challenge to Richard's betrayal
of his office, the play attends, increasingly, to the strategic composition
of language.

In the first stirrings of resistance against Richard, it is significant
that – in the hostile reactions of Northumberland, Ross and Willoughby
to Bolingbroke being 'Bereft and gelded of his patrimony' (237) – there
is a growing sensitivity to the political implications of words:

Ross: My heart is great, but it must break with silence
Ere't be disburdened with a liberal tongue.

Northumberland: Nay, speak thy mind, and let him ne'er speak more
That speaks thy words again to do thee harm.

Willoughby: Tends that thou wouldst speak to the Duke of
Hereford?
If it be so, out with it boldly, man.
Quick is mine ear to hear of good towards him.

(228–34)

Once agreement has been reached to speak securely, their grievances
can be rehearsed against the king's arbitrary rule and the consequent
vulnerability of 'our lives, our children, and our heirs' (245) to factional
whim. This critique of the 'degenerate King' (262) as a thief and a tyrant
allows a number of tactics to be developed that sustain further critical
reflection and the actions that might accompany it. Thus Northumberland's news of Bolingbroke's imminent return at the head of an armed
party is introduced tactfully:

> ...Even through the hollow eyes of Death
> I spy life peering, *but I dare not say*
> How near the tidings of our comfort is.

(270–2; emphasis added)

If Richard's regime is equated implicitly with death, this demands that the possibility of 'life' be embraced; but, again, the consequences of such a choice are presented indirectly. Ross urges Northumberland to disclose his knowledge in terms of their shared desires; hence, it has the quality of thought, something unspoken: 'Be confident to speak, Northumberland. / We three are but thyself, and, speaking so, / Thy words are but as thoughts. Therefore, be bold' (274–6). Richard's political betrayals are used to sanction the development of a flexible idiom in which inhibitions against open criticism of the king are overcome. Richard, however, is not to be resisted explicitly: the effect of Bolingbroke's return is conveyed conditionally through discreet metaphors of freedom restored, guilt exposed, and honour renewed:

> If, then, we shall shake off our slavish yoke,
> Imp out our drooping country's broken wing,
> Redeem from broking pawn the blemished crown,
> Wipe off the dust that hides our sceptre's gilt
> And make high majesty look like itself

(291–5)

This attentiveness to the accommodation of words and loyalties to new circumstances is present in Northumberland's elaborate compliment to the returned Bolingbroke's 'fair discourse' (2.3.6–18), a homage that is amply repaid: 'Of much less value is my company / Than your good words' (19–20). It is striking that Bolingbroke's speech is now denuded of chivalric fervour and is characterized by politic insinuation. Those who rally to his cause are greeted warmly with oblique hints of the material advantage that will accrue from their loyalty (45–67). Of course, the perspective from which Bolingbroke's return to the realm and his defiance of the king are perceived as treachery does not disappear from the play. It is reintroduced punctually with York's angry imputation of his 'gross rebellion and detested treason' (86–112). York's attack on his nephew's resort to arms is met by Bolingbroke's claim of a new status as the wronged 'Lancaster' and an appeal to his uncle's sense of the outrageous violation of family honour: 'I am a subject, / And I challenge law' (133–4). Bolingbroke's strategy is typified by this pragmatic arbitration; he does not formulate an alternative conception of treachery so much as amend York's dogmatism by revealing its limitations in the present context. This mitigation is adapted, persuasively, to the needs of both his supporters and his opponents.

Bolingbroke proves expert in complicating the judgements made concerning his actions. In the dispatching of Bushy and Greene to execution, he takes pains to 'unfold some causes of your deaths' (3.1.7) to legitimize his assertiveness. The transgression against chivalric honour incurred by his dispossession is stressed, as well as his protective care for the monarch. The tacit implication, however, is that they are guilty of treason to Bolingbroke as instruments of Richard's corrupt will. The personal judgement they are subjected to enhances his right and status as 'a prince by fortune of my birth, / Near to the King in blood' (16–17).[21] Again, Bolingbroke's speech is equivocal in having an implicit, but not exclusively critical, potential. Northumberland's curt reference to 'Richard' (3.3.6–14) may betray many of the attitudes of those loyal to him, but such indiscretion is entirely alien to Bolingbroke's political tact. His public standing is increased by the use of suggestion: just as the king once sabotaged Bolingbroke's authority by superseding his chivalric entitlement to dispense justice, so 'Lancaster' rhetorically depletes Richard's authority by tempering the monarchical concept of treason. In a remarkable speech, Bolingbroke delegates to Northumberland an address to Richard in which he uses the formulation 'King Richard' on five occasions (31–67). At the outset, this testifies to the 'allegiance and true faith of heart' that governs his loyalty to 'his most royal person' (37; 38). This seemingly sacrosanct pledge is immediately qualified: it is contingent upon the repeal of his sentence and the restoration of his lands. What accompanies this is a threat of violence: the retribution he will visit in a 'crimson tempest' on the 'fresh green lap of fair King Richard's land' (46; 47). Force is collocated promptly with persuasion in Bolingbroke's political lexicon. In an informal coda, he engages in what appears to be an elaborate parody of Richard's imminent metaphorical projection of the 'thund'ring shock' that should accompany their encounter:

> Be he the fire, I'll be the yielding water;
> The rage be his, whilst on the earth I rain
> My waters – on the earth and not on him.
> March on, and mark King Richard how he looks.

(58–61)

The profane potential of these words are given more implication by the seditious pun on 'rain'; notably, Bolingbroke's response to the king's appearance is equally divested of reverence:

> See, see, King Richard doth himself appear,
> As doth the blushing discontented sun
> From out the fiery portal of the east,
> When he perceives the envious clouds are bent
> To dim his glory and to stain the track
> Of his bright passage to the Occident.
>
> (62–7)

This satirical account of Richard's poetic, and political, self-conception dispenses with the king's charisma.[22]

The ambiguous implications of Bolingbroke's address help establish the grounds for his ascendancy; his strategic refusal to behave as a unified political subject makes manifest that an absolute claim to authority can be subject to qualification and change.[23] Again in *Richard II*, the kernel of this strategy is formed by its relationship to treachery. Bolingbroke's linguistic cunning allows him to rebut Richard's charge, 'That every stride he makes upon my land / Is dangerous treason' (92–3). By maintaining, principally through Northumberland, that his wants have a strictly limited scope – his own 'Enfranchisement' and the restoration of his 'lineal royalties' (114; 113) – Bolingbroke manages to assert simultaneously his own royal blood and his sense of justice, with what degree of good or bad faith, it is impossible to evaluate. Although Richard longs to 'send / Defiance to the traitor, and so die' (129–30), his bitter resignation to 'come at traitor's calls' recognizes (even as it satirizes) the power of 'King Bolingbroke' (181; 173).

3

Shakespeare's interest in treason is intrinsic to his understanding of the discursive practices of early modern authority. Historical study has demonstrated that treason statutes, and the trials and executions that accompanied them, were carefully regimented by Tudor governments: as many defendants pointed out, their prosecution acted to confirm an already assumed guilt.[24] The public exposure of the traitor was expected to reveal an adherence to the heinous beliefs itemized in the treason act of 1571: 'that the Queene...is an Heretyke Schesmatyke Tyraunt Infidell or an Usurper of the Crowne' (13 Elizabeth c. 1). In the ritualized judgement and punishment of treason against the monarch, and in the citation of such procedures and their assumptions in other settings such as the theatre, the populace was encouraged to absorb orthodox political antipathies and inhibitions. However, there were significant debates in Tudor culture concerning both the impartiality of treason trials and the adequacy of the law itself, disputes whose implications are absorbed by both Holinshed and Shakespeare's play. In particular, there were marked differences concerning the status of verbal and written expression as proof of a treasonous temperament, the 'transgressive imagining' Karen Cunningham has detailed as an innovatory interpretation of political betrayal.[25] Current critical thinking has interpreted treason not simply as a matter of external juridical control, but as a discourse that sought to influence political consciousness: 'a tranquil and orderly society seemed to depend not merely upon the "outward observance" and "external conformity" of its subjects, but upon their "heartfelt love" and "sincere conviction"'.[26]

Certainly the legislative pursuit of the 'imagining' of treason had material effect on the conduct of late Elizabethan treason trials. Here, as John Barrell reminds us, we need to recollect the 'purposive sense' of evil contrivance that also accrued to this term in the sixteenth century.[27] Such an implication manifests itself in trials where the majesty of sovereignty was testified to by the prosecution of words that constituted actions against royal prerogative. A representative case, proximate to Shakespeare's play, is the arraignment of Sir John Perrot, the Lord Deputy of Ireland in 1592.[28] This precisely reproduces the prohibitions against injurious forms of political reflection and expression, the treasonous 'Pryntinge Wrytinge Cyphryng Speache Wordes or Sayinges', prohibited in the 1571 act. Perrot is 'not charged with not executing her majesty's commandments, but with contemptuous speeches used against her majesty in the matter' (1319). His offence is proved by hostile interpretation of his irreverent words and the debased imaginings they express: 'which imagination itself was in itself High-Treason, albeit the same proceeded not to any overt fact: and the heart being possessed with the abundance of his traitorous imagination, and not being able so to contain itself, burst forth in vile and traitorous Speeches, and from thence to horrible and heinous actions' (1318). As one witness defined it: 'he spoke as though the kingdom were his own, and not the queen's' (1319).

Such a politically charged legal process, however, was subject to challenge. Catholic polemicists are an especially rich source of criticism of Elizabethan legal policy towards treason, as Curt Breight has noted.[29] An apposite example would be Cardinal Allen's citation of the terms cited by Tudor treason law as, in fact, evidence of the truths the government sought to extirpate from public discourse: 'she [Elizabeth] ys so notoriously knowne, termed and taken for an heretike, as well at home as abrode, that she was glad to provide by a special acte of parliament, that none should call her heretike, Schismatike, Tyrante, usurper, or infidell, under pain of highe treason'.[30] The capacity to question the interests informing prosecutions for treason was widespread. Camden, for example, provides important evidence of a contemporary capacity to demystify the political interests served by the treason trial; his account of Perrot's indictment emphasizes how partisan motivations could operate under the guise of justice. Sir Christopher Hatton and a circle of Perrot's adversaries at court 'laboured tooth and nayle to put him from his place, as a man over-proud. And so farre was the matter brought, that when they found an informer or two in *Ireland*, though *Hatton* were now dead, they called him in the moneth of April to his tryall, *Burghley* Lord Treasurer labouring to the contrary.'[31] Even in the most carefully orchestrated arraignments, there could be volatile moments where the crown's evidence could be disputed by a competing account of its distorted and malevolent character. Essex questioned the motivations of those proceeding against him, accusing Cecil of treasonable sympathies for a Spanish succession: 'I can prove thus much from sir Robert Cecil's own mouth; that he, speaking to one of his fellow-counsellors, should say, That none in the world but the infanta of Spain had right to the crown of England.' The proof for Cecil's disaffection is based on verbal testimony, but a witness promptly testifies that he 'never did hear Mr Secretary use any such words', and the distinction between treasonous and loyal speech is reaffirmed to Cecil's satisfaction: 'The difference between you and me is great; for I speak in the person of an honest man, and you, my lord, in the person of a Traitor.'[32]

In *Richard II*, language is consistently adduced as evidence of a character's treasonous disposition, from Richard's opening inquiry to Gaunt concerning his son's motivations, but the play is equally attentive to the historical and political necessities which accompany this. Even in the feudal atmosphere of the play's early scenes, Bolingbroke is accused of treacherous speech by his opponent, although the proof of this is to be decided in combat. However, there is a distinctive emphasis on the apprehension of verbal treachery and how this arises from the means Bolingbroke uses to assume the throne. Again, treason is identified as the key political medium through which sovereignty is expressed (as well as challenged); the accession of the new king is commingled with that of Aumerle for the assassination of the Duke of Gloucester.

Unquestionably, there is intention in this: reopening the circumstances surrounding Gloucester's death further besmirches Richard's authority and uncovers the corruption Bolingbroke has been impelled to contain. Furthermore, the once reviled Bagot is the chief and, presumably, suborned witness; another powerful indication of the aim of this proceeding.
   Bolingbroke initiates the action against Aumerle:

> Now, Bagot, freely speak thy mind,
> What thou dost know of noble Gloucester's death,
> Who wrought it with the King, and who performed
> The bloody office of his timeless end.

> (4.1.2–5)

Significantly, the accusations that follow have little of the earlier chivalric insistence on the dishonour intrinsic to specific actions. The testimony is not simply evidence of a treasonable assault on a member of the royal family, but proof of his disloyal temperament. Bagot, and subsequently the appellant knights, recount their recollections of what Aumerle said:

> My Lord Aumerle, I know your daring tongue
> Scorns to unsay what once it hath delivered.
> In that dead time when Gloucester's death was plotted,
> *I heard you say*, 'Is not my arm of length,
> That reacheth from the restful English court
> As far as Calais, to mine uncle's head?'
> Amongst much other talk, that very time,
> *I heard you say* that you had rather refuse
> The offer of an hundred thousand crowns
> Than Bolingbroke's return to England –
> Adding withal how blest this land would be
> In this your cousin's death.

> (8–19; emphases added)

Bagot's indictment resembles the protocols of the Elizabethan treason trial: the reckless words of the accused prove his malicious ambition. Strikingly, given the character of Bolingbroke's earlier political strategy, Aumerle's treachery is proved by his equivocal language, his use of words which are an implicit claim of kingly stature and which culminate in the compassing of Bolingbroke's death.[33]

Despite Aumerle's attempts to discredit Bagot, he is repeatedly confronted with hostile accounts of his disloyal conversations and those of his confederates:

> By that fair sun which shows me where thou stand'st,
> *I heard thee say – and vauntingly thou spak'st it –*
> That thou wert cause of noble Gloucester's death.
> ...
> As I intend to thrive in this new world,
> Aumerle is guilty of my true appeal.
> Besides, *I heard the banished Norfolk say*
> That thou, Aumerle, dids't send two of thy men
> To execute the noble Duke at Calais.
>
> (36–8; 79–83; emphases added)

It is not simply what Aumerle, or Mowbray, is accused of saying but also the 'vaunting' manner in which it was spoken. It is difficult, however, to identify conclusive proof in this; the rhetorical nature of the allegations is palpable. Surrey, an apparently reliable witness, was also 'in presence' during the disputed conversations; he testifies for the accused, and we have no evidence to evaluate the rival claims. Instead, the issue of Aumerle's treachery is displaced by the Bishop of Carlisle's shocking intervention to insist that the real enactment of treason has just been witnessed in Bolingbroke's sudden decision to 'ascend the regal throne' (4.1.114–50). Carlisle reaffirms the political proprieties of speech – 'I speak to subjects, and a subject speaks' (133) – and the ordained hierarchy that has been violated by the deposition of 'the figure of God's majesty' (126). Carlisle's rival testimony continues to envisage what cannot be seen directly in his prophecy of the 'tumultuous wars' (141) that subsequently consume the kingdom, a form of seditious speculation which results in his immediate arrest for treason.

To help interpret the significance of these accusations and counter-accusations, it is important to register again the investigative nature of *Richard II*'s treatment of authority. The play is alert to the origins of Bolingbroke's action against utterance as those of a protagonist inured to the adaptation of principle to necessity. Such a perspective sheds light on the new king's use of contrivance to consolidate his power, a tendency that is notoriously visible in Richard's subversive self-deposition. This scene is laden with inference concerning the imperative for an orchestrated spectacle compressed in Bolingbroke's terse instructions to: 'Fetch hither *Richard*, that in common view / He may surrender. So we shall proceed / Without suspicion' (156–8; italics added). Again, there is a significant emphasis on verbal testimony; Richard's public resignation of the crown should naturalize Bolingbroke's authority by infusing it with both inevitability and rectitude. This tactical production of a criminal self is, of course, drastically undermined by Richard's poetic intensification of the deprivation to which he is being subjected and by his competing use of equivocal speech to imply that political interests exist within judicial procedures. Contrary to his penitent demeanour in Holinshed, where he reads out and signs, in public, the statement of his own deposition,[34] Richard refuses to confirm the legal forms that would guarantee his own subjection by using Bolingbroke's tactics of self-abnegation and indeterminate statement:

> Mine eyes are full of tears; I cannot see.
> And yet salt water blinds them not so much
> But they can see a sort of traitors here.
> Nay, if I turn mine eyes upon myself,
> I find myself a traitor with the rest;
> For I have given here my soul's consent
> T'undeck the pompous body of a king,
> Made Glory base and Sovereignty a slave,
> Proud Majesty a subject, State a peasant.
>
> (244–52)

The groundlessness of Bolingbroke's authority appears in the absurdity with which the deposed king expresses his new loyalty (214–22). Richard divulges his understanding of the actual treason being committed: the 'truth' of the scene is shown to be composed in the interests of new-made sovereignty. Partly, this is established by the historical process the audience has witnessed in the play with its conflicting formulations of treason. Bolingbroke's accession has been predicated on a reappraisal of social obligations that demonstrate his entitlement to act as a self-constituted source of authority. The consequence of this is that 'King Bolingbroke' constrains the same kind of politically destabilizing speech which might qualify his own entitlement to power, specifically the use of insinuation to disclose the pragmatic origins of his jurisdiction (and which is deployed with such dialectical force by Richard).

Richard's coded ridicule is reinforced within the play by a new strain of absurdity in its closing phase. As a number of critics have argued, there is a strong taint of the ridiculous over Aumerle's involvement in the conspiracy against Bolingbroke.[35] Of course, it is the treason committed by Richard's imprisonment and killing that distances an audience from Bolingbroke's 'new world'. The sinister allusion that secures Richard's death embodies the same tactics of intimation that secured his authority. Just as Bolingbroke deployed a versatile political register in achieving power, so the play arouses a similarly fluid range of reactions to that authority. It is precisely this latitude of reflection that treason is being mobilized to regiment, but it is vulnerable to the conditional political insight that brought it into being. As the drama proves, such practical deliberation can also decipher the limitations, discontinuity and deficiencies that attend the achievement of political ascendancy.

Still, in important respects, the foiling of Aumerle's plot is a tribute to the success of Bolingbroke's kingship with its impressive combination of toleration with force. Yet there is a double-edged aspect to this. Partly, the incongruous nature of the conclusion is reinforced by its fugitive resemblance to the play's opening events: the accusations that accompany the preparations for Aumerle's trial by combat are also followed by an act of dispossession that questions the monarch's legitimacy, and this incurs another conspiracy against the king. The play appears to visit Bolingbroke with the return of intractable political problems. In light of the new king's earlier concern with the symptomatic appearance of disloyal expression, it is significant that Aumerle's offence is committed and betrayed by a piece of writing. Similarly, the scale of his treason is diminished by its manifest lack of sophistication, and its crassness is emphasized by its discovery in the York household.

This diminution in the efficacy of treason is connected both to the practice of Bolingbroke's sovereignty and the historical conditions that underpin it. York's impulse to betray his own son is a signal, in however serio-comic a fashion, of a compulsive loyalty derived from highly unstable circumstances. It is this which revokes his earlier allegiances both to Richard and to kinship and honour. Clearly, it is fundamental to Bolingbroke's success that he has transcended existing obligations and impressed on his new subjects the necessity of conformity to his will and maintenance of his favour. In identifying the recapitulation of events and situations in the play, it is significant that York's protective loyalty to the king is now expressed by both informing upon and then demanding the death of his son.[36] However, York's eloquent compassion for Richard in his public humiliation is juxtaposed to his abrupt, even insensate, commendation of the necessity that dictates they have become Bolingbroke's 'sworn subjects' (5.2.37–40). The apprehension of Aumerle's conspiracy by his father continues to plot a dynamic relationship between treason and sovereignty as political quantities prone to alteration. More pressingly, there is an increasingly debased quality to the formation of loyalties. The obligation demanded by the new regime – embodying the easily recognizable injunction that to fail to report treason is itself treason – is rendered as disturbing and divisive and the reductive conception of honour to which York appeals has a similarly degraded aspect: 'Mine honour lives when his dishonour dies, / Or my shamed life in his dishonour lies. / Thou kill'st me in his life: giving him breath, / The traitor lives, the true man's put to death' (5.3.69–72). Such a tortuous set of paradoxes and inversions in the language of treason register the degree to which loyalty derives from a circumstantial historical process whose fluctuations are embodied in York.

In his final, as well as his first soliloquy, the imprisoned Richard II reflects on the extraordinary displacement that has deprived him of power. He summons up habits of thought that appear convincing, only to expose their partiality and limitation. Given the brute reality with which deposition has contradicted his own self-conception as a monarch, the king explores how any settled physical state can be overturned and how any process of thought is self-deceiving to the extent that it ignores the possibility of negation. Just as his ambitious fantasies of escape are cancelled by the prison walls, so even 'thoughts of things divine, are intermixed / With scruples and do set the word itself / Against the word' (5.5.12–14). Of course, the Duchess of York has just used the same phrase in berating her husband's cynical use of the term pardon to prevent the bestowing of pardon on Aumerle: 'That sets the word itself against the word!' (5.3.121). This verbal formulation describes the subtle and pervasive dramatic process by which apparently self-consistent terms and concepts are qualified and divided against themselves in *Richard II*. As Richard acknowledges in the moments prior to his death, there is a painful correspondence between sovereignty and treason, as if one condition produces the other which haunts and dispossesses it: 'Sometimes am I king; / Then treasons make me wish myself a beggar, / And so I am' (5.5.32–4). In a macabre way, treason and sovereignty depend on and describe each other, and such proximity is most strikingly manifested in rendering the other provisional: if a king can become a beggar, Richard has witnessed how a traitor can become a king. Like its soliloquizing protagonist, *Richard II* seems drawn to such paradoxical and enquiring modes in its consideration of political values, especially as they are established and contested through language. There is no starker instance of the questions the play has raised concerning the authority treason threatens and locates than in its final paradoxical spectacle of the new and treason-tainted king confronted by the body of the betrayed and the betrayer.

In a recent essay, David Norbrook argues that criticism of *Richard II* should attend more carefully to the motivations of the Essex conspirators and their revival of the play on the day before their rising: 'the 1601 performance was a significant pointer to elements in the play's political rhetoric'.[37] In conclusion, it is worth pursuing briefly this suggestion to reflect on the play's concern with treachery in relation to the rebellion with which it has long been associated. To modern sensibilities, the inclusiveness of the text, and the demands it makes for complex modulations in emotional and political response, render it a bizarre choice either for incendiary propaganda or for ideological material likely to strengthen rebellious resolve. If Mervyn James is correct, *Richard II* could hardly have offered the inspiration provided by John Hayward's *The First Part of the Life and Reign of King Henry IV* (1599), where 'history became a field for the play of the heroic energy of the autonomous political will, seeking to dominate events by its command of the politic arts'.[38] If the temperament of Essex has been accurately evoked – 'a confused jumble of fears, rages, sly plottings and crude irrational outbursts of emotions, culminating in the tragic and dismal fiasco of the 8 February rebellion'[39] – it may be misguided to impute, either to the earl or his circle, any subtlety of interest, beyond that of an apparently successful deposition, in the spectacle of Shakespeare's play.

However, if the interest of Essex and his followers in the history of Richard II is undoubted, their attitude towards it is less clear. When the earl accused Robert Cecil of supporting a catholic succession, he implied Cecil's sympathy for Robert Parson's notorious tract *A conference about the next succession* (1595). Parson's key argument for the Spanish claim was based on the legality of Richard II's deposition, and, hence, the primacy of the Lancastrian line, an argument Essex repudiates as treasonous.[40] As Paul Hammer points out, an emphasis on the military complexion of the circle has tended to simplify its nature, primarily by obscuring the earl's erudition. His following was renowned as a centre for intense, if hardly disinterested, scholarly enquiry, centred upon an 'intellectually high-powered' secretariat, 'a remarkable concentration of scholarly talent'.[41] In this ethos, a more sophisticated rationale might be admitted for the conspirators' interest in Shakespeare's play, especially its disputative stance towards treason as a category relative to authority. The earl's complaint that his reputation was distorted by 'the false glass of others' information'[42] certainly resonates with *Richard II*'s concern with the ensnarement treason presented for public figures and the means by which reputations are divested of, as well as invested with, integrity. Moreover, even the play's dialectical openness may have appealed to their demand for the right of unprejudiced judgement, an impartial appraisal of the often complex and misunderstood realities that could be obscured by the rhetorical flare of treason allegations. The fullness and lucidity with which *Richard II* considers the intensive political mediation intrinsic to the attribution of treason may have been the source of a more complex interest from the Essex circle in the fate of both its protagonists.

In *Richard II*, Shakespeare subjects to searching critical attention one of the principal categories that determined early modern political action and expression. This involves examining the limitations of both the play's rival monarchs and their successive attempts to constrain unwelcome language and reflection. As Paula Blank has suggested, this play demonstrates the vividness of Shakespeare's interest in an ethic of free speech as well as the pressures that militated against this.[43] The political discourse upon which Shakespeare drew to maintain this wariness towards dominant definitions of both rumour and treason will now be explored in relation to *Henry V*, a work often deemed to celebrate the virtues of the King's English.

6
Henry V and the Reformation of the Word

There is an obvious reason for concluding this study with Shakespeare's *Henry V*. If Bale's *King Johan*, is often seen as a point of origin for the history play, *Henry V* can be seen as something like its end. Performed in the closing years of Elizabeth's reign, it marks Shakespeare's final engagement with the English medieval past. Moreover, elements within the play reinforce this mood of culmination. The choric speeches that precede and conclude act five are suffused with the sense of an epic endeavour coming to a close. These events are of such magnitude as to be almost beyond representation: that 'due course of things / Which cannot in their huge and proper life / Be here presented.'[1] Yet, the play's resolution is as contentious as any other aspect of its presentation of events. Notoriously, the final Chorus also contains a reminder of the future awaiting England under *Henry VI*: 'Whose state so many had the managing / That they lost France and made his England bleed' (Epilogue, 11–12). An equal wariness might qualify the assumption that Shakespeare's apparent relinquishment of the genre marked the exhaustion of its possibilities: the history play continued to thrive far more vigorously than is often imagined and the dramatist's own interest in historical material changed rather than terminated.[2] *Henry V* is better seen as continuing Shakespeare's enquiry into the ends of history rather than representing its end.

One feature of the play does help, however, to provide a fitting conclusion to this study: its recapitulation and development of Shakespeare's concern with the challenges presented by turbulent language. This concluding chapter will argue that both the dramatic structure and political concerns of *Henry V* are also informed by this continuing preoccupation with 'delinquent' speech and habits of thought. In this instance, however, the emphasis falls upon how such discourses are pursued as subjects fit for reform. In Shakespeare's account, it is through his reformation of the word that *Henry V* attempts both to perfect himself and to release the best potentialities of the nation.

As this study has already demonstrated, this topic is a key political interest of many history plays. *Henry V* could be interpreted as a comprehensive revision of Bale's *King Johan* where the godly monarch overcomes intense opposition, unites his subjects and succeeds in creating faith in his own integrity.[3] This heroic enterprise also involves the mastery of verbal threats from treacherous counsel, foreign derision, defeatist sentiment and hostile speculation. If sceptical accounts of authority and its troubling relationship to threatening speech pervade the historical drama of the 1590s, *Henry V* appears to answer these in an orthodox way. For example, the play shares the romance form of Greene's *James IV*; both works celebrate marriage as a way of defusing national enmities. Yet Shakespeare's drama turns the utopian potential of romance in a very different direction. In contrast to Greene's dispassionate approach to national feeling, *Henry V* presents the King's English triumphing over foreign or irresponsible speakers. Moreover, the speech of Shakespeare's monarch is no longer a source of instability that requires correction, but the agent of such reform. Throughout, Henry V succeeds in enhancing his presence within his subjects' habits of thought and expression and in refining the way this is conducted. Indeed, if these emphases are symptomatic of Shakespeare's desire to reform contemporary historical theatre, this impulse may well extend to his own work. As many commentators have noted in relation to *Henry IV, Parts 1 and 2*, Hal's political triumph is also achieved over a world of unregenerate speech, hostile perceptions and festive licence.[4] A deepening association with the language and values of spiritual reform marks this hard-won achievement, yet, it is complicated throughout by notorious ambiguities in presentation.[5] *Henry V* concentrates upon the monarch's charismatic oratory and his rhetorical ascendancy is enhanced by the responsibility he also undertakes for the correction, improvement and, on occasion, the silencing of deficient speech.

One context for *Henry V*'s engagement with the process of reform lies with the enduring sixteenth-century interest in the improvement of language and the contribution this made to a newly expansive sense of English as a discourse of civility and empire. The status of the vernacular, the possibility of its advancement, and the discrimination of a 'standard', even superior, form of English – the literate speech of the court, the Home Counties and the higher social classes – became increasingly prominent subjects for debate during this period.[6] Anna Bryson has explored how the command of a 'pleasing' discourse became an important symbol of status; this was accompanied by an increasing intolerance of what were 'perceived as distortions of voice, indecencies of vocabulary attributed to the lower classes'.[7] A notable symptom of this growing emphasis on 'proper' forms of English was manifested in elaborate schemes of national linguistic reform proposed by humanists such as Sir Thomas Smith, John Hart and Alexander Gill. These sought to bring the heteroglot variety of written and spoken English under the regulation prescribed by its most literate and 'well-spoken' members. John Hart explained that 'perfait speche' is the prerogative of 'the lettered': 'yet the rest naturally utter their mindes the one to the other, though painfulli with circumstances, and litell other discretion than chidlre: therwith contenting, and flattering theim selves they think no speech so good as that they use'.[8] The contrasts *Henry V* draws between gentle and plebeian speech and between the language of the court, other 'dialects' and French have been perceived as reinforcing these new modes of English urbanity and civility.[9] From this viewpoint, the play promotes both an exclusivist ideal of an English empire united by a common language and by the agency of a royal hero who comes to speak for the nation.[10]

This chapter will challenge, however, accounts of the play that stress its elevation of a courtly and imperial form of English. It will argue that the early modern debate concerning language has been seen too readily as providing a conservative ethos for its political reflection. This issue can be reopened by exploring the complexity of humanist discourse on the vernacular as well *Henry V*'s own intricate engagement with these issues. Consideration of this topic was far from uniform in the sixteenth century: the idea that language should be improved or standardized was disputed as was the issue of how it might be corrected and to what end. Contemporary criticism has often assumed that a 'top-down' thesis of language reform prevailed in the sixteenth century, an acceptance that appropriate forms of speech (and writing) needed to be imposed from 'above' or from 'outside' on recalcitrant, unruly and marginal speakers. Yet this was hardly a complete or uncontested process; the social role of language was open to a variety of arguments concerning its most fitting condition and purposes. As we shall see, humanists such as Richard Mulcaster opposed the idea of dominion being exercised over speech. Language was also conceived in the period as variegated and mutable and as the summation of its speakers' usages; any attempt to regulate or reform this would involve both cultural diminishment and political threat.

Furthermore, the complex formal composition of *Henry V* allowed Shakespeare to explore a range of viewpoints concerning the fate of language at the hands of those who sought its reform. The emphasis of this chapter falls again, therefore, on the political implications of dramatic form in Shakespeare's history plays. As with *King John* and *Richard II*, we need to attend as carefully to the rhetorical conception of the drama as to its most influential speakers. Marion Trousdale has argued that the rhetorical structures of Shakespeare's plays were designed both to convey and to provoke variegated responses and to elicit as wide-ranging an experience of history as possible. Shakespeare's method is to 'open up' or 'unfold' the history 'suggesting some of the topics that lie within it...the language used is questioned and then discussed'.[11] This imperative has an important bearing upon the King's English in *Henry V* as each act of the play presents successive linguistic, as well as practical, challenges that its protagonist must overcome. This allows Shakespeare to create a complex historical context in which the contrast and correspondences between 'superior' and 'inferior' idioms expose the limitations as well as the strengths of each; in this way, the king's speech is held to account from 'below'. One of the subtlest areas of the play's historical reflection – as well as its complex rhetorical structure – is that the very language with which the reform of speech is conducted is also subject to sustained critical examination from the viewpoint of common or customary speech. The play suggests that as Henry's regal discourse develops in conviction, range and fluency, reactions to this also require qualification and restraint.

Richard Mulcaster and the language question

'No one turns Shakespeare himself,' remarks Patrick Collinson 'into a chapter of the English Reformation.'[12] Yet Shakespeare's *Henry V* has featured prominently in a widespread reappraisal of how protestant spiritual ideals and social values were absorbed into and expressed by sixteenth-century literature and drama.[13] This ideological context has served to emphasize the play's doctrinal and political orthodoxy. On this view, the dramatist's concern with 'reformation' is cognate with the desires of his protagonist; both attempt to transform and enlarge an audience's understanding of the king's significance. Thus, Shakespeare's selective treatment of his sources signals his intentions towards his hero.[14] Equally, the play's epic tenor has often been interpreted and performed as a monarchist and patriotic spectacle: 'a propaganda play on National Unity: heavily orchestrated for the brass'.[15]

The interpretation of language in *Henry V* has bolstered this tradition of reading. The king is perceived, understandably enough, as the most exalted of speakers, a paradigm of eloquence in action. 'A General', counselled Leonard Digges in his *Stratioticos* (1579) – a work that Shakespeare recollected in his creation of Fluellen[16] – 'ought first in his owne person so to reforme all disordered appetites, that his life may serve as a mirrour to the whole Armie howe to reforme themselves'. The control of speech is central to this endeavour of personal and collective reform. A general should be 'no vain Vaunter, neyther to vendicate wholye to himselfe the prayse of good successe, but to impute the same firste to God, secondly to his Captaines and Souldiours that serve under him'.[17] Henry V's language and leadership embody precisely these virtues. Selfless, disciplined, inspirational, this king is able to vanquish the hostile words and perceptions of his enemies as decisively as physical threats. 'O that we now had here,' remarks the despondent Westmorland in the moments before Agincourt, 'But one ten thousand of those men in England / That do no work to-day!' (4.3.16–18). It is this statement, one that glances mischievously at the audience, that provokes Henry's inspirational address on the momentous destiny awaiting those 'happy few' on Crispin Crispian day (18–67). As so often, the king's speech corrects mistaken perceptions, inspires audacity and resolution, and fosters a newly rewarding dialogue between monarch and subject:

King: Thou dost not wish more help from England, coz?

Westmorland: God's will, my liege, would you and I alone,
             Without more help, could fight this royal battle!

                                                    (4.3.73–5)

The play does present, however, a variety of voices that remain indifferent or opposed to the king's promulgation of a unifying national discourse, those who comment, sometimes unknowingly, in an abrasive manner upon this ideal: Pistol, Nym, the Dauphin and the French courtiers, Katherine and Fluellen. Evaluating Henry's correction of these seemingly intransigent or unresponsive voices has been a central issue in critical debate. One context that helps in the arbitration of this issue can be drawn from the period's rhetorical tradition and, especially, its debate over the status of the vernacular. Much of this material might be cited to confirm the king's linguistic credit. Henry's versatile, compelling oratory is presented in terms comparable to those used by Thomas Wilson concerning the elect orator in his *Arte of Rhetorique* (1553). Wilson portrays the ideal rhetorician by drawing repeated analogies 'between secular and sacred eloquence, between the would-be improver of his fellow Englishmen and the worthy minister of the Word'.[18] Hence, stressing his role as a reformer expands the conventional emphasis in the classical rhetorical tradition upon the orator's part in creating social order and civility. For Wilson, the spiritually enlightened rhetorician enlarges the sense of responsibility we should feel for others; this in turn helps facilitate harmonious relationships within the commonwealth. By his own dedicated example, the orator helps to edify the principle of vocation; equally, by reproving selfish and uncivil impulses, the eloquent speaker helps to preserve hierarchy, social cohesion and the obedience these principles require. Ultimately, the orator helps to draw others towards wisdom and hence towards God. Without this important office, Wilson asks, who would accept their ordained place – 'Who woulde digge and delve from morne till evening?' – and who would pursue any enterprise larger than their own interests:

> Yea, who woulde for his kynges pleasure adventure and hasarde his life, if witte hadde not so wonne men, that they thought nothing more needfull in this world, nor anye thing whereunto they were more bounden: then here to live in their duty, and to traine their whole lyfe accordynge to their callynge.

The inspirational figure who can win acceptance of these goals is 'not onlye to be taken for a singuler manne, but rather to be counted for halfe a God'.[19] As we shall see, the king is presented as a paragon of reformed rhetoric in precisely this mode in the play's opening scene.

Similarly, among proponents of language reform, a strong sense of the monarch's responsibility for exalting language was often detectable. As Martin Elsky suggests, a 'linguistic responsibility' was imputed to monarchs and a connection made 'between morally disposed political power and the verbal health of a nation'.[20] Alexander Gill reminded James I that 'Leaders, Kings, and Emperors, have sought eagerly to sustain elegance and grace in their native language' and that Edward III, Henry V's illustrious ancestor, revealed his excellence in prohibiting law-French as much as in his military triumphs against the old enemy.[21] A mounting anxiety has been perceived amongst humanists concerning the contemporary state of English. Many deplored the vast increase in neologism and loan words, the proliferation of underworld and professional argots, and the ongoing babel of regional dialects.[22] Those who sought the reform of language looked back with nostalgia to a time when purity of speech was pervasive and sought to renew this ideal. *Henry V* can be interpreted as cognate both with this attempt to 're-form' English and with the disdain that pervaded literate Tudor society towards subordinate forms of speech. John Hart recommended that 'the vicious parts' of language should be 'cut away, as are the idle or offensive members in a politike common welth'.[23] The play and its protagonist undoubtedly realize this goal, 'cutting away', in both literal and symbolic terms, those who express themselves in 'poor' English. As Stephen Greenblatt argues, speakers of dialect in the play are included as 'puppets jerked on the strings of their own absurd accents'.[24]

We need to maintain, however, an awareness of the complexity of the debate provoked by language in sixteenth-century culture. The contemporary criticism that alerts us to the ideological agenda of Tudor language reform does also risk composing a homogeneous 'voice' for a humanist 'speech community'. One influential contributor to these debates was the Cumbrian-born Richard Mulcaster, headmaster of the Merchant Taylors' School (1561–86) and St Paul's (1596–1608) and one of the period's most celebrated pedagogues; his students included Edmund Spenser and Thomas Kyd. Mulcaster's reflections upon English in his *The First Part of the Elementarie* (1582) allow us to consider *Henry V*'s relationship to a language debate that was far from ideologically uniform. Indeed, in this work the reform of language was subjected to a wide-ranging and politically informed critique. Mulcaster's principal engagement, however, is with those advocates of spelling reform who sought to rationalize the unruly condition of English spelling. They perceived orthography as dominated by custom; this had resulted in the preservation of obsolete spellings even when letters no longer matched the sound of words. For Thomas Smith and John Hart, 'custom...may merely represent the end product of human folly, whereas reason must be the instrument of reform'.[25] Smith lamented that 'Great is the force, great the weight, enormous the authority of custom and usage.' The consequences of this had drastic consequences for language, but adhering to custom, Smith argues, also had an impact well beyond the linguistic sphere:

So that without blame, and as it were by right it can cause wrong to be praised and good slighted, right to be despised and sin practised, justice to be disowned and unjustice maintained, your own goods to be lost and other men's detained by you.[26]

The linguistic solution proposed by Smith and like-minded humanists, put crudely, was to make spelling correspond more accurately to a 'rational' or received idea of pronunciation. In contrast to this, Mulcaster defends custom and emphasizes that language exists as a set of conventionally agreed upon norms.[27] The implications of his argument bear scrutiny as they help to provide a new context for the treatment of language and its reform in *Henry V*.

For both Mulcaster and his opponents, the very idea of language use is 'intimately connected with concepts of political legitimacy and the common weal'.[28] The *Elementarie* appeals for limitations on prerogative, for custom to be defended, and for a variety of idioms and usages to flourish. In this respect, Mulcaster 'sometimes speaks as if language is the public possession of the national commonweal'.[29] The *Elementarie* criticizes the idea that the sound of words should determine their pronunciation or spelling; those in favour of such a reform support an autocratic view of language as thriving best under the sway of sole governance. In contrast, Mulcaster argues that the history of language teaches us a very different lesson: '*sound* upon great cause, was deposed from his monarchie, as no fit person to rule the pen alone' and it exists now 'like a restrained not banished *Tarquinius* desiring to be restored to his first and sole monarchie'.[30] Hence, the 'imperiousnesse' of sound must be resisted for 'the generall good of the hole province of writing' (p. 67); this requires the admission of reason, consent and custom to the governance of language. 'Custom' is a crucial term for Mulcaster. It is often misunderstood as simply common usage and hence prone to debasement and corruption; it should be perceived as 'that, which is grounded at the first, upon the best and fittest reason, and is therfor to be used, bycause it is the fittest' (p. 72). Furthermore, customary speech is the wellspring of 'fitting' speech: 'For speche being our instrument at will, for our common dealings, why should not that be the right therein, which is of commonest note and best understood' (p. 101). This idea allows Mulcaster to launch his critique of all those who seek the reform of language. This defies 'the authoritie of the peple which speak it', and it requires custom to be disparaged, innovation to be lauded, and the prerogative of sound, that 'vile usurper', to be restored (p. 80; p. 94). Speech and writing should be open and free in their usages, ready to alter and expand; it is this capacity that Mulcaster christens as the 'true *prerogative* and libertie of English speakers' (p. 160).[31]

'For the common weal is the measure of everie mans being, which if anie one respect not, he is not to live in it' (p. 12). Mulcaster's emphasis upon the commonwealth allowed him to formulate a thoroughgoing critique of the desire to reform common or customary speech. Indeed, the *Elementarie* values the latter as providing the real authority for how language should be spoken and disparages any prospect of sole governance over a variety of idioms and usage. As James L. Calderwood acknowledges, such an insight into speech was familiar to Shakespeare. He notes that in *Richard II*, for example, the relationship between word and referent is revealed not to be fixed or determined solely by Richard's dictat, but as dependent upon 'informal covenants among speakers. Kings and meanings rule by custom.'[32] In *Henry V*, agreements (or even disagreements) among speakers question, as well as endorse, Henry's invitation to support the legitimacy of his actions. This permits other forms of 'customary' language to qualify historical understanding and, especially, to take a critical view of the reform of speech. Such a probing response to the 'verbal health' of a monarch and his impact upon national life and discourse can also be perceived in Reformation historiography. 'Never tyrant more cruel' ran the marginal gloss in the 1563 edition of *Actes and Monuments*, as Foxe described Henry V's hounding of lollardy once he accepted the church's support for his invasion of France. This persecution was turned upon vernacular language as much as the bodies of and beliefs of 'heretics':

> the king made this most blasphemous and cruel act, to be as a law for ever: That whatsoever they were that should read the Scriptures in the mother tongue (which was then called Wickliff's learning), they should forfeit land, cattle, life, and goods, from their heirs for ever, and so be condemned for heretics to God, enemies to the crown, and most arrant traitors to the land. (*A & M*, p. 275)

In Foxe, the king's language and behaviour passes out of sympathetic consideration when he is shown to share the views of his clergy and to ignore the popular voice. In the remainder of this chapter, it will be argued that such a perspective is also present in *Henry V*, a text where even the act of locating the reformed voice is not straightforward.

Reforming speech in *Henry V*

The issue of language and its correction is vivid throughout Shakespeare's play and it is conceived dynamically within it. This motif finds expression within a variety of contexts and it is shaped by the motivations of different speakers. The significance of this pervasive concern with language is stressed by the play's insistent staging of verbal differences and conflicts.[33] What matters as much as Agincourt is the outcome of its lengthy sequence of orations, disputes, diplomatic exchanges, petitionings, acts of translation, judgements and negotiations. Even in the heated circumstances of the siege at Harfleur, Henry's four captains find time for a 'linguistic turn'. Fluellen pursues Macmorris for 'a few disputations with you as partly touching or concerning the disciplines of the wars, the Roman wars, in the way of argument, look you, and friendly communication?' The valiant captain Jamy is dismayed at the latter's dismissal of this as a wasteful distraction: 'Marry, I wad full fain heard some question 'tween you twa' (3.2.96–9; 119–20).

As this example suggests, the play is engaged not only with rhetorical oppositions, but also with a specific stance towards these: identifying and correcting deficiencies in the speech and attitudes of others. Yet, as is also evident here, the pervasiveness as well as the mutable appearance of linguistic reform invites a varied consideration of its equity and decorum. Later in the play we see Fluellen pursuing an argument over the quality of thought and language but in more desperate circumstances. Pistol seeks the support of his more powerful voice to save Bardolph from execution for the theft of a 'pax of little price': 'Therefore go speak – the Duke will hear thy voice...Speak, Captain, for his life, and I will thee requite' (3.6.45; 49). For Fluellen, the critical issue here is the proper definition of Fortune (3.6.29–37). This obtrusive concern with linguistic propriety discloses a gap between the motives informing common speech and those who evaluate it for its perceived deficiencies.

If we turn now to the opening of the play, we can grasp in more detail the complex presence of both the 'reformed' voice in *Henry V* and of those who seek to correct speech. The opening Chorus, for example, rapidly calls its own linguistic exuberance to account, begging 'pardon, gentles all' for:

> The flat unraised spirits that hath dared
> On this unworthy scaffold to bring forth
> So great an object.

> (Prologue, 8–11)

The passing moment of hubris requires an acknowledgement that theatrical power depends upon a communal imaginative effort: the 'humble patience' of an audience who, in the quality of their attention at least, are 'gentles all'. The Chorus, therefore, introduces us to *Henry V*'s double perspective upon language by its simultaneous indulgence and demystification of rhetorical display. This establishes a mode of critical scrutiny towards speech that is of great importance for the play. Whatever the fervour of the rhetorical discourse we encounter it as accompanied by a more thoughtful estimate of its scope and motivations.[34] In this way, the play absorbs a key Reformation concern with scrutinizing language by turning it upon those speakers who are engaged most extensively in reforming their own speech as well as the words of others.

The intricacy of the play's consideration of this issue is apparent in its opening depiction of the new king in relation to both the reports we hear of him and by direct presentation. The former emphasizes Henry's reformed eloquence; the latter the gravity of his linguistic expectations of others. These two sequences will now be examined in some detail to compose a framework for interpreting the play's treatment of reformed and reforming speech. In the Archbishop of Canterbury's account, we are invited both to remember and to reinterpret Henry's unredeemed preference for 'courses vain', and for 'companies unlettered, rude, and shallow' (1.1.54; 55). Through this account we discover the magnitude of Henry's personal transformation, how 'wildness, mortified in him' seemingly at the instant of his father's death and 'Consideration like an angel came / And whipped th'offending Adam out of him' (28–9):

> Never was such a sudden scholar made,
> Never came reformation in a flood
> With such a heady currence scouring faults,
> Nor never Hydra-headed wilfulness
> So soon did lose his seat, and all at once,
> As in this king.

> (1.1.32–7)

The new king's conversion is made immediately apparent in his language: it bestows upon him a seemingly instantaneous and unstudied mastery of different idioms and these are granted compelling power:

> Hear him but reason in divinity
> And, all-admiring, with an inward wish
> You would desire the king were made a prelate.
> Hear him debate of commonwealth affairs,
> You would say it hath been all in all his study.
> List his discourse of war, and you shall hear

> A fearful battle rendered you in music.
> Turn him to any cause of policy,
> The Gordian knot of it he will unloose,
> Familiar as his garter, that, when he speaks,
> The air, a chartered libertine, is still,
> And the mute wonder lurketh in men's ears
> To steal his sweet and honeyed sentences
>
> (1.1.38–50)

In all areas of humane discourse, the new king is endowed with a preternatural competence born of his spiritual renovation. This reduces his auditors to a state of mute astonishment and it foments their desire to imitate their new monarch and to enrich their own discourse from his rhetorical *copia*. The ground for Henry's evaluation of the speech of others derives from his own far-reaching experience of reformation.

This helps to establish Henry's rhetorical presence in the terms suggested by Thomas Wilson's ideal of the elect orator. Yet this arresting account of elevated speech does not quite evoke unquestioning admiration. By stressing the king's piety and new sense of vocation, the archbishop also engages in a form of self-persuasion designed to aid his circumvention of the proposed appropriation of church lands. For those in the audience familiar with Foxe, his discourse would be profoundly tainted as one of those malign figures who 'put the king in remembrance to claim his right in France... Thus were Christ's people betrayed every way, and their lives bought and sold by these most cruel thieves' (*A & M*, p. 275). Oddly, Canterbury's dialogue with Ely implicates them both in 'reformed' attitudes despite their sectional interests. Both speakers improve upon and correct the other's estimation of the king's great change and arrive at a fuller sense of the event and its implications. Ely reminds his superior that the king's redemption only appears to be miraculous by his analogy of the strawberry's hidden maturation beneath 'baser' fruit. Equally, the prince must have 'obscured his contemplation / Under the veil of wildness' (1.1.63–4). Canterbury concedes this more material perspective and, by deciphering Henry's *sprezzatura*, he arrives at a key instance of reformed insight: 'It must be so, for miracles are ceased, / And therefore we must needs admit the means / How things are perfected' (67–9). This is an instance of what Huston Diehl has identified as an imperative of the period's protestant theatrical aesthetics: 'arousing suspicion of the marvelous and fostering a skepticism about received beliefs'.[35] Such a perception is all the more provocative by being placed in the mouths of Catholic clergy. The arch-bishop is able subsequently to embrace a more realistic appraisal of the king's sympathies towards the church: 'He *seems* indifferent, / Or rather swaying more upon our part / Than cherishing th'exhibitors against us' (72–4; emphasis added). Retrieving the detail of this dialogue demonstrates how the play both deploys Wilson's ideal of the elect orator and qualifies this by contrasting forms of rhetorical enquiry and historical assessment. These are far less conclusive or reverential in their evaluation of the king's sacrosanct qualities. Furthermore, the presence of reformed understanding is far from predictable; it emerges here in the voices of those least likely to possess it.

Such complication in response also affects the direct presentation of the king's language: the rhetorical circumstances in which it finds articulation restrain assent to it. Initially, however, the heightened expectations aroused by Henry's speech are satisfied not least by the rigorous linguistic and moral expectations he holds towards others. As Thomas Wilson commended, the king not only lives up to the awesome obligations of his office, but he demands that his subjects embrace a fuller sense of their duties. Henry emphasizes to the Archbishop of Canterbury, his care for speech: what motivates it, its truthfulness, and the obligations it may impose upon others. To the latter, the king emphasizes the solemn duty that attends his account of Salic law; this he must 'justly and religiously unfold', avoiding any attempt to 'fashion, wrest or bow your reading...whose right / Suits not in native colours with the truth' (1.2.10; 14; 16–17). Canterbury should speak under the hearing of God and weigh every word in full awareness of his respons-ibility for the bloodshed incumbent to war:

> Under this conjuration speak, my lord,
> For we will hear, note, and believe in heart
> That what you speak is in your conscience washed
> As pure as sin with baptism.

> (1.2.29–32)

The archbishop now unravels the long skein of corrupted reasoning deriving from Salic law and recovers – according to venerable humanist practice – the origins and contexts that truly define its meaning. Yet subjecting his own discourse to a similar form of analysis would hardly vindicate Henry's desire for uncontaminated speech. The Archbishop's critique of specious claims of legitimacy is being addressed, for example, to the heir of a usurper. More proximately, we are only too aware of the archbishop's own desire for a distracting war. Predominantly, these awkward details involve the limitations of the king's subjects or 'extradramatic' material at the margins of remembrance. The scene does broaden, however, to qualify any straightforward acceptance of royal, courtly or ecclesiastical speech as the deliberations continue regarding the just motivations for war.

   After Canterbury's address, both the clergy and aristocracy engage in a choric persuasion that Henry must realize his historical destiny as a warrior-king. Throughout, the monarch's concern for responsible speech is emphasized by his acting as a sceptical interlocutor towards a variety of arguments that drift away from the laboriously established ground of Salic law. Ely couches his advice, for example, in a chivalric idiom where the equity of the cause is only remotely felt:

> Awake remembrance of these valiant dead,
> And with your puissant arm renew their feats.
> You are their heir, you sit upon their throne,
> The blood and courage that renowned them.
> Runs in your veins, and my thrice-puissant liege
> Is in the very May-morn of his youth,
> Ripe for exploits and mighty enterprises.

> (115–121)

These admonitions stress that Henry must live up to the expectations of his office and that these must be addressed in a timely fashion; his legitimacy will be vindicated through chivalric action. What matters in this historical vision is the need to revivify the martial spirit of the nation, not issues of convoluted legalism. Henry is heir to the much more significant legacy of his warlike ancestors and only his success in imitating their endeavours will allow him to evade historical oblivion. As the king puts it:

> Either our history shall with full mouth
> Speak freely of our acts, or else our grave
> Like Turkish mute shall have a tongueless mouth,
> Not worshipped with a waxen epitaph.

> (231–4)

Henry's achievements need to be recorded in a vernacular that will be exalted by them. This will mark the difference between his discourse and the merely barbarous and servile. It is this aspiration that motivates his decision for action, although this is charged with a new spirit of enmity provoked by the Dauphin's gibe. Yet the rhetorical process by which this conclusion is arrived at qualifies its reception. Each cause for action has a contestable relationship to the others: a military campaign will help defeat secular ambitions to appropriate church land; it is legally and morally justified; there are irresistible historical expectations that the king must live up to; such an endeavour will produce greater social unity and outface historical oblivion; it will allow Henry, in response to the Dauphin's scorn, 'To venge me as I may, and to put forth / My rightful hand in a well-hallowed cause' (293–4). None of these motives, with the partial exception of the first, is specious, but they are offered pragmatically in a way which tends to supersede each previous statement. More significantly, the king comes to embrace a chivalric idiom that has passed through some compromised speakers, especially Canterbury and Ely. As the persuasions to action mount in intensity, the archbishop reminds the audience, at least, of his less than dispassionate impulses:

> O let their bodies follow, my dear liege,
> With blood and sword and fire to win your right;
> In aid whereof we of the spiritualty
> Will raise your highness such a mighty sum
> As never did the clergy at one time
> Bring in to any of your ancestors.
>
> (130–5)

In this way, the scene also involves a 'fall' in the integrity and value of the language that we hear; we are reminded that even the most convincing discourse can proceed in the interest of deeply 'unreformed' motivations. Hence, King Henry's initial scruples over language and motive are 'corrected' but in less than ideal ways.

Perhaps this reading is over-subtle in its treatment of a scene where the impetus for war grows steadily more convincing and we come to admire the audacity which inspires this consensus. Furthermore, there are certainly stark contrasts drawn in *Henry V* between the King's English and others who are less rhetorically gifted and more stridently lacking in integrity. Whatever the subtle rhetorical counterpoints and qualifications found in its opening act, the play does develop into a drama of compelling differences. Clear verbal and ethical distinctions are drawn between the English court and the vainglorious French one and between Henry, his military commanders, and that remnant of the London underworld that subsists, disgracefully, at the margins of his campaign. Being contrasted so forcibly with the 'linguistically disadvantaged' augments the king's achievement of a commanding language.[36]

Linguistic impoverishment marks those commoners who are determined to join Henry's army. The absence of Falstaff's incandescent and subversive wit is palpable in contrast to the cacophony of verbal blunders, malapropisms and misunderstandings that characterize his followers. Nym's stunted prose is both laboured and vacuous and the world of Eastcheap seems devoid of warmth or communal spirit. Pistol's mangled rendition of the 'mighty line' catches fire only in crude animosity and the absurdity of his quarrel with Nym is conveyed through a series of half-literate, inflammatory exchanges. In short, the language we hear is largely quarrelsome and profane.

Furthermore, an even deeper contrast is developed between vulgar speakers and the monarch by the elision of this scene with the apprehension of the traitors. Here, Henry's potency as a reformed orator is enhanced by his ability to discriminate between distinct forms of deficient language:

> Enlarge the man committed yesterday
> That railed against our person. We consider
> It was excess of wine that set him on,
> And on his more advice we pardon him.
>
> (2.2.40–3)

This tolerance of one form of delinquent speech helps Henry to expose the most heinous form of verbal, moral and political corruption: treachery. In his oration against Scroop, the king expounds upon the sacredness of his own person which he distinguishes, very much like Richard II, as the unique object of treasonous speculation: 'this revolt of thine, methinks, is like / Another fall of man' (141–2). Scroop's treason can be explained only in terms of demonic temptation that results in the purest form of evil: unmotivated destruction. The devil who seduced him 'Hath got the voice in hell for excellence' by providing Scroop 'no instance why thou shouldst do treason / Unless to dub thee with the name of traitor' (113; 119–120). Henry's serious regard for the responsibilities incumbent to speech, and their grotesque distortion in Scroop's dialogue with the devil, also involves him in the reform of his own

attitudes. As his anger escalates, the king arrives at a more dispassionate motive for judgement as he delivers the traitors over to summary
execution:

> Touching our person seek we no revenge,
> But we our kingdom's safety must so tender,
> Whose ruin you have sought, that to her laws
> We do deliver you.
>
> (175–8)

Throughout this scene, Henry again conceives the integrity of language
in a manner that was deeply embedded in the early modern rhetorical
tradition and, especially, in its ideal of reformed eloquence which stressed
'the interdependency of speech and right living'.[37] In this view, speech
was construed as 'the very measure of the soul' and the deleterious
consequences of corrupt speech on thought and morals were perceived
as leading to such 'spiritual calamities as falsehood, treason, heresy, and
atheism'.[38] It is this kind of evaluation that informs Henry's own earlier
and rigorous account of his 'wilder days' as a period of moral exile,
a dangerous time of 'barbarous license' where he neither valued himself
nor held any larger conception of his responsibilities to England. Such
forms of self and national neglect can degenerate into treacherous
speculation and conspiracy. Again, this is cognate with the conception
of language promoted by protestant humanists such as Roger Ascham
and his understanding of what occurs 'when apt and good words began
to be neglected':

> then also began ill deeds to spring, strange manners to oppress
> good orders, new and fond opinions to strive with old and true
> doctrine...right judgment of all things to be perverted, and so virtue
> with learning is contemned and study left off. Of ill thoughts cometh
> perverse judgment; of ill deeds springeth lewd talk.[39]

As with the opening scene, however, we need to recognize how these
rhetorical ideals and ethical contrasts are embodied in a dramatic
process: this forms its own argument through pointed counter-
statements as well as equivocal correspondences and oblique commentary. In other words, the play's dramatic language is not simply
a supplement to the king's speech, but a discourse that exceeds his
power to regulate it. In this way, Henry's moral status remains open to

question. This can be demonstrated by considering briefly the play's representation of the French and by returning to the depiction of its lowlife characters.

'Yet forgive me, God, / That I do brag thus!' (3.6.149–50), Henry remarks to Montjoy concerning the pride he takes in his army. Yet, this typical gesture of self-correction and moderation is delivered cuttingly: 'This your air of France / Hath blown that vice in me. I must repent' (150–1). Henry's conceit of adulterated French air spreading its contagion is certainly vindicated elsewhere in the play. It is most marked in the scene immediately following this statement: in the absurd verbal superfluity of the Dauphin. Vain, prolix, xenophobic and uncharitable, the Dauphin's speech is the antithesis of his English opponent and functions as a paradigm of linguistic excess and the ethical misdirection that accompanies this. In his notorious reflections on his beloved horse before Agincourt, we witness precisely how when apt words are neglected so 'right judgment of all things' becomes perverted (3.7.11–18; 20–4; 27–9; 31–40). Yet critical accounts of the play's representation of the French have tended, at times, to make their national discourse synonymous with the Dauphin's.[40] In fact, the French court is a complex 'speech community' that subjects the latter's hubris, in this scene, to ironic disparagement, and, in an earlier presentation, to revision and reform. It is equally typical of *Henry V* that apparently antithetical verbal and moral positions also disclose an underlying correspondence. In the closing scene of act two, the contrast we might expect between enemy arrogance and English resolution is belied by the mature scrutiny the French undertake of this new military threat. Here, it is the Dauphin who manifests an attitude often mistaken for the play's, with his 'breezy confidence that appropriates and manipulates foreignness almost as if it were a commodity'.[41] This is corrected from two historical perspectives: the Constable's clear-eyed acceptance of Henry's reformation (2.4.29–40) and the French king's tragic recollection of Cressy. This deliberation allows the French to arrive at a considered response to English power and to subordinate the Dauphin's reckless misjudgement of Henry as a 'vain, giddy, shallow, humorous youth' (2.4.28). In contrast to this, the French king confronts a painful historical legacy of defeat at the hands of the Black Prince whose father:

> ...smiled to see him,
> Mangle the work of nature and deface
> The patterns that by God and by French fathers
> Had twenty years been made. This is a stem

> Of that victorious stock; and let us fear
> The native mightiness and fate of him.
>
> (2.4.59–64)

This unflinching recollection of catastrophe allows the French court to correct superficial impressions, engage seriously with a political challenge, and to arrive at a just resolution. This assured process of rhetorical deliberation equals that of the English court and it bears out Lisa Hopkins's observation that *Henry V* puts pressure on the distinction between self and other to the point where it is not always possible to designate the French as alien.[42] The convergence between English and French discourse will be returned to later, but it is accompanied by a similar disjunction in the representation of the disreputable characters of the play where, again, the complexity of what is spoken contradicts expectations. Again the distinctions between degraded and responsible speech prove to be less consistent than might be expected and, instead, the play creates parallels and resemblances between remote or divergent spheres of speech.

Thus, important aspects of the 'poor' English we hear in the play comment forcibly on the more elevated sphere of action. In one sense the glaring contrast between the king's imposing language in 'the traitor's scene' and the crass squabble between Nym and Pistol over the Hostess is all to the latter's credit. Yet, the latter also contains the discussion of Falstaff's illness and death, with its direct allusion to another friendship betrayed. This is evoked in the Hostess's broken English who is sure, at least, of Falstaff's redemption in 'Arthur's bosom' after he 'babbled of green fields' (2.3.10; 16–17). Finally, Falstaff's speech is reduced to gibberish and then to silence. However, this seemingly insufficient reformation makes the completed process of Henry's conversion less sacrosanct. It becomes the occasion for critical reflection among all those who remember it: 'The King hath run bad humours on the knight, that's the even of it' (2.1.121–2). In this respect, the 'lowlife' characters succeed in flooding the play with the recollection of lived experience that is being set aside at 'higher' levels of the play.[43] Even the capacity of the French king to confront painful historical memories is not always reciprocated within Henry's national-historical crusade. When Fluellen reports the execution of Bardolph 'for robbing a church...if your majesty know the man' (3.6.100–1), the king reminds his followers once again that their speech and action must be carefully tempered: 'none of the French' should be 'upbraided or abused in disdainful

language' (3.6.109; 110). This sermonizing response does leave important aspects of Henry's previous identity and experience unaccounted
for. Even in the unimpeachably loyal discourse of Fluellen we find a
memorable example of the king's exposure to forms of recollection that
discomfit his ethical status. In the famous passage where Fluellen com-
pares his king to Alexander, this potentially absurd analogy suddenly
clarifies around one significant detail: Alexander 'did in his ales and his
angers, look you, kill his best friend Clytus...so also Harry Monmouth,
being in his right wits and his good judgements, turned away the
fat knight with the great-belly doublet' (4.7.37–8; 45–7). Fluellen can
remember Falstaff's physical presence and the nature of his speech
('jests, and gipes, and knaveries, and mocks') but not his name;
Gower supplies it: 'Sir John Falstaff' (48; 50). Here, the very distinction Fluellen makes between two actions – Alexander's intemperance
and Henry's probity – blurs the boundary between them as each has
the same dreadful consequence. Hence, the most emphatic sign of
Henry's reformation reappears in a manner calculated to reawaken its
ambivalence.[44]

When Henry wishes that 'history shall with full mouth / Speak freely
of our acts', he assumes that one version of events will prevail, heroic in
texture and uniform in evaluation. Yet *Henry V* includes a variety of
voices and accents that question the fullness of the king's own habits of
recollection as well as his unfolding presentation of events. As English
passes through many different types of idiom and forms of expression,
the value of these cannot be easily stratified. The play shares Mulcaster's
sense of language as a communal possession as well as his wariness
towards any exalted form of discourse that would regulate its variety. In
this play, foreign and 'irresponsible' speakers can take on surprising
qualities helping them to elude denigration. In the sphere of verbal
accident or confusion, in slips of the tongue, or in disorderly speech,
counter-statements are made in contrast to Henry's desire for uniformity
and reformation. Hence, unregenerate or apparently unedifying speech
is also given access to powerful forms of reflection, or to displays of
loyalty, or to degrees of personal intimacy that make more illustrious
discourses appear less imposing. This aspect of the play intensifies as it
reaches its climacteric at Agincourt.

On the night before the battle, Henry's appetite for moralizing *exempla*
is unabated. Even the forbidding presence of enemy troops can be
elucidated as didactic material, functioning as 'our outward consciences /
And preachers to us all, admonishing / That we should dress us fairly
for our end' (4.1.8–10). In this mood, *Henry V* has been interpreted as

reaching the zenith of his authority as a godly monarch prior to his ultimate vindication in battle. David Womersley suggests that this scene presents the king's arrival at a state of grace in a specifically protestant idiom.[45] The key passage here is Henry's agonized soliloquy where he makes a vow to amend, turning to God the more intensely he sees through the trivial mediatory practices that constitute ceremony:

> And what art thou, thou idol ceremony?
> What kind of god art thou, that suffer'st more
> Of mortal griefs than do thy worshippers?
> What are thy rents? what are thy comings-in?
> O ceremony, show me but thy worth!
> What is thy soul, O adoration?
> Art thou aught else but place, degree and form,
> Creating awe and fear in other men
>
> (4.1.237–44)

It is against this perception that the play measures the hostile voice of Michael Williams, whose critical scrutiny of the king's enterprise turns upon his own acute sense of an ending:

> But if the cause be not good, the King himself hath a heavy reckoning to make when all those legs and arms and heads chopped off in a battle shall join together at the latter day and cry all 'We died at such a place', some swearing, some crying for a surgeon, some upon their wives left poor behind them, some upon the debts they owe, some upon their children rawly left. I am afeard there are few die well that die in a battle, for how can they charitably dispose of anything when blood is their argument? Now if these men do not die well it will be a black matter for the King, that led them to it, who to disobey were against all proportion of subjection. (134–46)

For Womersley, this speech needs to be read in the context of popular protestant catechisms and dialogues. It represents the untutored voice of spiritual confusion, where Henry as 'the true Protestant' 'tries to make his men accept the difficult, but authentically Protestant doctrine, that every man must take responsibility for working out his own salvation'.[46] As the king encounters the spiritually obtuse this further refines his powers of self-correction; equally, seeing Henry beleaguered by, and ultimately triumphing over, uncomprehending or antagonistic voices increases the scale of his ultimate triumph.

Yet Womersley's perception of Williams as the deficient speaker of protestant pedagogical writing is not the only context available to us from the Reformation. Indeed, the latter argument might be weighed against the massive cultural authority of Foxe's *Actes and Monuments* and the priority this grants to 'the colloquial language of the common person'.[47] As Huston Diehl has argued, Foxe's work valorized individuals who were defiant, questioning and unwavering in the face of authority, those who 'express doubts, refuse to accept unexamined doctrines, insist on their own authority to interpret texts, apply empirical criteria, and resist coercion'.[48] This characterization sounds very like Williams. Foxe admonishes his reader to be wary of the world and to distrust its deceptive surfaces. In this respect, Henry's appearance in disguise does place his avowals of honest and open speech under some strain: 'For though I speak it to you, I think the King is but a man, as I am...By my troth, I will speak my conscience of the King' (4.1.101–2; 118–19). Given the disguised Henry's diminution in rhetorical and social status, however, the gulf between monarch and subject is also drastically reduced; this allows Williams the freedom to refuse assent to Henry's proposition that his cause is indeed just and honourable: 'That's more than we know' (129). This painfully reopens an issue that has long been closed in the play. Williams's evocation of the victims of war, cited above, projects a bleaker sense of an ending to that envisaged elsewhere and it personifies and moralizes upon the fate of the nation in a very different idiom to that of the king. This speech might well be cited as a *locus classicus* of the play's commitment to a variegated consideration of its subject matter and to its questioning of even the most powerful discourse used within it. Moreover, it also bears out the force of Mulcaster's awareness of common speech being able to claim its own authority in the face of those who would govern it. As many commentators have noted, Henry's response to this represents the first time in the play where he is rhetorically discommoded. The correspondences he draws between a father and a prodigal son and the merchant and servant, have only a dubious relationship to William's argument (147–58). Moreover, it also exposes some discomfiting insights into his conception of his followers as either so guilty that war acts as God's 'beadle' or, if they are shriven, 'dying so, death is to him advantage' (179–80). Such casuistry prepares us for Henry's rhetorical slip that he 'will never trust his word after' if he finds the king has ransomed himself (194). Here the King's English finds itself badly exposed from

a popular viewpoint; its illogic is unmasked, its sense of timeliness
gone awry. As David Scott Kastan suggests, the king's moral 'absolutism'
affects his capacity to hear others and, hence, to speak to them in
a fitting manner.[49] This illuminates the discordant notes and strained
emphases in the king's subsequent soliloquy on the false idol of ceremony. Hence his disparagement of his interlocutors – he speaks of
'greatness' being 'subject to the breath of every fool' (231–2) – sits oddly
with the fulsomeness that usually accompanies his effusions over his
followers and his own reiterated modesty. Again Henry's sense of the
burdensome responsibilities attributed to the king – 'Our debts, our
careful wives, / Our children and our sins' (228–9) – seems to evade
the burden of Williams's words. The king's thoughts now turn to the
degraded condition of his subjects. These appear as personified in
his demeaning vision of the speechless 'wretch', the 'slave' who with
'body filled and vacant mind' 'in gross brain little wots / What watch
the King keeps to maintain the peace, / Whose hours the peasant best
advantages' (265; 266; 279–81). In this extraordinary scene, the play
succeeds in further complicating understanding of the location and
identity of virtuous language. Royal speech not only fails to regulate
those perceptions that challenge it, but it is also exposed as lacking
comprehensive ethical awareness.

In evaluating the presentation of speech in *Henry V*, it is important, on
the one hand, not to idealize an 'underworld' of opposition to the king,
but to recognize that critical insight and moral perceptiveness can be
articulated in forms of English which appear inauspicious or devoid of
status. On the other hand, it is important not to derogate or celebrate
Henry's speech *tout court* as either exalted or as pervaded by his bad
faith. Its stature, like so many forms of the play's English, expands and
diminishes in unpredictable ways, especially as it is captured pursuing
the reform of the self or others. The fitness of the king's language for
this task is one of the play's great questions. The nobility of Henry's
speech also encompasses the savagery expressed at Harfleur (3.3.1–43)
and the pathos of being made a victim of such impulses is conveyed
most memorably in the words of a French speaker, in Burgundy's
anti-pastoral lament for the ruin of France (5.2.23–67). This speech
is made all the more cutting by its allusion to barbarism as intrinsic
to the enactment and the consequences of military conquest, as a
brutalized population sinks to the condition of those 'soldiers' that
'nothing do but meditate on blood' (59; 60). An ability to maintain
a clear distinction between English and French speakers comes under

further pressure in the play's conclusion. Here, Henry and Burgundy establish a dialogue after the wooing of Katherine but of a disturbingly obscene kind whose punning nature excludes her comprehension (5.2.278–315). Yet the French princess is the last of the play's insufficient speakers of English who, in turn, expose the limits of their betters. As Karen Newman has noted 'Katherine's speech, with its mispronunciations, consistently deflects Henry's questions and solicitations'; this successful interference with his intentions thwarts his exchange so that her 'linguistic disadvantage' also 'becomes a strategy of equivocation and deflection'.[50]

For Richard Mulcaster, any attempt to reform speech needed to be scrutinized with care as a commonwealth should include a variety of idioms. Similarly, a consideration of English could be used to propound the need for a restricted sense of a monarch's influence upon language and wariness towards any monopolising of its resources. Such attitudes also find a place in *Henry V*'s critical examination of the King's English and its relationship to the other 'Englishes' to which it is opposed. Ideas of reformation, as well as Reformation ideals, are perceived from a variety of viewpoints in relation to the correction of speech; the latter process is shown to be informed by a diverse and equivocal range of motivations. The play is made vital by the variety of idioms within it; these acquire and lose influence in ways that are not easily determinable by social status or, indeed, nationality. Consequently, the play emphasizes the need to restrain the scope of the King's English.

As we have seen in *King John*, attending to the formal complexity of Shakespeare's history plays also allows new contexts to be explored for their interpretation. In relation to the topic of disorderly speech and its control, it is evident that Shakespeare's works ask radical questions of the categories that defined such language and the equity of its regulation. His historical drama enquires into, rather than reinforces, received ideas concerning degraded, inflammatory, or 'fallen' speech. In *King John*, an idiom as disreputable as rumour is also perceived as a source of historical insight. *Richard II* arouses suspicions concerning the king's claim to speak for the nation and, hence, to define linguistic transgressions against it; these doubts are as powerful as those provoked by the 'fallen' political order that succeeds him. In *Henry V*, we have seen how a spirit of contradiction is also at work in the play's treatment of language, an impulse that questions the king's correction and self-correction of speech. Yet Shakespeare is also the heir and the contemporary of a complex tradition of historical drama. The political sophistication of the latter can also be demonstrated by considering its searching account of how specific forms of language are designated as either threatening or sustaining the commonwealth. Identifying continuities of interest across the diverse corpus of early modern historical drama is one way to enrich our understanding of its complexity as well as that of its most illustrious practitioner.

Notes

Introduction

1. F. P. Wilson observed influentially that there was 'no certain evidence that any popular dramatist before Shakespeare wrote a play based on English history', in *Marlowe and the Early Shakespeare* (Oxford: Clarendon Press, 1953), p. 106.
2. G. K. Hunter, *English Drama 1586–1642: the Age of Shakespeare* (Oxford: Clarendon Press, 1997), p. 156. See also his earlier essay, 'Truth and Art in History Plays', *Shakespeare Survey*, 42 (1990): 15–24. A critical emphasis upon the distinctively Elizabethan ethos of the genre dates back, at least, to Felix E. Schelling's *The English Chronicle Play: a Study in the Popular Historical Literature Environing Shakespeare* (London: Macmillan, 1902).
3. For some searching criticism of Ribner's approach, see Robert Ornstein, *A Kingdom for a Stage: the Achievement of Shakespeare's History Plays* (Cambridge, Mass.: Harvard University Press, 1972), ch. 1, esp. pp. 4–5.
4. See the dismissive treatment of *all* sixteenth-century historiography prior to Shakespeare's plays in Paola Pugliatti's, *Shakespeare the Historian* (London and Basingstoke: Macmillan, 1996), pp. 29–41. For an important corrective to such a view, see Steve Longstaffe, 'What is the English History Play and Why are They Saying Such Terrible Things About It?', *Renaissance Forum* 2: 2 (September 1997), 1–16. Available at http://www.hull.ac.uk/renforum/v2no2/longstaf.htm.
5. Irving Ribner, *The English History Play in the Age of Shakespeare* (London: Methuen, rev edn, 1965), p. 12; p. 8.
6. See D. R. Woolf, *Reading History in Early Modern England* (Cambridge: Cambridge University Press, 2000), esp. ch. 2.
7. Alexander Leggatt, *Shakespeare's Political Drama: the History Plays and the Roman Plays* (London and New York: Routledge, 1988), p. ix.
8. David Scott Kastan, 'The Shape of Time: Form and Value in the Shakespearean History Play', *Comparative Drama*, 7 (1973): 259–77, 269. See also his '"To Set a Form upon that Indigest": Shakespeare's Fictions of History', *Comparative Drama*, 17 (1983): 1–16; *Shakespeare and the Shapes of Time* (London and Basingstoke: Macmillan, 1982), chs 2 and 3. Kastan's thesis has been extended in interesting ways by Benjamin Griffin, *Playing the Past: Approaches to English Historical Drama, 1385–1600* (Woodbridge: D. S. Brewer, 2001), ch. 4.
9. Jonathan Hart, *Theater and World: the Problematics of Shakespeare's History* (Boston: Northeastern University Press, 1992), pp. 97–8.
10. Patricia Parker, *Literary Fat Ladies: Rhetoric, Gender, Property* (London and New York: Methuen, 1987), p. 94; p. 95.
11. See Richard Helgerson, *Forms of Nationhood: the Elizabethan Writing of England* (Chicago and London: University of Chicago Press, 1992), ch. 5; Jean E. Howard and Phyllis Rackin, *Engendering a Nation: a Feminist Account of Shakespeare's English Histories* (London and New York: Routledge, 1997).

12. Thomas Dekker, *O per se O. Or a new Cryer of Lanthorne and Candle-light* (1612), sig. A3v. Cited in Bruce R. Smith, *The Acoustic World of Early Modern England: Attending to the O-Factor* (Chicago and London: University of Chicago Press, 1999), p. 292.

13. For recent accounts of Renaissance rhetoric, see Victoria Kahn, *Rhetoric, Prudence and Skepticism in the Renaissance* (Ithaca: Cornell University Press, 1985); Thomas O. Sloane, *Donne, Milton, and the End of Humanist Rhetoric* (Berkeley, Los Angeles, London: University of California Press, 1985); Brian Vickers, *In Defense of Rhetoric* (Oxford: Clarendon Press, 1988); Quentin Skinner, *Reason and Rhetoric in the Philosophy of Hobbes* (Cambridge: Cambridge University Press, 1996), pp. 19–211; Jennifer Richards, *Rhetoric and Courtliness in Early Modern Literature* (Cambridge: Cambridge University Press, 2003).

14. Cicero, *De Officiis*, trans. Walter Miller (London: Heinemann, 1913), I.xvi.50.

15. Neil Rhodes, *The Power of Eloquence and English Renaissance Literature* (Hertfordshire: Harvester Wheatsheaf, 1992), pp. 31–4. See also Brian Vickers, '"The Power of Persuasion": Images of the Orator, Elyot to Shakespeare', in *Renaissance Eloquence: Studies in the Theory and Practice of Renaissance Rhetoric*, ed. James J. Murphy (Berkeley, Los Angeles, London: University of California Press, 1983), pp. 411–35.

16. Michaela Paasche Grudin, *Chaucer and the Politics of Discourse* (Columbia, South Carolina: University of South Carolina Press, 1996), esp. pp. 1–13; Edwin D. Craun, *Lies, Slander and Obscenity in Medieval Literature: Pastoral Rhetoric and the Deviant Speaker* (Cambridge: Cambridge University Press, 1997); Lynn Forest-Hill, *Transgressive Language in Medieval English Drama: Signs of Challenge and Change* (Aldershot: Ashgate, 2000).

17. See, for example, Margreta de Grazia, 'Shakespeare's View of Language: an Historical Perspective', *SQ*, 29 (1978): 374–88.

18. James L. Calderwood, *Metadrama in Shakespeare's Henriad: 'Richard II' to 'Henry V'* (Berkeley, Los Angeles, London: University of California Press, 1979); Joseph A. Porter, *The Drama of Speech Acts: Shakespeare's Lancastrian Tetralogy* (Berkeley, Los Angeles, London: University of California Press, 1979).

19. Calderwood, *Metadrama*, p. 38; Porter, *Drama of Speech Acts*, p. 47.

20. Porter, *Drama of Speech Acts*, p. 123; p. 124.

21. Calderwood, *Metadrama*, p. 168.

22. In relation to *Richard II*, see David Scott Kastan, 'Proud Majesty Made a Subject: Shakespeare and the Spectacle of Rule', *SQ*, 37 (1986): 459–75; David Norbrook, 'The Emperor's New Body? *Richard II*, Ernst Kantorowicz, and the Politics of Shakespeare Criticism', *Textual Practice*, 10 (1996): 329–57. For a sophisticated reading of *Henry IV*, see Lorna Hutson, 'Not the King's Two Bodies: Reading the "Body Politic" in Shakespeare's *Henry IV*, Parts 1 and 2', in *Rhetoric and Law in Early Modern Europe*, ed. Victoria Kahn and Lorna Hutson (New Haven and London: Yale University Press, 2001), pp. 166–98.

23. Peter Burke, 'Introduction', *The Social History of Language* (Cambridge: Cambridge University Press, 1987), ed. Peter Burke and Roy Porter, pp. 1–20, p. 13. Compare Andy Wood's observation: 'If we are to develop a richer appreciation of early modern social relations, the politics of speech ought therefore to lie at the heart of our enterprise.' '"Poore men woll speke one daye": Plebian Languages of Deference and Defiance in England,

c. 1520–1640', in *The Politics of the Excluded, c. 1500–1800*, ed. Tim Harris (Basingstoke: Palgrave, 2001), pp. 67–98, p. 71.

24. Penry Williams, *The Tudor Regime* (Oxford: Clarendon Press, 1979), pp. 375–94; G. R. Elton, *Policy and Police: the Enforcement of the Reformation in the Age of Thomas Cromwell* (Cambridge: Cambridge University Press, 1972); Adam Fox, *Oral and Literate Culture in England, 1500–1700* (Oxford: Clarendon Press, 2000). For drama, see Janette Dillon, *Language and Stage in Medieval and Renaissance England* (Cambridge: Cambridge University Press, 1998), ch. 4; Kenneth Gross, *Shakespeare's Noise* (Chicago: University of Chicago Press, 2001).

25. 'An Homelie agaynst Contencion and Braulynge,' in *Certain Sermons or Homilies 1547 and 'A Homily against Disobedience and Wilful Rebellion' (1570)*, ed. Ronald B. Bond (Toronto: University of Toronto Press, 1987), pp. 191–205, p. 191; p. 200.

26. Cyndia Susan Clegg, 'Archival Poetics and the Politics of Literature: Essex and Hayward Revisited', *Studies in the Literary Imagination*, 32 (1999): 115–23, 129.

27. See Stephen Greenblatt's influential essay, 'Invisible Bullets', in *Shakespearean Negotiations: the Circulation of Social Energy in Renaissance England* (Oxford: Clarendon Press, 1988), pp. 21–65.

28. Michel Foucault, *Discipline and Punish: the Birth of the Prison*, trans. Alan Sheridan (London: Allen Lane, 1979). Compare Foucault's suggestive remarks on 'disqualified knowledges' in 'Two Lectures', *Power/Knowledge: Selected Interviews and Other Writings 1972–1977*, ed. Colin Gordon, trans. Colin Gordon *et al.* (Brighton: Harvester Press, 1980), pp. 78–108, esp. pp. 81–3. For an application of Foucault's ideas to the history play, see Richard Wilson, *Will Power: Essays on Shakespearean Authority* (Hemel Hempstead: Harvester Wheatsheaf, 1993), esp. ch 1.

29. Foucault, *Discipline and Punish*, pp. 128–9.

30. Pierre Bourdieu, 'The Production and Reproduction of Legitimate Language', *Language and Symbolic Power*, ed. John B. Thompson, trans. Gino Raymond and Matthew Adamson (Cambridge: Polity Press, 1991), pp. 43–65, p. 46.

31. Louis Althusser, 'Ideology and Ideological State Apparatuses', in *Lenin and Philosophy and Other Essays* (London: New Left Books, 1971), pp. 127–86.

32. See Helgerson, *Forms of Nationhood*; Dillon, *Language and Stage*.

33. *Excitable Speech: a Politics of the Performative* (New York and London: Routledge, 1997), p. 12. Subsequent references are included in parentheses.

34. A. R. Braunmuller, '*King John* and Historiography', *ELH*, 55 (1988): 309–32, 314.

35. Ronald Knowles, *Shakespeare's Arguments With History* (Basingstoke: Palgrave, 2001), p. 3.

36. On the 'new humanism', see Richard Tuck, *Philosophy and Government, 1572–1651* (Cambridge: Cambridge University Press, 1993), chs 2 and 3. For its relevance to Shakespeare, see Martin Dzelzainis, 'Shakespeare and Political Thought', in *A Companion to Shakespeare*, ed. David Scott Kastan (Oxford: Blackwell, 1999), pp. 100–16.

37. Hutson, 'Not the King's Two Bodies', p. 180.

38. David Norbrook, ' "A liberal tongue": Language and Rebellion in *Richard II*', in *Shakespeare's Universe: Renaissance Ideas and Conventions*, ed. J. M. Mucciolo (Hants: Scolar Press, 1996), pp. 37–51, p. 41.

Notes   155

39. Paula Blank, 'Speaking Freely about Richard II', *Journal of English and Germanic Philology*, 96 (1997): 327–48, esp. 335–6.
40. Peter C. Herman, 'Henrician Historiography and the Voice of the People: the Cases of More and Hall', *Texas Studies in Literature and Language*, 39 (1997): 259–83; Thomas Betteridge, *Tudor Histories of the English Reformation, 1530–83* (Aldershot: Ashgate, 1999); Annabel Patterson, *Reading Holinshed's Chronicles* (Chicago: University of Chicago Press, 1994). For drama, see Ivo Kamps, *Historiography and Ideology in Stuart Drama* (Cambridge: Cambridge University Press, 1996); Marsha S. Robinson, *Writing the Reformation*: Actes and Monuments *and the Jacobean History Play* (Aldershot: Ashgate, 2002).

1. The Paradox of Sedition in John Bale's *King Johan*

1. Kamps, *Historiography and Ideology*, p. 54. For two interesting essays which dispute the influence of both Bale and the morality play on subsequent historical drama and emphasize instead the saint's play see David Scott Kastan, 'The Shape of Time', esp. pp. 264–5; Benjamin Griffin, 'The Birth of the History Play: Saint, Sacrifice, and Reformation,' *SEL, 1500–1900*, 39 (1999): 217–37.
2. Ribner, *The English History Play*, p. 36. Bale's use of historical argumentation is considered by Leslie P. Fairfield in *John Bale: Mythmaker for the English Reformation* (West Lafayette: Purdue University Press, 1976); his influence upon the development of a sovereign conception of English nationhood has been explored by Andrew Hadfield, *Literature, Politics and National Identity: Reformation to Renaissance* (Cambridge: Cambridge University Press, 1994), pp. 51–80 and Clare McEachern, *The Poetics of English Nationhood, 1590–1612* (Cambridge: Cambridge University Press, 1996), pp. 26–9. For general accounts of Bale's work, see Jesse W. Harris, *John Bale: a Study in the Minor Literature of the Reformation* (Illinois: Illinois Studies in Language and Literature, 1940); T. B. Blatt, *The Plays of John Bale: a Study of Ideas, Technique and Style* (Copenhagen: G. E. C. Gad, 1968); John N. King, *English Reformation Literature: the Tudor Origins of the Protestant Tradition* (Princeton: Princeton University Press, 1982), pp. 56–75 and Peter Happé, *John Bale* (New York: Twayne, 1996).
3. W. T. Davies, 'A Bibliography of John Bale', *Oxford Bibliographical Society, Proceedings and Papers* (Oxford: Oxford University Press, 1936–9), 5, 203– 46, 203.
4. Dillon, *Language and Stage*, p. 89.
5. For an excellent recent overview, see Paul Hamilton, *Historicism* (London and New York: Routledge, 1996).
6. David Hawkes, *Ideology* (London and New York: Routledge, 1996), p. 12.
7. James C. Siemon, *Shakespearean Iconoclasm* (Berkeley, Los Angeles, London: University of California Press, 1985), pp. 143–4.
8. As Lynn Forest-Hill notes, Sedition's role is augmented by two surprising decisions: first, Bale presents the Vice as a political rather than a moral evil and, second, he chooses not to make Usurped Power/the Pope the play's chief representative of corruption. See *Transgressive Language*, pp. 177–8.

9. In this respect, the influence of Bale's work on John Foxe would repay further attention. Huston Diehl's recent account of Foxe's intentions are cognate with the dramaturgy of *King Johan*; see *Staging Reform, Reforming the Stage: Protestantism and Popular Theatre in Early Modern England* (Ithaca and London: Cornell University Press, 1997), esp. p. 43.
10. The textual problem is discussed in the following editions: *King Johan by John Bale*, ed. J. H. P. Pafford and W. W. Greg, Malone Society (Oxford: Oxford University Press, 1931), pp. v–xxix; *John Bale's King Johan*, ed. Barry B. Adams (San Marino, California: Huntington Library, 1969), pp. 1–17; *The Complete Plays of John Bale*, ed. Peter Happé, 2 vols (Cambridge: D. S. Brewer, 1985–6), I, pp. 9–11; pp. 100–1; Greg Walker, *Plays of Persuasion: Drama and Politics at the Court of Henry VIII* (Cambridge: Cambridge University Press, 1991), pp. 170–8.
11. Christopher Haigh, *English Reformations: Religion, Politics, and Society under the Tudors* (Oxford: Clarendon Press, 1993), p. 169.
12. Paul Whitfield White, *Theatre and Reformation: Protestantism, Patronage, and Playing in Tudor England* (Cambridge: Cambridge University Press, 1993), pp. 12–41. Appropriately, a seditious outburst reported to Cromwell provides the primary evidence for *King Johan*'s date of production, see *The Miscellaneous Writings and Letters of Thomas Cranmer*, ed. J. E. Cox, Parker Society (Cambridge, 1846), pp. 387–8.
13. Peter Clark, *English Provincial Society from the Reformation to the Revolution: Religion, Politics and Society in Kent, 1500–1640* (Hassocks, Sussex: Harvester Press, 1977), p. 45.
14. See Elton, *Policy and Police*.
15. See Roger B. Manning, 'The Origins of the Doctrine of Sedition', *Albion*, 12 (1980): 99–121, 101.
16. Richard Morison, *A remedy for sedition* (1536), sig. D2^v.
17. For evidence of Cromwell's personal anxiety, see his urgent letter to the king in July 1533, describing how his spies had 'dogged to London' two Observant Friars, 'one of them a veray sedycious person', and requested that torture might be used in their examination as they were 'moche gyven to sedycyon', in R. B. Merriman, *Life and Letters of Thomas Cromwell*, 2 vols (Oxford, 1902), I, p. 279. Compare Cromwell's concern with 'sedicious wordes' at I, p. 112 and II, p. 279.
18. *TRP* I, 122 (1529). The association between religious dissent and sedition was longstanding, see Margaret Aston, 'Lollards and Sedition, 1381–1431', *P&P*, 17 (1960): 1–44.
19. *TRP*, I, 129 (1530); emphases added.
20. *LP*, XII, i, 892.
21. *LP*, XII, i, 200.
22. *LP*, VIII, 196, 278.
23. *LP*, XII, i, 892.
24. *Records of the Borough of Leicester, 1509–1603*, 7 vols, ed. Mary Bateson, revised by W. H. Stevenson and J. E. Stocks (Cambridge, 1905), III, pp. 31–2. The quotation has been modernized.
25. *LP*, IX, 179.
26. *LP*, VIII, 624; this case is cited by Susan Brigden, *London and the Reformation* (Oxford: Clarendon Press, 1989), p. 279. Seditious remarks by Friar Geoffery

Turner of the Grey Friars in London concerning King John are also recorded in April 1538; see *LP*, XIII, i, 658.

27. *LP*, VIII, 609. The priest involved, John Hale, also commented (reportedly) of Henry VIII: 'And if thou wilt deeply look upon his life, thou shalt find it more foul and more stinking than a sow, wallowing and defiling herself in any filthy place.' For 'endeavouring to excite sedition', Hale was tried and condemned for treason.

28. *LP*, IX, 1066 and XII, ii, 908.

29. *LP*, XIII, i, 1043. Friar Forest's 'inward man' was later exposed horribly at his burning in April 1538 as he defied attempts to make him abjure 'obsti-natlie and frowardlie...but standing yet stiff and proud in his malicious mynde...a seditious person to the Kinges leige people', in *Wriothesley's Chronicle*, ed. W. D. Hamilton, 2 vols, Camden Society (London, 1875), I, p. 78; p. 80.

30. All citations are to *King Johan by John Bale*, ed. J. H. P. Pafford and W. W. Greg, Malone Society (Oxford University Press, 1931). Speech headings have been standardized.

31. Ritchie D. Kendall provides an excellent analysis of the language of demonic play that Bale bestows on his vices and notes: 'It is a perilously illusive boundary that separates the old Bale from the new and the art of damnation from the art of salvation,' in *The Drama of Dissent: the Radical Poetics of Nonconformity, 1380–1590* (Chapel Hill and London: University of North Carolina Press, 1986), p. 119.

32. Betteridge, *Tudor Histories*, p. 36.

33. Walker, *Plays of Persuasion*, pp. 194–210.

34. 'The Confutation of Tyndale's Answer' (1533) in *The Complete Works of St. Thomas More*, (1963–97), ed. Louis A. Schuster *et al.*, 15 vols (New Haven and London: Yale University Press, 1973), VIII: Pt. i, p. 32. I owe this reference to Dr David Walker.

35. Brigden, *London and the Reformation*, p. 277.

36. *A & M*, p. 533.

37. *TRP*, I, 186 (1538).

38. *Actes and Monumentes* (1570), 2 vols, I, p. 1295.

39. Eamon Duffy, *The Stripping of the Altars: Traditional Religion in England: c. 1400–c. 1580* (New Haven and London: Yale University Press, 1992), p. 434.

40. Philip Hughes, *The Reformation in England*, 3 vols (London: Hollis and Carter, 1950–4), I, p. 365.

41. Paul Christianson, *Reformers and Babylon: English Apocalyptic visions from the Reformation to the Eve of the Civil War* (Toronto: University of Toronto Press, 1978), p. 19.

42. *The Image of Both Churches*, ed. H. Christmas, Parker Society (Cambridge, 1849), p. 427.

43. *A & M*, p. 611. Foxe also records Barnes's less oblique comment upon the justice of his execution in his prayer for Henry's life: 'and after him that godly prince Edward may so ragin [sic], that he may fynishe those thinges that his father hathe begonne', *ibid.*

44. *LP*, IX, 1059.

45. See *LP*, XVII, 177 and XXI, i, 1233.

46. *The vocacyon of Johan Bale* (1553), ed. Peter Happé and John N. King (Binghampton, New York: Medieval and Renaissance Texts and Studies, 1990), p. 74. Compare Bale's petitioning of Cromwell in January 1537 from the 'vileness, stink, penury, cold' of his imprisonment for heresy; here he laments the malicious fabrications of his parishioners: 'The articles they have gathered against my preaching were never my sayings, and they have twice altered them', *LP*, XII, i, 307.
47. Bale was ejected from his parish in Thorndon, Suffolk, for heretical preaching and, in the brief autobiography included in his *Catalogus* (1557–9), recollects how 'Deprived of all possessions, I was soon dragged from the pulpit to the courts of justice, first under Lee at York, and then under Stokesley at London: but the pious Cromwell who was in the confidence of King Henry always set me free on account of the comedies I had published', in *The Complete Plays of John Bale*, trans. Peter Happé, I, p. 147.
48. Beat Hodler, 'Protestant Self-Perception and the Problem of *Scandalum*: a Sketch', in *Protestant History and Identity in Sixteenth-Century Europe: the Medieval Inheritance*, 2 vols (Aldershot: Scolar 1996), ed. Bruce Gordon, I, pp. 23–30, p. 25.
49. *The Image of Both Churches*, p. 326.
50. At l. 1378, Sedition is also heard offstage to signify the imminent invasion of England. For an analysis of these changes see Peter Happé, 'Sedition in *King Johan*: Bale's Development of a "Vice"', *Medieval English Theatre*, 3 (1981): 3–6.
51. See Bernard Spivack's analysis of the Vice's 'exposition of himself' in *Shakespeare and the Allegory of Evil: the History of a Metaphor in Relation to His Major Villains* (New York and London: Columbia University Press, 1958), pp. 178–93.
52. 'Three Laws', in *The Complete Plays of John Bale*, II, ll. 1411–46.
53. Henry's instructions to Norfolk during the negotiations with the 'light and seditious' rebels provide a helpful gloss on the trickery that accompanies Sedition's execution: 'you would esteem no promise you should make to the rebels nor think your honor touched in the breach of it', *LP*, XI, 1226.
54. The circumstances surrounding John's surrender troubled Bale who added a lengthy interpolation to the 'A-text' in extenuation of the king. Barry B. Adams notes that this serves to dispel 'a strong suggestion of political compromise' in the original manuscript in his *John Bale's King Johan* (San Marino, California: Huntington Library, 1969), pp. 178–9.
55. Betteridge, *Tudor Histories*, p. 19.
56. See, for example, Homi K. Bhabha's reflections on the stereotype: 'the recognition and disavowal of "difference" is always disturbed by the question of its re-presentation or construction', in *The Location of Culture* (London and New York; Routledge, 1994), p. 81.
57. Stuart Clark, *Thinking with Demons: the Idea of Witchcraft in Early Modern Europe* (Oxford: Oxford University Press, 1997), p. 135. Compare Fredric Jameson's observation: 'my enemy can be thought of as being *evil* (that is, as other than myself and marked by some absolute difference), when what is responsible for his being so characterised is quite simply the *identity* of his own conduct with mine, the which...he reflects as in a mirror image', in *The Political Unconscious: Narrative as a Socially Symbolic Act* (London: Methuen, 1981), p. 118.

58. MacEachern, *The Poetics*, p. 28. See also David Scott Kastan's analysis of the 'unnerving parallelism' between the equally theatrical representation of godly rule and papal corruption in *King Johan* which implies both forces can be contested and reversed, in '"Holy Wurdes" and "Slypper Wit": John Bale's *King Johan* and the Poetics of Propaganda', in *Rethinking the Henrician Era: Essays on Early Tudor Texts and Contexts*, ed. Peter C. Herman (Urbana and Chicago: Illinois University Press, 1994), pp. 267–82.

2. The Language of Counsel in *Gorboduc*

1. Arthur B. Ferguson, *The Articulate Citizen and the English Renaissance* (Durham, North Carolina: Duke University Press, 1965), p. 191.

2. Kent Cartwright, *Theatre and Humanism: English Drama in the Sixteenth Century* (Cambridge: Cambridge University Press, 1999), p. 101.

3. *Proceedings in the Parliaments of Elizabeth I, 1558–1581*, ed. T. E. Hartley (Leicester: Leicester University Press, 1981), p. 35.

4. E. M. W. Tillyard, *Shakespeare's History Plays* (London: Chatto & Windus, 1944), p. 94.

5. Greg Walker, *The Politics of Performance in Early Renaissance Drama* (Cambridge: Cambridge University Press, 1998), pp. 196–221; p. 201.

6. Ribner, *The English History Play*, p. 37; pp. 45–6.

7. All quotations are to *Gorboduc or Ferrex and Porrex*, ed. Irby B. Cauthen, Jr. (London: Edward Arnold, 1970).

8. 'How to Tell a Flatterer from a Friend,' *Plutarch's Moralia*, trans. Frank Cole Babbit, 14 vols (London: William Heinemann, 1927), I, pp. 263–395, p. 267.

9. See *The Mirror for Magistrates*, ed. Lily B. Campbell (Cambridge: Cambridge University Press, 1938), pp. 318–45.

10. John Guy, 'Tudor Monarchy and its Critiques', in *The Tudor Monarchy*, ed. John Guy (London and New York: Edward Arnold, 1997), pp. 78–109, p. 99; emphasis in original.

11. See James Emmanuel Berg, '*Gorboduc* as a Tragic Discovery of "Feudalism"', *SEL*, 40 (2000): 199–226, 225–6, n. 28.

12. David Colclough, '*Parrhesia*: the Rhetoric of Free Speech in Early Modern England', *Rhetorica*, 17 (1999): 177–212.

13. Mortimer Levine, *The Early Elizabethan Succession Question, 1558–1568* (Stanford: Stanford University Press, 1966), p. 30. This view is still accepted in most recent accounts of the play, see Marie Axton's influential, *The Queen's Two Bodies: Drama and the Elizabethan Succession* (London: Royal Historical Society, 1977), pp. 11–25, 38–72; Jacqueline Vanhoutte, 'Community, Authority, and the Motherland in Sackville and Norton's *Gorboduc*', *SEL*, 40 (2000): 227–39, 227–8.

14. For a discussion of the sources of the play, see Cauthen, Jr., *Gorboduc*, pp. xiv–xvi.

15. Thomas Norton delivered an admonitory petition concerning the succession to the Commons at this time, deploring 'the perillous intermedlinges of forreyne princes with seditious, ambicious and factious subjectes at home', in Hartley, *Proceedings*, p. 91.

16. David Bevington, *Tudor Drama and Politics: a Critical Approach to Topical Meaning* (Cambridge, Mass.: Harvard University Press, 1968), p. 144; p. 145.

17. See Henry James and Greg Walker, 'The Politics of *Gorboduc*', *The English Historical Review*, 110 (1995): 109–21; Norman Jones and Paul Whitfield White, '*Gorboduc* and Royal Marriage Politics: an Elizabethan Playgoer's Report of the Premiere Performance', *ELR*, 26 (1996): 3–16. For other readings that emphasize the play's status as pro-Dudley propaganda, see Marie Axton, 'Robert Dudley and the Inner Temple Revels', *HJ*, 13 (1970): 563–78; Susan Doran, 'Juno Versus Diana: the Treatment of Elizabeth I's Marriage in Plays and Entertainments, 1561–1581', *HJ*, 38 (1995): 257–74.

18. James and Walker, 'The Politics of *Gorboduc*', 114. Leah Marcus criticises 'local reading' that depends on particular spectators in *Puzzling Shakespeare: Local Reading and its Discontents* (Berkeley, Los Angeles, London: University of California Press, 1988), esp. pp. 69–70. For reservations concerning the eyewitness account of *Gorboduc*, see Cartwright, *Theatre and Humanism*, p. 111; Mike Pincombe, 'Robert Dudley, *Gorboduc*, and "The Masque of Beauty and Desire": a reconsideration of the evidence for political intervention', *Parergon*, 20 (2003): 19–44.

19. John Guy, 'The Rhetoric of Counsel in Early Modern England', in *Tudor Political Culture*, ed. Dale Hoak (Cambridge: Cambridge University Press, 1995), pp. 292–310, p. 292.

20. Walker, *The Politics of Performance*, p. 65. As is well known, the play was performed for a second time at court on 18 January 1561/2.

21. Blair Worden, *The Sound of Virtue: Philip Sidney's* Arcadia *and Elizabethan Politics* (New Haven and London: Yale University Press, 1996), p. 196. For Sidney's comments on *Gorboduc*, see 'A Defence of Poetry', in *Miscellaneous Prose of Sir Philip Sidney*, ed. Katherine Duncan-Jones and Jan Van Dorsten (Oxford: Clarendon Press, 1973), p. 113.

22. F. W. Conrad, 'The Problem of Counsel Reconsidered: the Case of Sir Thomas Elyot', in *Political Thought and the Tudor Commonwealth: Deep Structure, Discourse and Disguise*, ed. P. A. Fideler and T. F. Mayer (London and New York: Routledge, 1992), pp. 75–107, p. 75.

23. See Peter Wentworth, *A pithie exhortation on to her Majestie for establishing her successor the crowne* (1598), p. 30. For an analysis of the circumstances surrounding this text in the context of Wentworth's career, see J. E. Neale, *Elizabeth I and Her Parliaments, 1584–1601* (London: Jonathan Cape, 1957), pp. 251–66.

24. For accounts of the ethos of the Inns of Court, see A. Wigfall Green, *The Inns of Court and Early English Drama* (New Haven: Yale University Press, 1931); Wilfrid R. Prest, *The Inns of Court under Elizabeth I and the Early Stuarts, 1590–1640* (London: Longman, 1972); J. H Baker, *The Third University of England: the Inns of Court and the Common-law Tradition* (London: Selden Society Lecture, 1990). For considerations of its educational and rhetorical culture, see R. J. Schoeck, 'Rhetoric and Law in Sixteenth-Century England', *SP*, 50 (1953): 110–27, and 'Lawyers and Rhetoric in Sixteenth-Century England', in *Renaissance Eloquence*, pp. 274–91; D. S. Bland, 'Rhetoric and the Law Student in Sixteenth-Century England', *SP*, 54 (1957): 489–508; W. R. Prest, 'The Learning Exercises at the Inns of Court, 1590–1640', *Journal of the Society of Public Teachers of Law*, 9 (1967): 310–13.

25. J. H. Baker, *Readings and Moots at the Inns of Court in the Fifteenth Century*, 2 vols, ed. Samuel E. Thorne and J. H. Baker (London: Selden Society, v. 105, 1990), II, pp. lxxii–lxxiii.
26. Compare the use of the term 'case' at 1.2.46; 4.2.29.
27. For the date and composition of Smith's dialogue, see Mary Dewar, *Sir Thomas Smith: a Tudor Intellectual in Office* (London: Athlone Press, 1964), pp. 84–7.
28. The dialogue survives in manuscript and is printed in John Strype, *The Life of the Learned Sir Thomas Smith* (Oxford, 1820) in Appendix III, pp. 184–259; the induction is printed in the main text at pp. 60–2, the quotation here from p. 61. Dewar notes that, although never printed, this text 'was one of the most widely copied tracts in Elizabethan England, read and re-read as men culled arguments from it in the wearying debate on Elizabeth's duty to marry and the problems involved in her choice', *Sir Thomas Smith*, p. 4.
29. See her famous statement of 10 February 1559, 'And in the end, this shalbe for me sufficient, that a marble stone shall declare that a Queene, having raigned such a tyme, lived and dyed a virgin', in Hartley, *Proceedings*, p. 45.
30. Compare Quintilian's observation: 'most rules are liable to be altered by the nature of the case, circumstances of time and place, and by hard necessity itself. Consequently, the all-important gift for an orator is a wise adaptibility since he is called upon to meet the most varied emergencies', in *Institutio Oratoria*, 4 vols, trans. H. E. Butler (London: Heinemann, 1922), 1, II.xiii.2.
31. Such an understanding was common in the period. See William Cecil's examination of political problems *pro* and *contra* as described by Stephen Alford, *The Early Elizabethan Polity: William Cecil and the British Succession Crisis, 1558–1569* (Cambridge: Cambridge University Press, 1998), p. 19.
32. This is a powerful strain of awareness in the play that adds to the atmosphere of catastrophe, see, 2.1.194–6; 2.2.75–9; 5.2.180–3.
33. Eric Rasmussen, 'The Implications of Past Tense Verbs in Early Elizabethan Dumb Shows', *English Studies*, 67 (1986): 417–19.
34. O. B. Hardison, Jr., *Prosody and Purpose in the English Renaissance* (Baltimore and London: Johns Hopkins University Press, 1989), p. 172. Hardison is stressing here, however, the authors' independence from Senecan influence. Compare Gordon Braden's observation that the foreshadowing found in Seneca's dramatic prologues 'is usually extensive but also incomplete, contradictory, and even wrong', in *Renaissance Tragedy and the Senecan Tradition: Anger's Privilege* (New Haven and London: Yale University Press, 1985), p. 40.
35. For Mark Breitenberg 'the characters add little more than a rhetorical version to the visual and verbal stories' presented by the Chorus and the dumb show, in 'Reading Elizabethan Iconicity: *Gorboduc* and the Semiotics of Reform', *ELR*, 18 (1988): 194–217, 213.
36. Butler, *Excitable Speech*, p. 2.
37. The pseudo-Ciceronian and extremely influential *Rhetorica ad Herennium* deals with the composition of a judicial oration in one's defence – especially 'the Shifting of the Question of Guilt' (I.xv.25) – in ways that provide an interesting gloss on Porrex's oration. See *[Cicero] Ad C. Herennium*, trans. Harry Caplan (London: Heinemann, 1954), I.xiv.24–xvi.26.
38. There are strong reasons for suspecting Ferrex's malicious intentions which are reported to Porrex at 2.2.6–28. The former also receives cynical counsel

to act exactly as his brother later testifies in 2.1.81–161. On the other hand, Ferrex signally rejects the counsel he is offered and, in the play's opening scene, is distinguished as a fair-minded, loyal and independent speaker.

39. William J. Bouwsma, *John Calvin: a Sixteenth-Century Portrait* (Oxford: Oxford University Press, 1988), pp. 143–9.

40. Plutarch, 'How to distinguish a flatterer from a friend', cited in F. W. Conrad, 'The Problem of Counsel Reconsidered', p. 103, n. 65.

41. His counsel is also a reductive version of Machiavellian thought. In his *Discorsi* on Livy, Machiavelli commends Romulus's murder of his brother Remus, but stresses that motive for such actions must be 'the common good' or else the result is 'tyranny', in *The Discourses* (Harmondsworth: Penguin, 1970, repr. 1974), ed. Bernard Crick and trans. Leslie J. Walker, p. 132.

42. C. O. McDonald, *The Rhetoric of Tragedy: Form in Stuart Drama* (University of Massachussetts Press, 1966), p. 33.

43. *Ibid.*, p. 104. McDonald's approach was developed in Joel B. Altman's outstanding study, *The Tudor Play of Mind: Rhetorical Inquiry and the Development of Elizabethan Drama* (Berkeley, Los Angeles and London: University of California Press, 1978). For Altman's discussion of *Gorboduc*, see pp. 249–59 and compare Kent Cartwright's reading of the play's 'destabilizing of certainty' in *Theatre and Humanism*, pp. 108–21.

44. For Norton's career, see Michael A. R. Graves, *Thomas Norton: the Parliament Man* (Oxford: Blackwell, 1994). Sackville's career would benefit from more sustained historical attention: see, C. H. Cooper and T. Cooper, *Athenae Cantabrigienses*, 3 vols (Cambridge, 1858–1913), II, pp. 484–92. For Sackville's practice of counsel see Rivkah Zim, 'Dialogue and Discretion: Thomas Sackville, Catherine de Medici and the Anjou Marriage Proposal 1571', *HJ*, 40 (1997): 287–310.

45. John Stow, *Annales, or, A general Chronicle of England* (1631), p. 635.

46. Elizabeth commented on such future uncertainties in her first speech to Parliament: 'For although I be never so carefull of your well doinges and mynd ever so to be, yet may my issue growe out of kinde, and become perhappes ungracious', in Hartley, *Proceedings*, p. 45.

47. Compare Thomas Elyot's subtle consideration of the fine distinction between flattering and friendly words in *The Boke Named the Governour* (1531; repr. Menston: Scolar Press, 1970), II.xiv, fol. 166r.

48. See, Timothy Hampton, *Writing from History: the Rhetoric of Exemplarity in Renaissance Literature* (Ithaca and London: Cornell University Press, 1990); Anthony Grafton and Lisa Jardine, ' "Studied for Action": How Gabriel Harvey Read his Livy', *P&P*, 129 (1990): 30–78.

49. *Orations, of Arsanes agaynst Philip the trecherous kyng of Macedone* (1568), sig. A iiir–v. For the dating and for Norton's authorship of this work, see Graves, *Thomas Norton*, pp. 41–3; for further consideration of Norton's attitudes towards history see Anthony Martin, 'The End of History: Thomas Norton's "v periodes" and the Pattern of English Protestant Historiography', in *John Foxe and his World*, ed. Christopher Highley and John N. King (Aldershot: Ashgate, 2002), pp. 37–53.

50. Sir Thomas North, *The Lives of the Noble Grecians and Romanes* (1579), sigs. iiiiv; iiiir.

51. Lorna Hutson, 'Fortunate travelers: reading for the plot in sixteenth-century England', *Representations*, 41 (1993): 83–103, 89.
52. *Ibid.*, 96.
53. This would concur with Victoria Kahn's sense of an increasing scepticism towards constructive persuasion and the reliability of prudential judgement in northern Europe during the sixteenth century, in *Rhetoric, Prudence, and Skepticism*, esp. pp. 46–54.
54. A. N. McLaren, *Political Culture in the Reign of Elizabeth I: Queen and Commonwealth, 1558–1585* (Cambridge: Cambridge University Press, 1999), p. 19. See also, C. H. McIlwain, *Constitutionalism: Ancient and Modern* (Ithaca: Cornell University Press, 1940).
55. Hartley, *Proceedings*, p. 45.
56. Franco Moretti stresses this feature of the play as part of his broader argument that 'English tragedy is nothing less than the negation and dismantling of the Elizabethan world picture', in 'The Great Eclipse: Tragic Form as the Deconsecration of Sovereignty', in *Signs Taken For Wonders: Essays in the Sociology of Literary Forms*, trans. David Miller (London and New York: Verso, rev. edn., 1988), pp. 42–82, esp. 43–8; the quotation here from p. 48. Strikingly, the most significant alteration between the two editions of *Gorboduc* in 1565 and 1570 involves the excision of eight lines from Eubulus's speech in 5.1; these commend passive obedience to monarchy and are included in Cauthen's edition at 5.1.42–9.
57. Hartley, *Proceedings*, p. 431.
58. Hampton, *Writing from History*, p. 206.
59. Hartley, *Proceedings*, p. 241. This was axiomatic to the period's understanding of the importance of debate; Thomas Elyot recommended that no adviser should be omitted: 'they all beinge herde, nedes must the counsaile be the more perfecte', *The Boke Named the Governour*, III, xxviii, fol. 255r. D. M. Dean and N. L. Jones have emphasized that 'liberty of speech' was perceived as central to the successful functioning of both houses of parliament. See their 'Introduction: Representation, Ideology and Action in the Elizabethan Parliaments', in *The Parliaments of Elizabethan England*, ed. D. M. Dean and N. L. Jones (Oxford: Basil Blackwell, 1990), pp. 1–13, p. 8.
60. J. G. A. Pocock, 'Verbalizing a Political Act: Towards a Politics of Speech', in *Language and Politics*, ed. Michael J. Shapiro (Oxford: Blackwell, 1984), pp. 25–43.

3. Language, Temperance and the Nation in Greene's *Scottish History*

1. *Greene's Groatsworth of Wit: Bought with a Million of Repentance* (1592), ed. D. Allen Carroll (Binghampton, New York: Medieval & Renaissance Texts & Studies, 1994), pp. 84–5.
2. *Ibid.*, pp. 1–31.
3. Scott McMillin and Sally-Beth MacLean, *The Queen's Men and their Plays* (Cambridge: Cambridge University Press, 1998), esp. ch. 7. For a review of the evidence that the Queen's Men performed *James IV*, see p. 92.

4. On Buc's tenure as Master of the Revels, see Richard Dutton, *Mastering the Revels: the Regulation and Censorship of English Renaissance Drama* (Basingstoke and London: Macmillan, 1991), ch. 8.
5. Buc's hand was identified by Samuel A. Tannenbaum, *Shaksperian Scraps and Other Elizabethan Fragments* (New York: Columbia University Press, 1933), p. 50. See also R. C. Bald, 'The *Locrine* and *George-a-Greene* Title-Page Inscription', *The Library*, 4th ser., 15 (1934–5): 289–305; Alan H. Nelson, 'George Buc, William Shakespeare, and the Folger *George a Greene*', *SQ*, 49 (1998): 74–83. On Buc, see Mark Eccles, 'Sir George Buc, Master of the Revels', in *Thomas Lodge and other Elizabethans*, ed. Charles J. Sisson (Cambridge, Mass.: Harvard University Press, 1933), pp. 411–506.
6. E. M. W. Tillyard, *Shakespeare's History Plays*, p. 105. For similarly negative judgements, see Bevington, *Tudor Drama*, pp. 208–9; Ribner, *The English History Play*, p. 25; p. 269; Pugliatti, *Shakespeare the Historian*, p. 35; Nicholas Grene, *Shakespeare's Serial History Plays* (Cambridge: Cambridge University Press, 2002), p. 191.
7. For an account of the play's sources, see Norman Sanders (ed.), *The Scottish History of James the Fourth* (London: Methuen, 1970), pp. xxix–xxxv.
8. The play's entry in the Stationer's Register in 1594, however, preserves its association with James IV: 'a booke entituled the Scottishe story of James the ffourthe slayne at Fflodden intermixed with a plesant Comedie presented by Oboron kinge of ffayres', cited in *The Scottish History of James the Fourth*, ed. A. E. H. Swaen and W. W. Greg, Malone Society Reprints (Oxford: Oxford University Press, 1921), p. v.
9. Ruth Hudson, 'Greene's *James IV* and Contemporary Allusions to Scotland', *PMLA*, 47 (1932): 652–67; Catherine Lekhal, 'The Historical Background of Robert Greene's "The Scottish History of James IV"', *Cahiers Elisabéthains*, 35 (1989): 27–45.
10. Paul Dean, 'Shakespeare's *Henry VI* Trilogy and Elizabethan "Romance" Histories: the Origins of a Genre', *SQ*, 33 (1982): 34–48.
11. *Ibid.*, esp. 36. For further discussion of romance histories, see Paul Dean, 'Chronicle and Romance Modes in *Henry V*', *SQ*, 32 (1981): 18–27. Compare Graham Holderness's observation that such drama offered 'a space of freedom from the event', in *Shakespeare Recycled: the Making of Historical Drama* (New York and London: Harvester Wheatsheaf, 1992), p. 19.
12. David Bevington notes that *James IV*'s apparently slapdash composition conveys the character of 'a man given to the most debilitating irregularity of life', in *Tudor Drama*, p. 224.
13. Anne Barton, 'The King Disguised: Shakespeare's *Henry V* and the Comical History', in *The Triple Bond: Essays in Honour of Arthur Colby Sprague*, ed. Joseph G. Price (Pennsylvania and London: Pennsylvania State University Press, 1975), pp. 92–117, p. 115; p. 116.
14. The issue of dating raises some uncertainties here. *Tamburlaine* can be safely assumed as an influence upon Greene, but the dates of Shakespeare's *Henry VI* plays are conjectural, as is the date of *James IV*. I have accepted the consensus that the latter can be dated 1590/1 and that Greene was likely to have known at least *The First Part of the Contention* if not more of the *Henry VI* sequence.
15. P. Z. Round, 'Greene's Materials for *Friar Bacon and Friar Bungay*', *Modern Language Review*, 21 (1926): 19–23.

16. This paragraph draws upon a broader consideration of the reputation of James IV, in 'Uncivil Monarchy: Scotland, England and the Reputation of James IV', in 'Early Modern Civil Discourses', ed. Jennifer Richards (Basingstoke: Palgrave Macmillan, 2003).

17. See Michel Foucault's influential *The Use of Pleasure: Volume 2 of The History of Sexuality*, trans. Robert Hurley (1985; repr. Harmondsworth: Penguin, 1992). For critical readings of temperance, see Stephen Greenblatt's influential analysis of Spenser's Legend of Temperance in *Renaissance Self-Fashioning: From More to Shakespeare* (Chicago: Chicago University Press, 1980), ch. 4; Lorna Hutson, 'Chivalry for Merchants; or, Knights of Temperance in the Realms of Gold', *Journal of Medieval and Early Modern Studies*, 26 (1996): 29–59.

18. Helen North, *Sophrosyne: Self-Knowledge and Self-Restraint in Greek Literature* (Ithaca: Cornell University Press, 1966).

19. Jennifer Richards, '"A wanton trade of living"?: Rhetoric, Effeminacy and the Early Modern Courtier', *Criticism*, 42 (2000): 185–206.

20. Werner Senn, 'Robert Greene's Handling of Source Material in *Friar Bacon and Friar Bungay*', *English Studies*, 54 (1973): 544–53, 546.

21. Charles Hieatt, 'A New Source for *Friar Bacon and Friar Bungay*', RES, NS, 32 (1981): 180–7, 185, 184. Hieatt is concerned here with Lyly's influence upon Greene.

22. Emrys Jones speculates that this episode was an important influence upon Shakespeare, especially the second scene of *Julius Caesar*, in *Scenic Form in Shakespeare* (Oxford: Clarendon Press, 1971), pp. 22–3.

23. T. McAlindon, *Shakespeare and Decorum* (Basingstoke: Macmillan, 1973), p. 11.

24. See Blair Worden, 'Favourites on the English Stage', in *The World of the Favourite*, ed. J. H. Elliot and L. W. B. Brockliss (New Haven and London: Yale University Press, 1999), pp. 159–83.

25. 1.1.183; 201; 278; 2.2.165.

26. *Perimedes the Blacke-Smith* (1588), sig. A3r.

27. *Greene's Groatsworth of Wit*, p. 81.

28. David Riggs, *Shakespeare's Heroical Histories*: Henry VI *and its Literary Tradition* (Cambridge, Mass.: Harvard University Press, 1971), p. 7.

29. McEachern, *The Poetics of English Nationhood*, p. 8.

30. Cartwright, *Theatre and Humanism*, p. 198. For a fuller consideration of the complex artistic relationship between Greene and Marlowe, see Una Ellis-Fermor, 'Marlowe and Greene: a Note on Their Relations as Dramatic Artists', *Studies in Honor of T. W. Baldwin*, ed. D. C. Allen (Illinois: University of Illinois Press, 1958), pp. 136–49.

31. Michael C. Schoenfeldt, *Bodies and Selves in Early Modern England: Physiology and Inwardness in Spenser, Shakespeare, Herbert, and Milton* (Cambridge: Cambridge University Press, 1999), p. 12.

32. Cicero, *De Officiis*, I.xxviii.98. Subsequent references in parentheses.

33. In his gloss upon this passage, Norman Sanders notes that Greene alludes here to two passages from Cicero's *De Senectute* and *De Divinatione*.

34. McAlindon, *Shakespeare and Decorum*, p. 8.

35. Jonathan Scott, *England's Troubles: Seventeenth-Century English Political Instability in European Context* (Cambridge: Cambridge University Press, 2000), p. 79; p. 78.

36. Thomas Elyot, *The Boke Named the Governour*, III, xix, fol. 224v.
37. If the author(s) of the *Groatsworth of Wit* testify accurately as to Greene's prejudices, it may be revealing that the line singled out for parody from *The True Tragedy of Richard Duke of York* [*Henry VI, Part 3*] (c. 1591/2) is the terrifying scene of York's mock-coronation and killing by the Lancastrians (1.4). Again, Greene's distaste for this kind of historical drama may spring from deeper sources than personal envy.
38. See Howard and Rackin, *Engendering a Nation*.
39. Helgerson, *Forms of Nationhood*, p. 3; p. 11.
40. See Dillon, *Language and Stage*, ch. 7.
41. See Cavanagh, 'Uncivil Monarchy'.
42. Anthony Esler, 'Robert Greene and the Spanish Armada', *ELH*, 32 (1965): 314–32.
43. Elyot, *The Governour*, I.xi, fol. 40r.
44. Mikhail Bakhtin, *Problems of Dostoyevsky's Poetics*, ed. and trans. Caryl Emerson (Manchester: Manchester University Press, 1984), p. 196.
45. Seneca, 'De Ira', in *Moral Essays*, trans. J. W. Basore, 3 vols (London: Heinemann, 1928), I: I.iv.2; iv.3.
46. *Ibid.*, III.ii.1; II.xv.5.
47. For example, Bohan's sons, Slipper and Nano, move freely between the different levels of the action and are agents in both of its plots. Subsequently, Ateukin recognizes them and is aware of Bohan's existence (1.2.118–19) and Oberon rescues Slipper from James's furious desire to execute him as a traitor for bearing the news of Ida's marriage (5.6.57). For further analysis of the interaction of frame and main plot, see A. R. Braunmuller, 'The Serious Comedy of Greene's *James IV'*, *ELR*, 3 (1973): 335–50.
48. Cited in, R.W. Hoyle, *The Pilgrimage of Grace and the Politics of the 1530s* (Oxford: Oxford University Press, 2001), p. 29.
49. See George Puttenham, *The Arte of English Poesie* (1589), ed. Gladys Doidge Willcock and Alice Walker (Cambridge: Cambridge University Press, 1936), p. 145.
50. Rackin, *Stages of History*, p. 29.
51. McMillin and MacLean, *The Queen's Men*, p. 155.

4.   Misreading History: Rumour in *King John*

1. For a comprehensive study, see Carole Levin, *Propaganda in the English Reformation: Heroic and Villainous Images of King John* (Lewiston, New York: Edwin Mellen Press, 1988).
2. The date of *King John* and its relationship to *The Troublesome Raigne* has been enduringly contentious; E. A. J. Honigmann returns to this issue and to the recent scholarship it has provoked in 'Shakespeare's Self-Repetitions and *King John'*, *Shakespeare Survey*, 53 (2000): 175–83. The consensus of opinion maintains that the play derives from *The Troublesome Raigne* and is to be dated 1595/6. Although this is far from resolved, its implications are not of great moment for the argument presented here.
3. Virginia Mason Vaughan, 'Between Tetralogies: *King John* as Transition', *SQ*, 35 (1984): 407–20. John F. Danby first suggested the play needed to be

perceived as transitional in *Shakespeare's Doctrine of Nature: a Study of* King Lear (London: Faber & Faber, 1968), pp. 68–80.

4. 'Introduction', *King John* (Oxford: Clarendon Press, 1989), pp. 1–93, p. 38; emphasis in original.

5. For some representative work, see Annabel Patterson's exploration of Shakespeare's sympathy for popular speech and action, in *Shakespeare and the Popular Voice* (Oxford: Basil Blackwell, 1989). For counter-readings, see, for example, Bevington, *Tudor Drama and Politics*, ch. 16; Wilson, *Willpower: Essays in Shakespearean Authority* (London: Harvester Wheatsheaf, 1993), esp. chs 1 and 2; Simon Hunt, '"Leaving Out the Insurrection": Carnival Rebellion, English History Plays, and a Hermeneutics of Advocacy', in *Renaissance Culture and the Everyday*, ed. Patricia Fumerton and Simon Hunt (Philadelphia: University of Pennsylvania Press, 1999), pp. 299–314.

6. See the discussion of George Cavendish's *The Life of Cardinal Wolsey* at pp. 85–6.

7. Rackin, *Stages of History*, p. 12.

8. See Levin, *Propaganda in the English Reformation*, pp. 55–104.

9. *A & M*, p. 64.

10. 'An Homelie against Disobedience and Wylfull Rebellion' (1570), in *'Certain Sermons or Homilies 1547*, ed. Ronald B. Bond, pp. 209–59, esp. pp. 242–4.

11. See *A breviat cronicle contaynynge all the kinges from Brute to this daye* (Canterbury?, 1551), cited in Thomas Betteridge, *Tudor Histories of the English Reformations, 1530–83*, p. 8.

12. Cited in John R. Elliot, 'Shakespeare and the Double Image of King John', *ShakS*, 1 (1965): 64–84, 68.

13. *Holinshed's Chronicles* detail the suspicions regarding John's cruelty towards Arthur at II: 286 and notes other reputed excesses at, for example, II: 298; 300; 319. In Roman Catholic polemic the reign was used to justify resistance to tyranny: see, for example, the comments in Cardinal Allen's *Defense of Sir William Stanley's Surrender of Deventry*, ed. Thomas Heywood (Chatham Society Publication, XXV, 1851), pp. 26–7.

14. See, Elliot, 'Shakespeare and the Double Image', 64–84.

15. For such readings, see, for example, Sigurd Burckhardt's influential '*King John*: the Ordering of this Present Time', in *Shakespearean Meanings* (Princeton: Princeton University Press, 1968), pp. 116–43; Douglas C. Wixson, '"Calm Words Folded Up in Smoke": Propaganda and Spectator Response in Shakespeare's *King John*', *ShakS*, 14 (1981): 111–27; Paola Pugliatti, *Shakespeare the Historian*, ch. 6. This tradition is contested by David Womersley, 'The Politics of Shakespeare's King John', *RES*, NS, 40 (1989): 497–515 ; Steve Longstaffe, 'The Limits of Modernity in Shakespeare's King John', *Shakespeare Yearbook*, 6 (1996): 91–118; Robert Weimann, 'Mingling Vice and Worthiness in *King John*', *ShakS*, 27 (1999): 109–33.

16. Penny Roberts, 'Arson, Conspiracy and Rumour in Early Modern Europe', *Continuity and Change*, 12 (1997): 9–29, 11. For further analysis, see Hans-Joachim Neubauer, *The Rumour: a Cultural History*, trans. Christian Braun (London and New York: Free Association Books, 1999).

17. *TRP*, I: 11. Subsequent references are included in parentheses.

18. Gross, *Shakespeare's Noise*, p. 18.

19. Fox, *Oral and Literate Culture*, p. 337; p. 339.

20. For an account of these, see ' "Possessed with Rumours": Popular Speech and *King John'*, *Shakespeare Yearbook*, 6 (1996): 171–94, esp. 180–1.
21. *LP*, 12; Pt. 2, 1256. Lyttelworke appeared in the pillory at Reading the following day 'and then and there whypped round about the same towne'.
22. See, for example, *Calendar of Assize Records: Surrey Indictments, Elizabeth I*, ed. J. S. Cockburn (London: HMSO, 1980), 2606, 2637; *Calendar of State Papers, Domestic, Elizabeth, 1598–1601*, ed. Mary Anne Everett Green (1869), CCLXXII, 49. Subsequently, *CSPD, Elizabeth*.
23. *TRP*, I: 168, 281, 329, 337; II: 389, 650.
24. 'Plays Confuted in Five Actions' (1582), in *Markets of Bawdrie: the Dramatic Criticism of Stephen Gosson*, ed. Arthur F. Kinney (Salzburg Studies in English Literature, 4, 1974), pp. 140–200, p. 164. The most famous instance of a collocation of theatre with rumour is, of course, the 'Induction' to *2 Henry IV*. For discussion of this, see Harry Berger Jr., 'Sneak's Noise, or, Rumour and Detextualization in *2 Henry IV'*, *Kenyon Review*, NS, 6 (1984): 58–78; Nick de Somogyi, *Shakespeare's Theatre of War* (Aldershot: Ashgate, 1998), pp. 131–85.
25. George Cavendish, *The Life and Death of Cardinal Wolsey*, ed. Richard S. Sylvester, Early English Text Society (Oxford: Oxford University Press, 1959), p. 3.
26. Carole Levin, ' "We shall never have a merry world while the Queene lyveth": Gender, Monarchy, and the Power of Seditious Words', in *Dissing Elizabeth: Negative Representations of Gloriana*, ed. Julia M. Walker (Durham, North Carolina and London: Duke University Press, 1998), pp. 77–95, p. 87. For further analysis of the misogyny inherent in criticism of Elizabeth, see Louis A. Montrose, 'Idols of the Queen: Policy, Gender, and the Picturing of Elizabeth I', *Representations*, 68 (1999): 108–61, esp. 118–20. These rumours are also discussed by Leah Marcus, *Puzzling Shakespeare*, pp. 70–1; Carole Levin, *'The Heart and Stomach of a King': Elizabeth I and the Politics of Sex and Power* (Philadelphia: University of Pennsylvania Press, 1994), ch. 4.
27. *Calendar of Assize Records: Kent Indictments, Elizabeth I*, ed. J. S. Cockburn (London: HMSO, 1979), 1 May 1568, 423.
28. *Calendar of Assize Records: Sussex Indictments, Elizabeth I*, ed. J. S. Cockburn (London: HMSO, 1975), 1 Jan. 1600, 1888; *CSPD, Elizabeth, 1581–90*, CXLVIII, 34. The speaker of the first rumour, Robert Fowler, also believed that the queen's other son was, less grandly, supposed 'to be the brother of Mr. Walwyn, late vicar of Wisborough Greene'.
29. *Calendar of Assize Records: Surrey Indictments, Elizabeth I*, ed. J. S. Cockburn (London: HMSO, 1980), 29 May 1585, 1602.
30. *Calendar of Assize Records: Essex Indictments, Elizabeth I*, ed. J. S. Cockburn (London: HMSO, 1978), 4 April 1590, 2128. The same rumour was recorded in June (2129); both rumour-mongers were sentenced to the pillory.
31. Cited in Adam Fox, 'Rumour, News and Popular Political Opinion in Elizabethan and Early Stuart England', *HJ*, 40 (1997): 597–620, 599.
32. *Calendar of Letters and State Papers, Spanish, 1558–1567*, ed. Martin A. S. Hume (1892), 270.
33. Chris Wickham, 'Gossip and Resistance Among the Medieval Peasantry', *P&P*, 160 (1998): 3–24, 18.

34. *CSPD, Elizabeth 1598–1601*, 28 December 1598, CCLXIX, 22.
35. For further details of the legal definition and prosecution of rumour-mongering (construed as sedition), see Roger B. Manning, 'The Origins of the Doctrine of Sedition', *Albion*, 12 (1980): 99–121; Joel B. Samaha, 'Gleanings from Local Criminal-Court Records: Sedition Amongst the "Inarticulate" in Elizabethan Essex', *Journal of Social History*, 8 (1975): 61–79.
36. Peter Stallybrass and Allon White, *The Politics and Poetics of Transgression* (London: Methuen, 1986), p. 19.
37. Ethan H. Shagan, 'Rumours and Popular Politics in the Reign of Henry VIII', in *The Politics of the Excluded, c. 1500–1800*, pp. 30–66, p. 31.
38. Gilbert Burnet, *The History of the Reformation of the Church of England*, ed. Nicholas Pocock (Oxford: Clarendon Press, 1865), 7 vols., VI, p. 223; p. 224. I owe this reference to Dr Alexandra Gillespie.
39. Fox, 'Rumour, News and Popular Political Opinion', p. 619. Compare Arlette Farge's suggestion that 'satirical and defamatory public judgements were a natural way of reacting orally to permanently truncated information'; such language granted 'public access to what was supposed to be secret. It was the converse of the flattery which ruled the society of court and princes', in *Subversive Words: Public Opinion in Eighteenth-Century France*, trans. Rosemary Morris (Cambridge: Polity Press, 1994), pp. 62–3.
40. James C. Scott, *Domination and the Arts of Resistance: Hidden Transcripts* (New Haven and London: Yale University Press, 1990), pp. 144–8.
41. For example, the claim 'that we should pretend to have all the gold in the hands of our subjects to be brought to our tower to be touched, and all their chattels being unmarked...and for license to eat wheat, bread, pig, goose, or capon', *TRP*, I: 168.
42. R. W. Hoyle, *The Pilgrimage of Grace and the Politics of the 1530s*, p. 91.
43. Scott, *Domination and the Arts of Resistance*, p. 145.
44. Simon Walker, 'Rumour, Sedition and Popular Protest in the Reign of Henry IV', *P&P*, 166 (2000): 31–65. Walker is drawing here on the categories formulated by James C. Scott's earlier study, *Weapons of the Weak: Everyday Forms of Peasant Resistance* (New Haven and London: Yale University Press, 1985), ch. 7.
45. Cavendish, *The Life and Death of Cardinal Wolsey*, p. 4. Ironically, according to R. H. Britnell, Cavendish's *Life* is itself 'little more than a loose succession of anecdotes and vignettes'. Cavendish 'wrote mostly from memory without verifying dates or the sequence of events, and he was not much interested in the sort of things historians ordinarily want to know', in 'Penitence and Prophecy: George Cavendish on the Last State of Cardinal Wolsey', *Journal of Ecclesiastical History*, 48 (1997): 263–81, 263. For other analyses of Cavendish's work, see Judith H. Anderson, *Biographical Truth: the Representation of Historical Persons in Tudor-Stuart Writing* (New Haven and London: Yale University Press, 1984), pp. 27–39 and Jonathan V. Crewe, *Trials of Authorship: Anterior Forms and Poetic Reconstruction from Wyatt to Shakespeare* (Berkeley, Los Angeles, Oxford: University of California Press, 1990), ch. 4.
46. *Calendar of Letters and State Papers, Spanish, 1558–1567*, ed. Martin A. S. Hume (1892), 22 January 1561, 122. The ambassador, Don Alvaro de la Quadra, stressed that he did not believe the latter rumour.

47. For a study of this complex relationship, see Adam Fox's analysis of the interaction between written and spoken rumours in *Oral and Literate Culture*, pp. 363–405.
48. Nicholas Sander, *The Rise and Growth of the Anglican Schism*, trans. David Lewis (1877), p. 99. William Cecil, Lord Burghley, countered Sander's arguments by circulating, in turn, the scandalous rumour concerning 'the strange manner' of the author's death as a papal legate 'wandering in the mountains in Ireland without succour, [he] died raving in a frenzy', *The Execution of Justice in England, by William Cecil*, ed. Robert M. Kinghorn (Ithaca, New York: Cornell University Press, 1965), p. 30.
49. Thomas Birch, *Memoirs of the Reign of Queen Elizabeth, From the Year 1581 till her Death*, 2 vols (1754), II, p. 81.
50. See the report by a client of the Earl, Edward Reynoldes, in *ibid.*, p. 100. Eventually the queen and Privy Council banned all publications about Cadiz and prepared its own official (although never published) account. For an analysis of this episode, see Paul E. J. Hammer, 'Myth-making: Politics, Propaganda and the Capture of Cadiz in 1596', *HJ*, 40 (1997): 621–42.
51. Quintilian, *Institutio Oratoria*, ed. and trans. Donald A. Russell (Cambridge, Mass.: Harvard University Press, 2001), 5 vols, II.5.3.
52. *Leicester's Commonwealth: the Copy of a Letter Written by a Master of Art of Cambridge (1584) and Related Documents*, ed. D. C. Peck (Athens, Ohio and London: Ohio University Press, 1985), p. 75.
53. *King John*, ed. L. A. Beaurline (Cambridge: Cambridge University Press, 1990), 4.2.120. All quotations are to this edition.
54. Lily B. Campbell, *Shakespeare's 'Histories': Mirrors of Elizabethan Policy* (San Marino, California: Huntington Library, 1947), p. 169.
55. In this respect, the play also diverges from *The Troublesome Raigne*. For discussions of this, see Brian Boyd, '*King John* and *The Troublesome Raigne*: Sources, Structure, Sequence', *Philological Quarterly*, 74 (1995): 37–56, esp. 47; Guy Hamel, '*King John* and *The Troublesome Raigne*: a Reexamination', in *King John: New Perspectives*, ed. Deborah T. Curren-Aquino (Newark: Delaware University Press, 1989), pp. 41–61.
56. Frank Whigham, *Ambition and Privilege: the Social Tropes of Elizabethan Courtesy Theory* (Berkeley, Los Angeles, London: University of California Press, 1984), p. 3.
57. *The Faerie Queene*, ed. A. C. Hamilton (London and New York: Longman, 1977), IV.i.28.
58. Rackin, *Stages of History*, p. 183.
59. For an important argument concerning this crucial textual issue see, L. A. Beaurline (ed.), *King John* (1990), pp. 189–92; Robert Lane, ' "The sequence of posterity": Shakespeare's *King John* and the Succession Controversy', *SP*, 92 (1995): 460–81, 477–81.
60. Lane, 'The sequence of posterity', 480.
61. Christopher Z. Hobson, 'Bastard Speech: the Rhetoric of "Commodity" in *King John*', *Shakespeare Yearbook*, 2 (1991): 95–114, 106. Michael Manheim observes that critics have overlooked 'the degree to which rather than simply being satir*ist*, he is also being satir*ized*', 'The Four Voices of the Bastard', in *King John: New Perspectives*, pp. 126–35, p. 127.

62. It is typical of the play's ironic structure that John's most forbidding enemy, the Dauphin, also resorts to anti-catholic polemic when the church eventually opposes his invasion of England, see 5.2.78–108.
63. Boyd, '*King John* and *The Troublesome Raigne*', 41. *Holinshed's Chronicles* acknowledge that 'writers make sundrie reports' concerning John's responsibility for Arthur's death and concludes: 'but verelie king John was had in great suspicion, whether worthilie or not, the lord knoweth', II: 286.
64. The centrality of Arthur's fate as shaping the play's historical interpretation of John's reign has been recognized since Adrien Bonjour's, 'The Road to Swinstead Abbey: a Study of the Sense and Structure of *King John*', *ELH*, 18 (1951): 253–74.
65. Emrys Jones, *The Origins of Shakespeare* (Oxford: Clarendon Press, 1977), p. 234.
66. See Marsha Robinson, 'The Historiographic Methodology of *King John*', in *King John: New Perspectives*, pp. 29–40, esp. p. 30; Robert C. Jones, 'Truth in *King John*', *SEL*, 25 (1985): 397–417.
67. For an alternative interpretation of these lines, see Longstaffe, 'The Limits of Modernity', 101–3.
68. Greenblatt, *Shakespearean Negotiations*, ch. 1.
69. Michel de Certeau, 'History: Science and Fiction', in *Heterologies: Discourse on the Other*, trans. Brian Massumi (Manchester: Manchester University Press, 1986), pp. 199–221, p. 200.
70. Pauline Kiernan, *Shakespeare's Theory of Drama* (Cambridge: Cambridge University Press, 1996), p. 128.

5. The Language of Treason in *Richard II*

1. Barbara Hodgdon, *The End Crowns All: Closure and Contradiction in Shakespeare's History* (Princeton: Princeton University Press, 1991), p. 130.
2. James L. Calderwood, *Metadrama in Shakespeare's Henriad*, p. 32.
3. Joseph A. Porter, *The Drama of Speech Acts*, p. 43. For a similar critique of Richard's language, see Ronald R. MacDonald, 'Uneasy Lies: Language and History in Shakespeare's Lancastrian Tetralogy', *SQ*, 35 (1984): 22–39, esp. 22–30.
4. See, for example, David Scott Kastan's influential 'Proud Majesty Made a Subject'. For a critique of such approaches, see Leeds Barroll, 'A New History for Shakespeare and His Time', *SQ*, 39 (1988): 441–64.
5. David Norbrook, 'The Emperor's New Body?', 329–57, 348–9.
6. '"By the choise and inuitation of al the realme": *Richard II* and Elizabethan Press Censorship', *SQ*, 48 (1997): 432–48, 444.
7. 'Traitor' occurs twenty-eight times in *Richard II*; there are thirteen uses of 'treason'. *Henry V* also has thirteen instances of the latter, although ten of these are concentrated in the 'traitor's scene' (2.2). A number of recent essays have analysed Shakespeare's interest in the 'vast discourse of treason that became an increasingly central response to difficult social problems in late Elizabethan and early Jacobean London', Curt Breight, '"Treason doth never prosper": *The Tempest* and the Discourse of Treason', *SQ*, 41 (1990): 1–28, 1. For recent discussions of this theme in historical drama, see Craig A.

Bernthal, 'Treason in the Family: the Trial of Thumpe v. Horner', *SQ*, 42 (1991): 44–54; Karen Cunningham, 'Female Fidelities on Trial: Proof in the Howard Attainder and *Cymbeline*', *RenD*, NS, 25 (1994): 1–31; Nina Levine, 'Lawful Symmetry: the Politics of Treason in 2 Henry VI', *RenD*, NS, 25 (1994): 197–218. The most comprehensive historical accounts remain John Bellamy's *The Tudor Law of Treason* (London: Routledge & Kegan Paul, 1979) and *The Law of Treason in the Later Middle Ages* (Cambridge: Cambridge University Press, 1970). See also, Lacey Baldwin Smith, *Treason in Tudor England: Politics and Paranoia* (London: Jonathan Cape, 1986); G. R. Elton, *Policy and Police*, pp. 263–326; Penry Williams, *The Tudor Regime*, pp. 375–94.

8. All citations are to the Arden 3 edition, *King Richard II*, ed. Charles R. Forker (London: Thomson Learning, 2002).

9. Victoria Kahn, *Machiavellian Rhetoric: From the Counter-Reformation to Milton* (Princeton: Princeton University Press, 1994), p. 5.

10. Annabel Patterson, *Reading Holinshed's* Chronicles , p. 159. This comment is part of a valuable analysis of treason law in relation to the significant, if highly anomalous, trial in 1554 of Sir Nicholas Throckmorton, pp. 154–83.

11. *Holinshed's Chronicles*, II: 738, 784, 791.

12. For an analysis of the blend of deference and aggression intrinsic to the judicial combat and its significance for Elizabethan concerns with the native rights of the nobility, see Richard C. McCoy, *The Rites of Knighthood: the Literature and Politics of Elizabethan Chivalry* (Berkeley and Los Angeles: University of California Press, 1989), esp. pp. 1–27.

13. Mervyn James, 'English Politics and the Concept of Honour, 1485–1642', in *Society, Politics and Culture: Studies in Early Modern England* (Cambridge: Cambridge University Press, 1986), pp. 308–415, p. 327.

14. Its most influential formulation is located in the famous statute of 1352, the progenitor of all subsequent legislation: 'When a Man doth compass or imagine the Death of our Lord the King, or of our Lady his [Queen] or of their eldest Son and Heir' (25 Edward III 5 c. 2). The act was revised, audaciously, under Cromwell's auspices for Henry VIII in 1534, to emphasize the harm to majesty incurred by hostile 'imagining'; those who 'malicyously wyshe will or desyre by wordes or writinge, or by crafte ymagen invent practyse or attempte, any bodely harme to be donne or commytted to the Kynges moste royall personne' (26 Henry VIII c. 13). It was this thesis of treason that became the period's dominant formulation and which was absorbed into the major component of Elizabethan legislation in 1571. For historical analysis, see Bellamy, *The Tudor Tudor Law of Treason*, pp. 31–4; Elton, *Policy and Police*, pp. 263–92, and Penry Williams, *The Tudor Regime*, pp. 375–89. For analyses of the significance of treason for Shakespearean drama, see Cunningham, 'Female Fidelities on Trial'; Katharine Eisaman Maus, *Inwardness and Theater in the English Renaissance* (Chicago: University of Chicago Press, 1995), pp. 104–27.

15. Robert Bartlett observes how the medieval trial by combat was a medium in which political differences between the aristocracy and the monarchy were expressed, in *Trial by Fire and Water: the Medieval Judicial Ordeal* (Oxford: Clarendon Press, 1986), esp. p. 126. Ute Frevert, develops this point: 'Instead of regarding their own honour as a mere derivative of that honour which

was personified by the prince as ruler and master, the sense of honour of the aristocracy retained a residue of habitual freedom and self-determination, to which they lent expression by engaging in duelling', *Men of Honour: a Social and Cultural History of the Duel*, trans. Anthony Williams (Cambridge: Polity Press, 1995), p. 15.

16. Joseph A. Porter is acute on Richard's tendency to refer to his own public self when apparently speaking of collective issues: 'throughout the play Richard generally uses "we" to mean a public identity which exists in the perception, consciousness, and thought of his audience – that-which-is perceived, as it is perceived by his public'; *The Drama of Speech Acts*, p. 31.

17. Compare the insistence of the 1352 treason act: 'that ought to be judged Treason which extends to our Lord the King, and His Royal Majesty' (25 Edward III 5 c. 2). Claire McEachern's remarks on the utility of personification in Elizabethan political discourse are also useful in interpreting 'a vocabulary of the monarch's private identity in the service of corporate identity', '*Henry V* and the Paradox of the Body Politic', *SQ*, 45 (1994): 33–56, 37.

18. The early phase of the play is intensely alert to the political divisions within medieval society. Peter G. Phialas emphasizes the significance of Edward III's kingship as a contrast to Richard's corruption of the office; 'The Medieval in *Richard II*', *SQ*, 12 (1961): 305–10; Graham Holderness argues that the play depicts the distinctive political ethos of 'a feudalism given cohesion and structure by the central authority of a king bound to his subjects by the reciprocal bonds of fealty', in *Shakespeare Recycled*, p. 64.

19. In terms of the 1352 treason act and subsequent Elizabethan legal practice – see below, note 28 – such a speculation could amount to a traitorous 'imagining' of a harmful act against the monarch, a feature that confirms Gaunt's break with orthodox loyalties.

20. As has been observed, this is a powerful constitutional statement of the necessity for a law-centred monarchy; see Donna B. Hamilton, 'The State of Law in *Richard II*', *SQ*, 34 (1983): 5–17.

21. In an (unconscious) acknowledgment of the equivocal implications of this scene, Leonard Tennenhouse asserts that Bolingbroke 'arrests Bushy and Green on charges of treason for assaulting the king's [that is, Richard's] body'; see his *Power on Display: the Politics of Shakespeare's Genres* (London: Methuen, 1986), p. 80. The rhetorical emphasis, however, is undoubtedly on their offences against Bolingbroke. Tennenhouse's general observation on the political process represented in Shakespeare's history plays helps in illuminating Bolingbroke's attitude towards treason: 'Together these chronicle history plays demonstrate, then, that authority goes to the contender who can seize hold of the symbols and signs legitimizing authority and wrest them from his rivals to make them serve his own interests'; p. 83.

22. The political implications of Bolingbroke's equivocal speech may well have carried more charge to an Elizabethan audience; Steven Mullaney discerns a widespread cultural sensitivity to ambiguous speech – 'the figure of treason itself' – as symptomatic of a politically disordered subject, in 'Lying Like Truth: Riddle, Representation and Treason in Renaissance England', *ELH*, 47 (1980): 32–47. Patricia Parker makes a similar argument in interpreting the 'motivated rhetoric' of, among other texts, Thomas Wilson's manual of logic, *The Rule of Reason* (1551), in *Literary Fat Ladies*, p. 100.

23. The relationship between Bolingbroke's making relative static assumptions and the authority this demonstrates can again be compared to Victoria Kahn's analysis of the form and content of Machiavelli's writing: a 'sophisticated rhetorical strategy, the aim of which is to destabilize or dehypostatize our conception of political virtue, for only a destabilized *virtù* can be effective in the destabilized world of political reality', in *Machiavellian Rhetoric*, p. 25.

24. See, for example, Mary, Queen of Scot's shrewd observation on the prejudicial nature of her trial: 'being already condemned by forejudgings, to give some shew and colour of a just and legal proceeding', *Cobbett's Complete Collection of State Trials*, ed. William Cobbett, Thomas Bayly Howell, Thomas Jones Howell and David Jardine, 34 vols (London, 1809–28), II: 1169–70.

25. Cunningham, 'Female Fidelities on Trial', esp. 2–4.

26. Maus, *Inwardness and Theater*, p. 24.

27. John Barrell, *Imagining the King's Death: Figurative Treason, Fantasies of Regicide 1793–1796* (Oxford: Oxford University Press, 2000), p. 32.

28. Subsequent quotations are from *State Trials*, 2:1315–34. For an insightful account of the legal procedures involved in proving treacherous interiority, see Karen Cunningham, '"A Spanish heart in an English body": the Ralegh Treason Trial and the Poetics of Proof', *Journal of Medieval and Renaissance Studies*, 22 (1992): 327–51.

29. Breight, 'Treason doth never prosper', 3–5.

30. *An admonition to the nobility and people of England and Ireland* (1588), sigs. A5v–A6r. For a detailed study of Elizabethan catholicism, see Peter Holmes, *Resistance and Compromise: the Political Thought of the Elizabethan Catholics* (Cambridge: Cambridge University Press, 1982), esp. pp. 129–65.

31. *The historie of the princesse Elizabeth* (1630), trans R. Norton, sigs. Eee3r + v. In a recent analysis, Hiram Morgan argues that Burghley orchestrated Perrot's downfall and that Camden sought to exculpate this 'despicable behaviour towards a fellow privy councillor', 'The Fall of Sir John Perrot', in *The Reign of Elizabeth I: Court and Culture in the Last Decade* ed. John Guy (Cambridge: Cambridge University Press, 1995), pp. 109–25, p. 125.

32. *State Trials*, 2:1351–2.

33. W. F. Bolton notes that Aumerle's figurative response to Bagot's accusation – 'mine honour soil'd / With the *attainder* of his slanderous lips' (4.1.23–4; emphasis added) – refers to the legal consequences of accusation (that is, the extinction of rights and capacities that followed the sentencing of a traitor); see, 'Ricardian Law Reports and *Richard II*', *ShakS*, 20 (1988): 53–66, 59–60.

34. *Holinshed's Chronicles*, II: 862–3.

35. Sheldon P. Zitner, 'Aumerle's Conspiracy', *SEL*, 14 (1974): 236–57. John Halverson argues that the tone of the whole play is more satirical and absurd than has been registered; 'The Lamentable Comedy of *Richard II*', *ELR*, 24 (1994): 343–69.

36. Compare Craig Bernthal's perceptive remarks on the conflict over treason between Thumpe and Horner in *2 Henry VI* as embodying 'the disquieting reality that people are not safe to speak their minds even in their own homes, that loyalty to the family and loyalty to the state are in fact at odds, and that, while a state cannot exist without stability in the family, the state's very efforts to purge itself of treason could undermine the harmony of

family life and, in the long run, the state itself', in 'Treason in the Family', 50.

37. David Norbrook, '"A liberal tongue"' , p. 38. Norbrook examines the Essex circle's interest in the play's aristocratic constitutionalism and 'the slow and painful process of formulating opposition', p. 41.

38. 'At a Crossroads of the Political Culture: the Essex revolt, 1601', in *Society, Politics and Culture: Studies in Early Modern England* (Cambridge: Cambridge University Press, 1986), pp. 416–65, 421. Louis Montrose argues that the motive of the conspirators in sponsoring a performance of the play was 'to rouse *themselves* to action', see, *The Purpose of Playing: Shakespeare and the Cultural Politics of the Elizabethan Theatre* (Chicago: University of Chicago Press, 1996,), pp. 66–75, p. 75.

39. Robert Lacey, *Robert, Earl of Essex: an Elizabethan Icarus* (London: Weidenfeld and Nicolson, 1971), pp. 261–2.

40. In '"By the choise and inuitation of al the realme"', Cyndia Susan Clegg discusses the implications of Parson's treatise for the play, esp. 437–42.

41. Paul Hammer, 'The Uses of Scholarship: the Secretariat of Robert Devereux, Second Earl of Essex', *English Historical Review*, 109 (1994): 26–51, 31. See also, Paul E. J. Hammer, *The Polarization of Elizabethan Politics: the Political Career of Robert Devereux, 2nd Earl of Essex, 1585–97* (Cambridge: Cambridge University Press, 1999), pp. 306–15; ch. 8.

42. Cited in Penry Williams, *The Later Tudors: England, 1547–1603* (Oxford: Clarendon Press, 1995), p. 372.

43. Paula Blank, 'Speaking Freely about Richard II'.

6. *Henry V* and the Reformation of the Word

1. Chorus, 5.0.4–6. All quotations are to *King Henry V*, ed. T. W. Craik, *The Arden Shakespeare* (1995; reprinted, London: Thomson Learning, 2001).

2. For some pertinent reflections on the myth of the history play's end after the Elizabethan period, see Longstaffe, 'What is the English History Play...?'.

3. David Womersley has interpreted Shakespeare's Henry V as conceived in the spirit of John Bale in 'Why is Falstaff Fat?', RES, NS, 47 (1996): 1–22, 8.

4. An interpretation renewed fulsomely in Tom McAlindon's *Shakespeare's Tudor History: a Study of* Henry IV, Parts 1 and 2 (Aldershot: Ashgate, 2001).

5. See, for example, the influential reading by Norman Rabkin, 'Rabbits, Ducks, and *Henry V*', SQ, 28 (1977): 279–96.

6. See, for example, E. J. Dobson, 'Early Modern Standard English', *Transactions of the Philological Society* (1955): 25–34; Paula Blank, *Broken English: Dialects and the Politics of Language in Renaissance Writings* (London and New York: Routledge, 1996); Cathy Shrank, 'Rhetorical Constructions of a National Community: the Role of the King's English in mid-Tudor Writing', in *Communities in Early Modern England: Networks, Place, Rhetoric*, ed. Alexandra Shepard and Phil Withington (Manchester: Manchester University Press, 2000), pp. 180–98.

7. Anna Bryson, *From Courtesy to Civility: Changing Codes of Conduct in Early Modern England* (Oxford: Clarendon Press, 1998), p. 159. For an account of humanist and protestant interest in the 'improvement' and standardization

of English, see Mike Pincombe, *Elizabethan Humanism: Literature and Learning in the later Sixteenth Century* (Harlow: Longman, 2001), esp. chs 3 and 4.

8. John Hart, 'The Opening of the unreasonable writing of our inglish toung' (1551), in *John Hart's Works on English Orthography and Pronunciation* (Stockholm: Almqvist and Wiksell, 1955–63), 2 pts., ed. Bror Danielsson, pt. 1, p. 115.

9. See Blank, *Broken English*, p. 51.

10. For recent examples of the political implications of the 'King's English' in *Henry V*, see Stephen Greenblatt's influential 'Invisible Bullets'; Michael Neill, 'Broken English and Broken Irish: Nation, Language, and the Optic of Power in Shakespeare's Histories', *SQ*, 45 (1994): 1–32; P. K. Ayers, ' "Fellows of Infinite Tongue": *Henry V* and the King's English', *SEL*, 34 (1994): 253–77; Dillon, *Language and Stage*, pp. 177–82; David Steinsaltz, 'The Politics of French Language in Shakespeare's History Plays', *SEL*, 42 (2002): 317–34.

11. Marion Trousdale, *Shakespeare and the Rhetoricians* (London: Scolar Press, 1982), p. 79.

12. Patrick Collinson, *The Birthpangs of Protestant England: Religious and Cultural Change in the Sixteenth and Seventeenth Centuries* (Basingstoke: Macmillan, 1988), p. 94.

13. Huston Diehl, *Staging Reform, Reforming the Stage: Protestantism and Popular Theater in Early Modern England* (Ithaca, New York: Cornell University Press, 1997).

14. See Karl P. Wentersdorf, 'The Conspiracy of Silence in *Henry V*', *SQ*, 27 (1976): 264–87. Jonathan Dollimore and Alan Sinfield have argued that the play is a form of (self-contradictory) ideological fantasy in 'History and Ideology: the Instance of *Henry V*', *Alternative Shakespeares*, ed. John Drakakis (London and New York: Routledge, 1985), pp. 206–27.

15. A. P. Rossiter, 'Ambivalence: the Dialectic of the Histories', in *Angel With Horns and Other Shakespeare Lectures*, ed. Graham Storey (London: Longman, 1961), pp. 40–64, p. 57.

16. See A. R. Humphreys (ed.), *Henry V* (Harmondsworth: Penguin, 1968), pp. 18–19.

17. Leonard Digges, *Stratioticos* (1579; repr. The English Experience, Amsterdam and New York: Da Capo Press, 1968), p. 137.

18. Janel M. Mueller, *The Native Tongue and the Word: Developments in English Prose Style, 1380–1580* (Chicago: University of Chicago Press, 1984), p. 348.

19. Thomas Wilson, *Arte of Rhetorique* (1553), ed. Thomas J. Derrick, The Renaissance Imagination, 1 (New York and London: Garland Publishing, 1982), p. 20.

20. Martin Elsky, *Authorizing Words: Speech, Writing, and Print in the English Renaissance* (Ithaca and London: Cornell University Press, 1989), p. 75.

21. Alexander Gill, *Logonomia Anglica* (1619), trans. Bror Danielsson and Arvid Gabrielson, 2 pts (Stockholm: Almqvist and Wiksell, 1972), pt. 2, p. 79.

22. See, for example, Paula Blank, ' "Niu ureiting": the Prose of Language Reform in the English Renaissance', in *The Project of Prose in Early Modern Europe and the New World*, ed. Elizabeth Fowler and Roland Greene (Cambridge: Cambridge University Press, 1997), pp. 31–47.

23. John Hart, 'An Orthographie' (1569) in *John Hart's Works*, pt. 1, p. 178.

24. Greenblatt, 'Invisible Bullets', p. 57.
25. Arthur B. Ferguson, *Clio Unbound: Perception of the Social and Cultural Past in Renaissance England* (Durham, North Carolina: Duke University Press, 1979), p. 323.
26. Sir Thomas Smith, 'De Recta et Emendata Linguae Graecae Pronuntiatione', in *Literary and Linguistic Works (1542, 1549, 1568)*, ed. Bror Danielsson (Stockholm: Almqvist and Wiksell, 1978), p. 77.
27. For discussions of the orthographical debate, see Ferguson, *Clio Unbound*, pp. 318–29; Elsky, *Authorizing Words*, pp. 43–56.
28. Elsky, *Authorizing Words*, p. 75.
29. *Ibid.*, p. 74. For further discussion of Mulcaster and his ideas concerning language, see Richard L. DeMolen, *Richard Mulcaster (c. 1531–1611) and Educational Reform in the Renaissance* (Nieuwkoop: De Graaf Publishers, 1991); Jonathan Goldberg, *Writing Matter: From the Hands of the English Renaissance* (Stanford: Stanford University Press, 1990), pp. 28–40.
30. Richard Mulcaster, *The First Part of the Elementarie* (1582) (repr. Menston Scolar Press, 1970), p. 66; p. 64. Subsequent references are included in parentheses.
31. Mulcaster's views can be compared to Gabriel Harvey's criticism of the quantitative movement. See Helgerson, *Forms of Nationhood*, esp. p. 28 and Richards, *Rhetoric and Courtliness*, ch. 5.
32. Calderwood, *Metadrama in Shakespeare's Henriad*, p. 22.
33. Compare Pugliatti, *Shakespeare the Historian*, pp. 140–1.
34. Compare A. Elizabeth Ross's observation that the Chorus's opening movement 'from inspiration to doubt' signals the play's intention to interrupt 'the full development of the bombastic style', in 'Hand-me-Down-Heroics: Shakespeare's Retrospective of Popular Elizabethan Heroical Drama in *Henry V*', in *Shakespeare's English Histories: a Quest for Form and Genre*, ed. John W. Velz (Binghampton, New York: Medieval and Renaissance Texts and Studies, 1996), pp. 171–203, p. 175.
35. Diehl, *Staging Reform*, p. 28.
36. Karen Newman, *Fashioning Femininity and English Renaissance Drama* (Chicago: University of Chicago Press, 1991), p. 101. Compare Rackin's observation that the 'linguistic deformities' of the insubordinate soldiery bespeaks 'their exclusion from the dominant official discourse of the King's English', p. 244.
37. Alvin Vos, ' "Good Matter and Good Utterance": the Character of English Ciceronianism', *SEL*, 19 (1979): 3–18, 12.
38. *Ibid.*, 9
39. Roger Ascham, *The Schoolmaster* (1570), ed. Lawrence V. Ryan (Ithaca, New York: Cornell University Press, 1967), p. 115.
40. For an instructive alternative to this, see David Womersley's subtle essay, 'France in Shakespeare's *Henry V*', *Renaissance Studies*, 9 (1995): 442–59.
41. Dillon, *Language and Stage*, p. 177.
42. Lisa Hopkins, 'Neighbourhood in *Henry V*', *Shakespeare and Ireland: History, Politics, Culture*, ed. Mark Thornton Burnett and Ramona Wray (Basingstoke: Macmillan, 1997), pp. 9–26, esp. p.11.
43. For (opposing) discussions of the play's treatment of memory, see Jonathan Baldo, 'Wars of Memory in *Henry V*', *SQ*, 47 (1996): 132–59;

Alison A. Chapman, 'Whose Saint Crispin's Day Is It?: Shoemaking, Holiday Making, and the Politics of Memory in Early Modern England', *Renaissance Quarterly*, 54 (2001): 1467–94.

44. For further (and opposing) discussion of this passage, see Judith Mossman, '*Henry V* and Plutarch's Alexander', *SQ*, 45 (1994); 57–73; Janet M. Speer, 'Princes, Pirates, and Pigs: Criminalizing Wars of Conquest in *Henry V*', *SQ*, 47 (1996): 160–77.
45. David Womersley, 'Why is Falstaff Fat?'
46. *Ibid.*, 15
47. Huston Diehl, *Staging Reform*, p. 42.
48. *Ibid.*, p. 31.
49. Kastan, *Shakespeare and the Shapes of Time*, pp. 64–5.
50. Newman, *Fashioning Femininity*, p. 106; p. 107.

Bibliography

Primary sources

Allen, William, Cardinal, *An admonition to the nobility and people of England and Ireland* (1588).
—— *Cardinal Allen's Defense of Sir William Stanley's Surrender of Deventry*, ed. Thomas Heywood (Chatham Society Publication, XXV, 1851).
Ascham, Roger, *The Schoolmaster (1570)*, ed. Lawrence V. Ryan (Ithaca, New York: Cornell University Press, 1967).
Baker, J. H. and Samuel E. Thorne, eds, *Readings and Moots at the Inns of Court in the Fifteenth Century*, 2 vols (London: Selden Society, v. 105, 1990).
Bale, John, *King Johan by John Bale*, ed. J. H. P. Pafford and W. W. Greg, Malone Society (Oxford: Oxford University Press, 1931).
—— *John Bale's King Johan*, ed. Barry B. Adams (San Marino, California: Huntington Library, 1969).
—— *The Complete Plays of John Bale*, ed. Peter Happé, 2 vols (Cambridge: D. S. Brewer, 1985).
—— *The Image of Both Churches*, ed. H. Christmas, Parker Society (Cambridge, 1849).
—— *The vocacyon of Johan Bale* (1553), ed. Peter Happé and John N. King (Binghampton, New York: Medieval and Renaissance Texts and Studies, 1990).
Bateson, Mary, ed., *Records of the Borough of Leicester, 1509–1603*, 7 vols, revised by W. H. Stevenson and J. E. Stocks (Cambridge, 1905).
Birch, Thomas, *Memoirs of the Reign of Queen Elizabeth, From the Year 1581 till her Death*, 2 vols (1754).
Bond, Ronald B., ed., *'Certain Sermons or Homilies 1547' and 'A Homily against Disobedience and Wilful Rebellion' (1570)* (Toronto: University of Toronto Press, 1987).
Brewer, J. S., *et al*. eds, *Letters and Papers, Foreign and Domestic, of the Reign of Henry VIII*, 21 vols, (1862–1932).
Burnet, Gilbert, *The History of the Reformation of the Church of England*, ed. Nicholas Pocock, 7 vols (Oxford, 1865).
Camden, William, *The historie of the princesse Elizabeth* (1630), trans. R. Norton.
Campbell, Lily B, ed., *The Mirror for Magistrates* (Cambridge: Cambridge University Press, 1938).
Cavendish, George, *The Life and Death of Cardinal Wolsey*, ed. Richard S. Sylvester, Early English Text Society (Oxford: Oxford University Press, 1959).
Cecil, William, *The Execution of Justice in England, by William Cecil*, ed. Robert M. Kinghorn (Ithaca: New York: Cornell University Press, 1965).
Cicero, *[Cicero] Ad Herennium*, trans. Harry Caplan (London: Heinemann, 1954).
—— *De Officiis*, trans. Walter Miller (London: Heinemann, 1913).
Cobbett, William, Thomas Bayly Howell, Thomas Jones Howell and David Jardine, eds, *Cobbett's Complete Collection of State Trials*, 34 vols (London, 1809–28).
Cockburn, J. S., ed., *Calendar of Assize Records: Sussex Indictments, Elizabeth I* (London: HMSO, 1975).

—— Calendar of Assize Records: Essex Indictments, Elizabeth I (London: HMSO, 1978).

—— Calendar of Assize Records: Kent Indictments, Elizabeth I (London: HMSO, 1979).

—— Calendar of Assize Records: Surrey Indictments, Elizabeth I (London: HMSO, 1980).

Cooper, C. H. and T. Cooper, Athenae Cantabrigienses, 3 vols (Cambridge, 1858–1913).

Cranmer, Thomas, The Miscellaneous Writings and Letters of Thomas Cranmer, ed. J. E. Cox, Parker Society (Cambridge, 1846).

Cromwell, Thomas, Life and Letters of Thomas Cromwell, ed. R. B. Merriman, 2 vols (Oxford, 1902).

Dekker, Thomas, O per se O. Or a new Cryer of Lanthorne and Candle-light (1612).

Digges, Leonard, Stratioticos (1579; repr. The English Experience, Amsterdam and New York: Da Capo Press, 1968).

Elyot, Sir Thomas, The Boke Named the Governour (1531; repr. Menston: Scolar Press, 1970).

Foxe, John, Actes and Monuments (1563).

Gill, Alexander, Logonomia Anglica (1619), trans. Bror Danielsson and Arvid Gabrielson, 2 pts (Stockholm: Almqvist and Wiksell, 1972).

Green, Mary Anne Everett, ed., Calendar of State Papers, Domestic, Elizabeth, 1598–1601 (1869).

Greene, Robert, Greene's Groatsworth of Wit: Bought with a Million of Repentance (1592), ed. D. Allen Carroll (Binghampton, New York: Medieval & Renaissance Texts & Studies, 1994).

—— The Scottish History of James the Fourth, ed. Norman Sanders (London: Methuen, 1970).

—— The Scottish History of James the Fourth, ed. A. E. H. Swaen and W. W. Greg, Malone Society Reprints (Oxford: Oxford University Press, 1921).

—— Perimedes the Blacke-Smith (1588).

Gosson, Stephen, 'Plays Confuted in Five Actions' (1582), in Arthur F. Kinney, ed., Markets of Bawdrie: the Dramatic Criticism of Stephen Gosson (Salzburg Studies in English Literature, 4, 1974), pp. 140–200.

Hart, John, John Hart's Works on English Orthography and Pronunciation, ed. Bror Danielsson, 2 pts (Stockholm: Almqvist and Wiksell, 1955–63).

Hartley, T. E., ed., Proceedings in the Parliaments of Elizabeth I, 1558–1581 (Leicester: Leicester University Press, 1981).

Holinshed, Raphael, Holinshed's Chronicles (1587), ed. Henry Ellis, 6 vols (London, 1807–8; repr. New York: AMS Press, 1965).

Hughes, P. L. and J. F. Larkin, eds, Tudor Royal Proclamations, 3 vols (New Haven: Yale University Press, 1964–9).

Hume, Martin A. S., ed., Calendar of Letters and State Papers, Spanish, 1558–1567 (London, 1892).

Machiavelli, Niccolo, The Discourses, ed. Bernard Crick, trans. Leslie J. Walker (Harmondsworth: Penguin, 1970; repr. 1974).

More, Thomas, 'The Confutation of Tyndale's Answer' (1533), in Louis A. Schuster et al., eds, The Complete Works of St. Thomas More (1963–97), 15 vols (New Haven and London: Yale University Press, 1973), 8: Pt. I.

Morison, Richard, A remedy for sedition (1536).

Mulcaster, Richard, *The First Part of the Elementarie* (1582; repr. Menston: Scolar Press, 1970).

Peck, D. C., ed., *Leicester's Commonwealth: the Copy of a Letter Written by a Master of Art of Cambridge (1584) and Related Documents* (Athens, Ohio and London: Ohio University Press, 1985).

Plutarch, 'How to Tell a Flatterer from a Friend', *Plutarch's Moralia*, trans. Frank Cole Babbit, 14 vols (London: William Heinemann, 1927), I, pp. 263–395.

Puttenham, George, *The Arte of English Poesie*, ed. Gladys Doidge Willcock and Alice Walker (Cambridge: Cambridge University Press, 1936).

Quintilian, *Institutio Oratoria*, ed. and trans. Donald A. Russell (Cambridge, Mass.: Harvard University Press, 2001), 5 vols.

—— *Institutio Oratoria*, trans. H. E. Butler (London: Heinemann, 1922), 4 vols.

Sackville, Thomas and Thomas Norton, *Gorboduc or Ferrex and Porrex*, ed. Irby B. Cauthen, Jr. (London: Edward Arnold, 1970).

Sander, Nicholas, *The Rise and Growth of the Anglican Schism*, trans. David Lewis (London, 1877).

Seneca, *De Ira*, in *Moral Essays*, 3 vols, trans. J. W. Basore (London: Heinemann, 1928), I.

Shakespeare, William, *Henry V*, ed. A. R Humphreys (Harmondsworth: Penguin, 1968).

—— *King Henry V*, ed. T. W. Craik, The Arden Shakespeare (1995; repr. London: Thomson Learning, 2001).

—— *King John*, ed. A. R. Braunmuller (Oxford: Clarendon Press, 1989).

—— *King John*, ed. L. A. Beaurline (Cambridge: Cambridge University Press, 1990).

—— *Richard II*, ed. Charles R. Forker, The Arden Shakespeare (London: Thomson Learning, 2002).

Sidney, Sir Philip, 'A Defence of Poetry', in *Miscellaneous Prose of Sir Philip Sidney*, ed. Katherine Duncan-Jones and Jan Van Dorsten (Oxford: Clarendon Press, 1973).

Smith, Sir Thomas, *Literary and Linguistic Works (1542, 1549, 1568)*, ed. Bror Danielsson (Stockholm: Almqvist and Wiksell, 1978).

Spenser, Edmund, *The Faerie Queene*, ed. A C. Hamilton (London and New York: Longman, 1977).

Stow, John, *Annales, or, A general Chronicle of England* (1631).

Strype, John, *The Life of the Learned Sir Thomas Smith* (Oxford, 1820).

Wentworth, Peter, *A pithie exhortation on to her Majestie for establishing her successor for the crowne* (1598).

Wilson, Thomas, *Arte of Rhetorique* (1553), ed. Thomas J. Derrick, The Renaissance Imagination, 1 (New York and London: Garland Publishing, 1982).

Wriothesley's Chronicle, ed. W. D. Hamilton, 2 vols, Camden Society (London, 1875).

Secondary sources

Alford, Stephen, *The Early Elizabethan Polity: William Cecil and the British Succession Crisis, 1558–1569* (Cambridge: Cambridge University Press, 1998).

Althusser, Louis, 'Ideology and Ideological State Apparatuses', in *Lenin and Philosophy and Other Essays* (London: New Left Books, 1971).

Altman, Joel B., *The Tudor Play of Mind: Rhetorical Inquiry and the Development of Elizabethan Drama* (Berkeley, Los Angeles and London: University of California Press, 1978).

Anderson, Judith H., *Biographical Truth: the Representation of Historical Persons in Tudor-Stuart Writing* (New Haven and London: Yale University Press, 1984).

Aston, Margaret, 'Lollards and Sedition, 1381–1431', *P&P*, 17 (1960): 1–44.

Ayers, P. K., '"Fellows of Infinite Tongue": *Henry V* and the King's English', *SEL*, 34 (1994): 253–77.

Axton, Marie, 'Robert Dudley and the Inner Temple Revels', *HJ*, 13 (1970): 563–78.

—— *The Queen's Two Bodies: Drama and the Elizabethan Succession* (London: Royal Historical Society, 1977).

Baker, J. H., *The Third University of England: the Inns of Court and the Common-law Tradition* (London: Selden Society Lecture, 1990).

Bakhtin, Mikhail, *Problems of Dostoyevsky's Poetics*, ed. and trans. Caryl Emerson (Manchester: Manchester University Press, 1984).

Bald, R. C., 'The *Locrine* and *George-a-Greene* Title-Page Inscription', *The Library*, 4th ser., 15 (1934–5): 289–305.

Baldo, Jonathan, 'Wars of Memory in *Henry V*', *SQ*, 47 (1996): 132–59.

Barrell, John, *Imagining the King's Death: Figurative Treason, Fantasies of Regicide 1793–1796* (Oxford: Oxford University Press, 2000).

Barroll, Leeds, 'A New History for Shakespeare and His Time', *SQ*, 39 (1988): 441–64.

Bartlett, Robert, *Trial by Fire and Water: the Medieval Judicial Ordeal* (Oxford: Clarendon Press, 1986).

Barton, Anne, 'The King Disguised: Shakespeare's *Henry V* and the Comical History', in Joseph G. Price, ed., *The Triple Bond: Essays in Honour of Arthur Colby Sprague* (Pennsylvania and London: Pennsylvania State University Press, 1975), pp. 92–117.

Bellamy, John, *The Law of Treason in the Later Middle Ages* (Cambridge: Cambridge University Press, 1970).

—— *The Tudor Law of Treason* (London: Routledge & Kegan Paul, 1979).

Berg, James Emmanuel, '*Gorboduc* as a Tragic Discovery of "Feudalism"', *SEL*, 40 (2000): 199–226.

Berger, Harry, Jr., 'Sneak's Noise, or, Rumour and Detextualization in *2 Henry IV*', *Kenyon Review*, NS, 6 (1984): 58–78.

Bernthal, Craig A., 'Treason in the Family: the Trial of Thumpe v. Horner', *SQ*, 42 (1991): 44–54.

Betteridge, Thomas, *Tudor Histories of the English Reformation, 1530–83* (Aldershot: Ashgate, 1999).

Bevington, David, *Tudor Drama and Politics: a Critical Approach to Topical Meaning* (Cambridge, Mass.: Harvard University Press, 1968).

Bhabha, Homi K., *The Location of Culture* (London and New York: Routledge, 1994).

Bland, D. S., 'Rhetoric and the Law Student in Sixteenth-Century England', *SP*, 54 (1957): 489–508.

Blank, Paula, *Broken English: Dialects and the Politics of Language in Renaissance Writings* (London and New York: Routledge, 1996).

—— '"Niu ureiting": the Prose of Language Reform in the English Renaissance', in Elizabeth Fowler and Roland Greene, eds, *The Project of Prose in Early Modern Europe and the New World* (Cambridge: Cambridge University Press, 1997), pp. 31–47.

—— 'Speaking Freely about Richard II', *Journal of English and Germanic Philology*, 96 (1997): 327–48.

Blatt, T. B., *The Plays of John Bale: a Study of Ideas, Technique and Style* (Copenhagen: G. E. C. Gad, 1968).

Bolton, W. F., 'Ricardian Law Reports and *Richard II*', *ShakS*, 20 (1988): 53–66.

Bonjour, Adrien, 'The Road to Swinstead Abbey: a Study of the Sense and Structure of *King John*', *ELH*, 18 (1951): 253–74.

Bourdieu, Pierre, 'The Production and Reproduction of Legitimate Language', in John B. Thompson, ed., *Language and Symbolic Power*, trans. Gino Raymond and Matthew Adamson (Cambridge: Polity Press, 1991), pp. 43–65.

Bouwsma, William J., *John Calvin: a Sixteenth-Century Portrait* (Oxford: Oxford University Press, 1988).

Boyd, Brian, '*King John* and *The Troublesome Raigne*: Sources, Structure, Sequence', *Philological Quarterly*, 74 (1995): 37–56.

Braden, Gordon, *Renaissance Tragedy and the Senecan Tradition: Anger's Privilege* (New Haven and London: Yale University Press, 1985).

Braunmuller, A. R., 'The Serious Comedy of Greene's *James IV*', *ELR*, 3 (1973): 335–50.

—— '*King John* and Historiography', *ELH*, 55 (1988): 309–332.

Breight, Curt, '"Treason doth never prosper": *The Tempest* and the Discourse of Treason', *SQ*, 41 (1990): 1–28.

Breitenberg, Mark, 'Reading Elizabethan Iconicity: *Gorboduc* and the Semiotics of Reform', *ELR*, 18 (1988): 194–217.

Brigden, Susan, *London and the Reformation* (Oxford: Clarendon Press, 1989).

Britnell, R. H., 'Penitence and Prophecy: George Cavendish on the Last State of Cardinal Wolsey', *Journal of Ecclesiastical History*, 48 (1997): 263–81.

Bryson, Anna, *From Courtesy to Civility: Changing Codes of Conduct in Early Modern England* (Oxford: Clarendon Press, 1998).

Burckhardt, Sigurd, *Shakespearean Meanings* (Princeton: Princeton University Press, 1968).

Burke, Peter, 'Introduction', in Peter Burke and Roy Porter, eds, *The Social History of Language* (Cambridge: Cambridge University Press, 1987), pp. 1–20.

Butler, Judith, *Excitable Speech: a Politics of the Performative* (New York and London: Routledge, 1997).

Calderwood, James L., *Metadrama in Shakespeare's Henriad: Richard II to Henry V* (Berkeley and Los Angeles: University of California Press, 1979).

Cartwright, Kent, *Theatre and Humanism: English Drama in the Sixteenth Century* (Cambridge: Cambridge University Press, 1999).

Cavanagh, Dermot, '"Possessed with Rumours": Popular Speech and *King John*', *Shakespeare Yearbook*, 6 (1996): 171–94.

—— 'Uncivil Monarchy: Scotland, England and the Reputation of James IV', in Jennifer Richards, ed., *Early Modern Civil Discourses* (London: Palgrave Macmillan, 2003).

Certeau, Michel de, 'History: Science and Fiction', in *Heterologies: Discourse on the Other*, trans. Brian Massumi (Manchester: Manchester University Press, 1986), pp. 199–221.

Chapman, Alison A., 'Whose Saint Crispin's Day Is It?: Shoemaking, Holiday Making, and the Politics of Memory in Early Modern England', *Renaissance Quarterly*, 54 (2001): 1467–94.

Christianson, Paul, *Reformers and Babylon: English Apocalyptic Visions from the Reformation to the Eve of the Civil War* (Toronto: University of Toronto Press, 1978).

Clark, Peter, *English Provincial Society from the Reformation to the Revolution: Religion, Politics and Society in Kent, 1500–1640* (Hassocks, Sussex: Harvester Press, 1977).

Clark, Stuart, *Thinking with Demons: the Idea of Witchcraft in Early Modern Europe* (Oxford: Oxford University Press, 1997).

Clegg, Cyndia Susan, ' "By the choise and inuitation of al the realme": *Richard II* and Elizabethan Press Censorship', *SQ*, 48 (1997): 432–48.

—— 'Archival Poetics and the Politics of Literature: Essex and Hayward Revisited', *Studies in the Literary Imagination*, 32 (1999): 115–23.

Colclough, David, '*Parrhesia*: the Rhetoric of Free Speech in Early Modern England', *Rhetorica*, 17 (1999): 177–212.

Collinson, Patrick, *The Birthpangs of Protestant England: Religious and Cultural Change in the Sixteenth and Seventeenth Centuries* (Basingstoke: Macmillan, 1988).

Conrad, F. W., 'The Problem of Counsel Reconsidered: the Case of Sir Thomas Elyot', in P. A. Fideler and T. F. Mayer, eds, *Political Thought and the Tudor Commonwealth: Deep Structure, Discourse and Disguise* (London and New York: Routledge, 1992), pp. 75–107.

Craun, Edwin D., *Lies, Slander and Obscenity in Medieval Literature: Pastoral Rhetoric and the Deviant Speaker* (Cambridge: Cambridge University Press, 1997).

Crewe, Jonathan V., *Trials of Authorship: Anterior Forms and Poetic Reconstruction from Wyatt to Shakespeare* (Berkeley, Los Angeles, Oxford: University of California Press, 1990).

Cunningham, Karen, ' "A Spanish heart in an English body": the Ralegh Treason Trial and the Poetics of Proof', *Journal of Medieval and Renaissance Studies*, 22 (1992): 327–51.

——'Female Fidelities on Trial: Proof in the Howard Attainder and *Cymbeline*', *RenD*, NS, 25 (1994): 1–31.

Curren-Aquino, Deborah T., ed., *King John: New Perspectives* (Newark: Delaware University Press, 1989).

Danby, John F., *Shakespeare's Doctrine of Nature: a Study of* King Lear (London: Faber & Faber, 1968).

Davies, W. T., 'A Bibliography of John Bale', *Oxford Bibliographical Society, Proceedings and Papers* (Oxford: Oxford University Press, 1936–9), 5, 203–46.

Dean, D. M. and N. L. Jones, 'Introduction: Representation, Ideology and Action in the Elizabethan Parliaments', in D. M. Dean and N. L. Jones, eds, *The Parliaments of Elizabethan England* (Oxford: Basil Blackwell, 1990). pp. 1–13.

Dean, Paul, 'Chronicle and Romance Modes in *Henry V*', *SQ*, 32 (1981): 18–27.

—— 'Shakespeare's *Henry VI* Trilogy and Elizabethan "Romance" Histories: the Origins of a Genre', *SQ*, 33 (1982): 34–48.

DeMolen, Richard L., *Richard Mulcaster (c. 1531–1611) and Educational Reform in the Renaissance* (Nieuwkoop: De Graaf Publishers, 1991).

Dewar, Mary, *Sir Thomas Smith: a Tudor Intellectual in Office* (London: Athlone Press, 1964).

Diehl, Huston, *Staging Reform, Reforming the Stage: Protestantism and Popular Theater in Early Modern England* (Ithaca and London: Cornell University Press, 1997).

Dillon, Janette, *Language and Stage in Medieval and Renaissance England* (Cambridge: Cambridge University Press, 1998).

Dobson, E. J., 'Early Modern Standard English', *Transactions of the Philological Society* (1955): 25–34.

Dollimore, Jonathan and Alan Sinfield, 'History and Ideology: the Instance of *Henry V*', in John Drakakis, ed., *Alternative Shakespeares* (London and New York: Routledge, 1985), pp. 206–27.

Doran, Susan, 'Juno Versus Diana: the Treatment of Elizabeth I's Marriage in Plays and Entertainments, 1561–1581', *HJ*, 38 (1995): 257–74.

Dutton, Richard, *Mastering the Revels: the Regulation and Censorship of English Renaissance Drama* (Basingstoke and London: Macmillan, 1991).

Dzelzainis, Martin, 'Shakespeare and Political Thought', in David Scott Kastan, ed., *A Companion to Shakespeare* (Oxford: Blackwell, 1999), pp. 100–16.

Eccles, Mark, 'Sir George Buc, Master of the Revels', in Charles J. Sisson, ed., *Thomas Lodge and Other Elizabethans* (Cambridge, Mass.: Harvard University Press, 1933), pp. 411–506.

Elliot, John R., 'Shakespeare and the Double Image of King John', *ShakS*, 1 (1965): 64–84.

Ellis-Fermor, Una, 'Marlowe and Greene: a Note on their Relations as Dramatic Artists', in D. C. Allen, ed., *Studies in Honor of T. W. Baldwin* (Illinois: University of Illinois Press, 1958), pp. 136–49.

Elsky, Martin, *Authorizing Words: Speech, Writing, and Print in the English Renaissance* (Ithaca and London: Cornell University Press, 1989).

Elton, G. R., *Policy and Police: the Enforcement of the Reformation in the Age of Thomas Cromwell* (Cambridge: Cambridge University Press, 1972).

Esler, Anthony, 'Robert Greene and the Spanish Armada', *ELH*, 32 (1965): 314–32.

Fairfield, Leslie P., *John Bale: Mythmaker for the English Reformation* (West Lafayette: Purdue University Press, 1976).

Farge, Arlette, *Subversive Words: Public Opinion in Eighteenth-Century France*, trans. Rosemary Morris (Cambridge: Polity Press, 1994).

Ferguson, Arthur B., *The Articulate Citizen and the English Renaissance* (Durham, North Carolina: Duke University Press, 1965).

—— *Clio Unbound: Perception of the Social and Cultural Past in Renaissance England* (Durham, North Carolina: Duke University Press, 1979).

Forest-Hill, Lynn, *Transgressive Language in Medieval English Drama: Signs of Challenge and Change* (Aldershot: Ashgate, 2000).

Foucault, Michel, *Discipline and Punish: the Birth of the Prison*, trans. Alan Sheridan (Harmondsworth: Penguin, 1979).

—— 'Two Lectures', *Power/Knowledge: Selected Interviews and Other Writings 1972–1977*, ed. Colin Gordon; trans Colin Gordon *et al.* (Brighton: Harvester Press, 1980), pp. 78–108.

—— *The Use of Pleasure: Volume 2 of The History of Sexuality*, trans. Robert Hurley (1985; repr. Harmondsworth: Penguin, 1992).

Fox, Adam, 'Rumour, News and Popular Political Opinion in Elizabethan and Early Stuart England', *HJ*, 40 (1997): 597–620.

—— *Oral and Literate Culture in England, 1500–1700* (Oxford: Clarendon Press, 2000).

Frevert, Ute, *Men of Honour: a Social and Cultural History of the Duel*, trans. Anthony Williams (Cambridge: Polity Press, 1995).

Goldberg, Jonathan, *Writing Matter: From the Hands of the English Renaissance* (Stanford: Stanford University Press, 1990).

Graves, Michael A. R., *Thomas Norton: the Parliament Man* (Oxford: Blackwell, 1994).

Grazia, Margreta de, 'Shakespeare's View of Language: an Historical Perspective', *SQ,* 29 (1978): 374–88.

Green, A. Wigfall, *The Inns of Court and Early English Drama* (New Haven: Yale University Press, 1931).

Greenblatt, Stephen, *Renaissance Self-Fashioning: From More to Shakespeare* (Chicago: University of Chicago Press, 1980).

—— *Shakespearean Negotiations: the Circulation of Social Energy in Renaissance England* (Oxford: Clarendon Press, 1988).

Grene, Nicholas, *Shakespeare's Serial History Plays* (Cambridge: Cambridge University Press, 2002).

Griffin, Benjamin, 'The Birth of the History Play: Saint, Sacrifice, and Reformation', *SEL,* 39 (1999): 217–37.

—— *Playing the Past: Approaches to English Historical Drama, 1385–1600* (Woodbridge: D. S. Brewer, 2001).

Gross, Kenneth, *Shakespeare's Noise* (Chicago: University of Chicago Press, 2001).

Grudin, Michaela Paasche, *Chaucer and the Politics of Discourse* (University of South Carolina Press, 1996).

Guy, John, 'Tudor Monarchy and its Critiques', in John Guy, ed., *The Tudor Monarchy* (London: Edward Arnold, 1997), pp. 78–109.

—— 'The Rhetoric of Counsel in Early Modern England', in Dale Hoak, ed., *Tudor Political Culture* (Cambridge: Cambridge University Press, 1995), pp. 292–310.

Hadfield, Andrew, *Literature, Politics and National Identity: Reformation to Renaissance* (Cambridge: Cambridge University Press, 1994).

Haigh, Christopher, *English Reformations: Religion, Politics, and Society under the Tudors* (Oxford: Clarendon Press, 1993).

Halverson, John, 'The Lamentable Comedy of *Richard II*', *ELR,* 24 (1994): 343–69.

Hamel, Guy, '*King John* and *The Troublesome Raigne*: a Reexamination', in *King John: New Perspectives*, pp. 41–61.

Hamilton, Donna B., 'The State of Law in *Richard II*', *SQ,* 34 (1983): 5–17.

Hamilton, Paul, *Historicism* (London and New York: Routledge, 1996).

Hammer, Paul E. J., 'The Uses of Scholarship: the Secretariat of Robert Devereux, Second Earl of Essex', *English Historical Review,* 109 (1994): 26–51.

—— *The Polarization of Elizabethan Politics: the Political Career of Robert Devereux, 2nd Earl of Essex, 1585–1597* (Cambridge: Cambridge University Press, 1999).

Hampton, Timothy, *Writing from History: the Rhetoric of Exemplarity in Renaissance Literature* (Ithaca and London: Cornell University Press, 1990).

Happé, Peter, 'Sedition in *King Johan*: Bale's Development of a "Vice"', *Medieval English Theatre,* 3 (1981): 3–6.

—— *John Bale* (New York: Twayne, 1996).

Hardison, O. B., Jr., *Prosody and Purpose in the English Renaissance* (Baltimore and London: Johns Hopkins University Press, 1989).

Harris, J. W., *John Bale: a Study in the Minor Literature of the Reformation* (Illinois: Illinois Studies in Language and Literature, 1940).

Hart, Jonathan, *Theater and World: the Problematics of Shakespeare's History* (Boston: Northeastern University Press, 1992).

Hawkes, David, *Ideology* (London and New York: Routledge, 1996).
Helgerson, Richard, *Forms of Nationhood: the Elizabethan Writing of England* (Chicago: University of Chicago Press, 1992).
Herman, Peter C., 'Henrician Historiography and the Voice of the People: the Cases of More and Hall', *Texas Studies in Literature and Language*, 39 (1997): 259–83.
Hieatt, Charles, 'A New Source for *Friar Bacon and Friar Bungay*', *RES*, NS, 32 (1981): 180–7.
Hobson, Christopher Z.,'Bastard Speech: the Rhetoric of "Commodity" in *King John*', *Shakespeare Yearbook*, 2 (1991): 95–114.
Hodgdon, Barbara, *The End Crowns All: Closure and Contradiction in Shakespeare's History* (Princeton: Princeton University Press, 1991).
Hodler, Beat, 'Protestant Self-Perception and the Problem of *Scandalum*: a Sketch', in Bruce Gordon, ed., *Protestant History and Identity in Sixteenth-Century Europe: the Medieval Inheritance*, 2 vols (Aldershot: Scolar 1996).
Holderness, Graham, *Shakespeare Recycled: the Making of Historical Drama* (Hertfordshire: Harvester Wheatsheaf, 1992).
Holmes, Peter, *Resistance and Compromise: the Political Thought of the Elizabethan Catholics* (Cambridge: Cambridge University Press, 1982).
Honigmann, E. A. J., 'Shakespeare's Self-Repetitions and *King John*', *Shakespeare Survey*, 53 (2000): 175–83.
Howard, Jean E. and Phyllis Rackin, *Engendering a Nation: a Feminist Account of Shakespeare's English Histories* (London and New York: Routledge, 1997).
Hoyle, R. W., *The Pilgrimage of Grace and the Politics of the 1530s* (Oxford: Oxford University Press, 2001).
Hopkins, Lisa, 'Neighbourhood in *Henry V*', in Mark Thornton Burnett and Ramona Wray, eds, *Shakespeare and Ireland: History, Politics, Culture* (Basingstoke: Macmillan, 1997), pp. 9–26.
Hudson, Ruth, 'Greene's *James IV* and Contemporary Allusions to Scotland', *PMLA*, 47 (1932): 652–67.
Hughes, Philip, *The Reformation in England*, 3 vols (London: Hollis and Carter, 1950–4).
Hunt, Simon, ' "Leaving Out the Insurrection": Carnival Rebellion, English History Plays, and a Hermeneutics of Advocacy', in Patricia Fumerton and Simon Hunt, eds, *Renaissance Culture and the Everyday* (Philadelphia: University of Pennsylvania Press, 1999), pp. 299–314.
Hunter, G. K., *English Drama 1586–1642: the Age of Shakespeare* (Oxford: Clarendon Press, 1997).
——'Truth and Art in History Plays', *Shakespeare Survey*, 42 (1990): 15–24.
Hutson, Lorna, 'Fortunate Travelers: Reading for the Plot in Sixteenth-century England', *Representations*, 41 (1993): 83–103.
—— 'Chivalry for Merchants; or, Knights of Temperance in the Realms of Gold', *Journal of Medieval and Early Modern Studies*, 26 (1996): 29–59.
—— 'Not the King's Two Bodies: Reading the "Body Politic" Shakespeare's *Henry IV*, Parts 1 and 2', in Victoria Kahn and Lorna Hutson, eds, *Rhetoric and Law in Early Modern Europe* (New Haven and London: Yale University Press, 2001), pp. 166–98.
James, Henry and Greg Walker, 'The Politics of *Gorboduc*', *The English Historical Review*, 110 (1995): 109–21.

James, Mervyn, 'At a Crossroads of the Political Culture: the Essex Revolt, 1601', in *Society, Politics and Culture: Studies in Early Modern England* (Cambridge: Cambridge University Press, 1986), pp. 416–65.

—— 'English Politics and the Concept of Honour, 1485–1642', in *Society, Politics and Culture*, pp. 308–415.

Jameson, Fredric, *The Political Unconscious: Narrative as a Socially Symbolic Act* (London: Methuen, 1981).

Jones, Emrys, *Scenic Form in Shakespeare* (Oxford: Clarendon Press, 1971).

—— *The Origins of Shakespeare* (Oxford: Clarendon Press, 1977).

Jones, Norman and Paul Whitfield White, '*Gorboduc* and Royal Marriage Politics: an Elizabethan Playgoer's Report of the Première Performance', *ELR*, 26 (1996): 3–16.

Jones, Robert C., 'Truth in *King John*', *SEL*, 25 (1985): 397–417.

Kahn, Victoria, *Rhetoric, Prudence, and Skepticism in the Renaissance* (Ithaca and London: Cornell University Press, 1985).

—— *Machiavellian Rhetoric: From the Counter-Reformation to Milton* (Princeton: Princeton University Press, 1994).

Kamps, Ivo, *Historiography and Ideology in Stuart Drama* (Cambridge: Cambridge University Press, 1996).

Kastan, David Scott, 'The Shape of Time: Form and Value in the Shakespearean History Play', *Comparative Drama*, 7 (1973): 259–77.

—— *Shakespeare and the Shapes of Time* (London and Basingstoke: Macmillan, 1982).

—— ' "To Set a Form upon that Indigest": Shakespeare's Fictions of History', *Comparative Drama*, 17 (1983): 1–16.

—— 'Proud Majesty Made a Subject: Shakespeare and the Spectacle of Rule', *SQ*, 37 (1986): 459–75.

—— ' "Holy Wurdes" and "Slypper Wit": John Bale's *King Johan* and the Poetics of Propaganda', in Peter C. Herman, ed., *Rethinking the Henrician Era: Essays on Early Tudor Texts and Contexts* (Urbana and Chicago: Illinois University Press, 1994), pp. 267–82.

Kendall, Ritchie D., *The Drama of Dissent: the Radical Poetics of Nonconformity, 1380–1590* (Chapel Hill and London: University of North Carolina Press, 1986).

Kiernan, Pauline, *Shakespeare's Theory of Drama* (Cambridge: Cambridge University Press, 1996).

King, John N., *English Reformation Literature: the Tudor Origins of the Protestant Tradition* (Princeton: Princeton University Press, 1982).

Knowles, Ronald, *Shakespeare's Arguments With History* (Basingstoke: Palgrave, 2001).

Lacey, Robert, *Robert, Earl of Essex: an Elizabethan Icarus* (London: Weidenfeld and Nicolson, 1971).

Lane, Robert, ' "The sequence of posterity": Shakespeare's *King John* and the Succession Controversy', *SP*, 92 (1995): 460–81.

Leggatt, Alexander, *Shakespeare's Political Drama: the History Plays and the Roman Plays* (London and New York: Routledge, 1988).

Lekhal, Catherine, 'The Historical Background of Robert Greene's "The Scottish History of James IV"', *Cahiers Elisabéthains*, 35 (1989): 27–45.

Levin, Carole, *Propaganda in the English Reformation: Heroic and Villainous Images of King John* (Lewiston, New York: Edwin Mellen Press, 1988).

—— ' "We shall never have a merry world while the Queene lyveth": Gender, Monarchy, and the Power of Seditious Words', in Julia M. Walker, ed., *Dissing Elizabeth: Negative Representations of Gloriana* (Durham, North Carolina and London: Duke University Press, 1998), pp. 77–95.

—— *'The Heart and Stomach of a King': Elizabeth I and the Politics of Sex and Power* (Philadelphia: University of Pennsylvania Press, 1994).

Levine, Mortimer, *The Early Elizabethan Succession Question, 1558–1568* (Stanford: Stanford University Press, 1966).

Levine, Nina, 'Lawful Symmetry: the Politics of Treason in *2 Henry VI*', RenD, NS, 25 (1994): 197–218.

Longstaffe, Steve, 'The Limits of Modernity in Shakespeare's *King John*', *Shakespeare Yearbook*, 6 (1996): 91–118.

—— 'What is the English History Play and Why are They Saying Such Terrible Things About It?', *Renaissance Forum*, 2: 2 (September 1997), 1–16. Available at http://www.hull.ac.uk/renforum/v2no2/longstaf.htm.

MacDonald, Ronald R., 'Uneasy Lies: Language and History in Shakespeare's Lancastrian Tetralogy', SQ, 35 (1984): 22–39.

Manheim, Michael, 'The Four Voices of the Bastard', in *King John: New Perspectives*, pp. 126–35.

Manning, Roger B., 'The Origins of the Doctrine of Sedition', *Albion*, 12 (1980): 99–121.

Marcus, Leah, *Puzzling Shakespeare: Local Reading and its Discontents* (Berkeley, Los Angeles, London: University of California Press, 1988).

Maus, Katharine Eisaman, *Inwardness and Theater in the English Renaissance* (Chicago: University of Chicago Press, 1995).

McAlindon, T., *Shakespeare and Decorum* (London and Basingstoke: Macmillan, 1973).

—— *Shakespeare's Tudor History: a Study of Henry IV, Parts 1 and 2* (Aldershot: Ashgate, 2001).

McCoy, Richard C., *The Rites of Knighthood: the Literature and Politics of Elizabethan Chivalry* (Berkeley and Los Angeles: University of California Press, 1989).

McDonald, C. O., *The Rhetoric of Tragedy: Form in Stuart Drama* (Massachussetts: University of Massachussetts Press, 1966).

McEachern, Clare, '*Henry V* and the Paradox of the Body Politic', SQ, 45 (1994): 33–56.

—— *The Poetics of English Nationhood, 1590–1612* (Cambridge: Cambridge University Press, 1996).

McLaren, A. N., *Political Culture in the Reign of Elizabeth I: Queen and Commonwealth, 1558–1585* (Cambridge: Cambridge University Press, 1999).

McMillin, Scott and Sally-Beth MacLean, *The Queen's Men and their Plays* (Cambridge: Cambridge University Press, 1998).

Montrose, Louis, *The Purpose of Playing: Shakespeare and the Cultural Politics of the Elizabethan Theatre* (Chicago: University of Chicago Press, 1996).

—— 'Idols of the Queen: Policy, Gender, and the Picturing of Elizabeth I', *Representations*, 68 (1999): 108–61.

Moretti, Franco, 'The Great Eclipse: Tragic Form as the Deconsecration of Sovereignty', in *Signs Taken For Wonders: Essays in the Sociology of Literary Forms*, trans. David Miller (London and New York: Verso, rev. ed., 1988), pp. 42–82.

Morgan, Hiram, 'The Fall of Sir John Perrot', in John Guy, ed., *The Reign of Elizabeth I: Court and Culture in the Last Decade* (Cambridge: Cambridge University Press, 1995), pp. 109–25.

Mossman, Judith, '*Henry V* and Plutarch's Alexander', *SQ*, 45 (1994): 57–73.

Mueller, Janel M., *The Native Tongue and the Word: Developments in English Prose Style, 1380–1580* (Chicago: University of Chicago Press, 1984).

Mullaney, Steven, 'Lying Like Truth: Riddle, Representation and Treason in Renaissance England', *ELH*, 47 (1980): 32–47.

Neill, Michael, 'Broken English and Broken Irish: Nation, Language, and the Optic of Power in Shakespeare's Histories', *SQ*, 45 (1994): 1–32.

Nelson, Alan H., 'George Buc, William Shakespeare, and the Folger *George a Greene*', *SQ*, 49 (1998): 74–83.

Neubauer, Hans-Joachim, *The Rumour: a Cultural History*, trans. Christian Braun (London and New York: Free Association Books, 1999).

Newman, Karen, *Fashioning Femininity and English Renaissance Drama* (Chicago: University of Chicago Press, 1991).

Norbrook, David, '"A liberal tongue": Language and Rebellion in *Richard II*', in J. M. Mucciolo, ed., *Shakespeare's Universe: Renaissance Ideas and Conventions* (Hants: Scolar Press, 1996), pp. 37–51.

—— 'The Emperor's New Body? *Richard II*, Ernst Kantorowicz, and the Politics of Shakespeare Criticism', *Textual Practice*, 10 (1996): 329–57.

North, Helen, *Sophrosyne: Self-Knowledge and Self-Restraint in Greek Literature* (Ithaca: Cornell University Press, 1966).

Ornstein, Robert, *A Kingdom for a Stage: the Achievement of Shakespeare's History Plays* (Cambridge, Mass.: Harvard University Press, 1972).

Parker, Patricia, *Literary Fat Ladies: Rhetoric, Gender, Property* (London: Methuen, 1987).

Patterson, Annabel, *Shakespeare and the Popular Voice* (Oxford: Basil Blackwell, 1989).

—— *Reading Holinshed's* Chronicles (Chicago: University of Chicago Press, 1994).

Phialas, Peter G., 'The Medieval in *Richard II*', *SQ*, 12 (1961): 305–10.

Pincombe, Mike, *Elizabethan Humanism: Literature and Learning in the Later Sixteenth Century* (Harlow: Longman, 2001).

Pocock, J. G. A., 'Verbalizing a Political Act: Towards a Politics of Speech', in Michael J. Shapiro, ed., *Language and Politics* (Oxford: Blackwell, 1984), pp. 25–43.

Porter, Joseph A., *The Drama of Speech Acts: Shakespeare's Lancastrian Tetralogy* (Berkeley and Los Angeles: University of California Press, 1979).

Prest, W. R., 'The Learning Exercises at the Inns of Court, 1590–1640', *Journal of the Society of Public Teachers of Law*, 9 (1967): 310–13.

—— *The Inns of Court under Elizabeth I and the Early Stuarts, 1590–1640* (London: Longman, 1972).

Pugliatti, Paola, *Shakespeare the Historian* (London and Basingstoke: Macmillan, 1996).

Rabkin, Norman, 'Rabbits, Ducks, and *Henry V*', *SQ*, 28 (1977): 279–96.

Rackin, Phyllis, *Stages of History: Shakespeare's English Chronicles* (London: Routledge, 1990).

Rasmussen, Eric, 'The Implications of Past Tense Verbs in Early Elizabethan Dumb Shows', *English Studies*, 67 (1986): 417–19.

Rhodes, Neil, *The Power of Eloquence and English Renaissance Literature* (Hertfordshire: Harvester Wheatsheaf, 1992).

Ribner, Irving, *The English History Play in the Age of Shakespeare* (Princeton: Princeton University Press, 1957; rev. ed. London: Methuen, 1965).

Richards, Jennifer, ' "A wanton trade of living"?: Rhetoric, Effeminacy and the Early Modern Courtier', *Criticism*, 42 (2000): 185–206.

—— *Rhetoric and Courtliness in Early Modern Literature* (Cambridge: Cambridge University Press, 2003).

Riggs, David, *Shakespeare's Heroical Histories*: Henry VI *and its Literary Tradition* (Cambridge, Mass.: Harvard University Press, 1971).

Roberts, Penny, 'Arson, Conspiracy and Rumour in Early Modern Europe', *Continuity and Change*, 12 (1997): 9–29.

Robinson, Marsha, 'The Historiographic Methodology of *King John*', in *King John: New Perspectives*, pp. 29–40.

—— *Writing the Reformation*: Actes and Monuments *and the Jacobean History Play* (Aldershot: Ashgate, 2002).

Ross, A. Elizabeth, 'Hand-me-Down-Heroics: Shakespeare's Retrospective of Popular Elizabethan Heroical Drama in *Henry V*', in John W. Velz, ed., *Shakespeare's English Histories: a Quest for Form and Genre* (Binghampton, New York: Medieval and Renaissance Texts and Studies, 1996), pp. 171–203.

Rossiter, A. P., 'Ambivalence: the Dialectic of the Histories', in Graham Storey, ed., *Angel With Horns: and Other Shakespeare Lectures* (London: Longman 1961), pp. 40–64.

Round, P. Z., 'Greene's Materials for *Friar Bacon and Friar Bungay*', *Modern Language Review*, 21 (1926): 19–23.

Samaha, Joel B., 'Gleanings from Local Criminal-Court Records: Sedition Amongst the "Inarticulate" in Elizabethan Essex', *Journal of Social History*, 8 (1975): 61–79.

Schelling, Felix E., *The English Chronicle Play: a Study in the Popular Historical Literature Environing Shakespeare* (London: Macmillan, 1902).

Schoeck, R. J., 'Rhetoric and Law in Sixteenth-Century England', *SP*, 50 (1953): 110–27.

—— 'Lawyers and Rhetoric in Sixteenth-Century England', in James J. Murphy, ed., *Renaissance Eloquence: Studies in the Theory and Practice of Renaissance Rhetoric* (Berkeley, Los Angeles and London: University of California Press, 1983), pp. 274–91.

Schoenfeldt, Michael C., *Bodies and Selves in Early Modern England: Physiology and Inwardness in Spenser, Shakespeare, Herbert, and Milton* (Cambridge: Cambridge University Press, 1999).

Scott, Jonathan, *England's Troubles: Seventeenth-Century English Political Instability in European Context* (Cambridge: Cambridge University Press, 2000).

Scott, James C., *Domination and the Arts of Resistance: Hidden Transcripts* (New Haven and London: Yale University Press, 1990).

—— *Weapons of the Weak: Everyday Forms of Peasant Resistance* (New Haven and London: Yale University Press, 1985).

Senn, Werner, 'Robert Greene's Handling of Source Material in *Friar Bacon and Friar Bungay*', *English Studies*, 54 (1973): 544–53.

Shagan, Ethan H., 'Rumours and Popular Politics in the Reign of Henry VIII', in Tim Harris, ed., *The Politics of the Excluded, c. 1500–1800* (Basingstoke: Palgrave, 2001), pp. 30–66.

Shrank, Cathy, 'Rhetorical Constructions of a National Community: the Role of the King's English in mid-Tudor Writing', in Alexandra Shepard and Phil Withington, eds, *Communities in Early Modern England: Networks, Place, Rhetoric* (Manchester: Manchester University Press, 2000), pp. 180–98.

Siemon, James C., *Shakespearean Iconoclasm* (Berkeley, Los Angeles, London: University of California Press, 1985).

Skinner, Quentin, *Reason and Rhetoric in the Philosophy of Hobbes* (Cambridge: Cambridge University Press, 1996).

Sloane, Thomas O., *Donne, Milton, and the End of Humanist Rhetoric* (Berkeley, Los Angeles, London: University of California Press, 1985).

Smith, Bruce R., *The Acoustic World of Early Modern England: Attending to the O-Factor* (Chicago: University of Chicago Press, 1999).

Smith, Lacey Baldwin, *Treason in Tudor England: Politics and Paranoia* (London: Jonathan Cape, 1986).

Somogyi, Nick de, *Shakespeare's Theatre of War* (Aldershot: Ashgate, 1998).

Speer, Janet M., 'Princes, Pirates, and Pigs: Criminalizing Wars of Conquest in *Henry V*', *SQ*, 47 (1996): 160–77.

Spivack, Bernard, *Shakespeare and the Allegory of Evil: the History of a Metaphor in Relation to His Major Villains* (New York and London: Columbia University Press, 1958).

Stallybrass, Peter and Allon White, *The Politics and Poetics of Transgression* (London: Methuen, 1986).

Steinsaltz, David, 'The Politics of French Language in Shakespeare's History Plays', *SEL*, 42 (2002): 317–34.

Tannenbaum, Samuel A., *Shakesperian Scraps and Other Elizabethan Fragments* (New York: Columbia University Press, 1933).

Tennenhouse, Leonard, *Power on Display: the Politics of Shakespeare's Genres* (London: Methuen, 1986).

Tillyard, E. M. W., *Shakespeare's History Plays* (London: Chatto & Windus, 1944).

Trousdale, Marion, *Shakespeare and the Rhetoricians* (London: Scolar Press, 1982).

Tuck, Richard, *Philosophy and Government, 1572–1651* (Cambridge: Cambridge University Press, 1993).

Vanhoutte, Jacqueline, 'Community, Authority, and the Motherland in Sackville and Norton's *Gorboduc*', *SEL*, 40 (2000): 227–39.

Vaughan, Virginia Mason, 'Between Tetralogies: *King John* as Transition', *SQ*, 35 (1984): 407–20.

Vickers, Brian, *In Defense of Rhetoric* (Oxford: Clarendon Press, 1988).

—— ' "The Power of Persuasion": Images of the Orator, Elyot to Shakespeare', in James J. Murphy, ed., *Renaissance Eloquence: Studies in the Theory and Practice of Renaissance Rhetoric* (Berkeley, Los Angeles and London: University of California Press, 1983), pp. 411–35.

Vos, Alvin, ' "Good Matter and Good Utterance": the Character of English Ciceronianism', *SEL*, 19 (1979): 3–18.

Walker, Greg, *Plays of Persuasion: Drama and Politics at the Court of Henry VIII* (Cambridge: Cambridge University Press, 1991).

—— *The Politics of Performance in Early Renaissance Drama* (Cambridge: Cambridge University Press, 1998).

Walker, Simon, 'Rumour, Sedition and Popular Protest in the Reign of Henry IV', *P&P*, 166 (2000): 31–65.

Weimann, Robert, 'Mingling Vice and Worthiness in *King John*', *ShakS*, 27 (1999): 109–33.

Wentersdorf, Karl P., 'The Conspiracy of Silence in *Henry V*', *SQ*, 27 (1976): 264–87.

Whigham, Frank, *Ambition and Privilege: the Social Tropes of Elizabethan Courtesy Theory* (Berkeley, Los Angeles, London: University of California Press, 1984).

White, Paul Whitfield, 'Patronage, Protestantism, and Stage Propaganda in Early Elizabethan England', *The Yearbook of English Studies*, 21 (1991): 39–52.

—— *Theatre and Reformation: Protestantism, Patronage, and Playing in Tudor England* (Cambridge: Cambridge University Press, 1993).

Wickham, Chris, 'Gossip and Resistance Among the Medieval Peasantry', *P&P*, 160 (1998): 3–24.

Williams, Penry, *The Tudor Regime* (Oxford: Clarendon Press, 1979).

—— *The Later Tudors: England, 1547–1603* (Oxford: Clarendon Press, 1995).

Wilson. F. P., *Marlowe and the Early Shakespeare* (Oxford: Clarendon Press, 1953).

Wilson, Richard, *Willpower: Essays in Shakespearean Authority* (London: Harvester Wheatsheaf, 1993).

Wixson, Douglas C., '"Calm Words Folded Up in Smoke": Propaganda and Spectator Response in Shakespeare's *King John*', *ShakS*, 14 (1981): 111–27.

Womersley, David, 'The Politics of Shakespeare's King John', RES, NS, 40 (1989): 497–515.

—— 'France in Shakespeare's *Henry V*', *Renaissance Studies*, 9 (1995): 442–59.

—— 'Why is Falstaff Fat?', *RES*, NS, 47 (1996): 1–22.

Wood, Andy, '"Poore men woll speke one daye": Plebian Languages of Deference and Defiance in England, c. 1520–1640', in *The Politics of the Excluded*, pp. 67–98, p. 71.

Woolf, D. R., *Reading History in Early Modern England* (Cambridge: Cambridge University Press, 2000).

Worden, Blair, *The Sound of Virtue: Philip Sidney's* Arcadia *and Elizabethan Politics* (New Haven and London: Yale University Press, 1996).

—— 'Favourites on the English Stage', in J. H. Elliot and L. W. B. Brockliss, eds, *The World of the Favourite* (New Haven and London: Yale University Press, 1999), pp. 159–83.

Zim, Rivkah, 'Dialogue and Discretion: Thomas Sackville, Catherine de Medici and the Anjou Marriage Proposal 1571', *HJ*, 40 (1997): 287–310.

Zitner, Sheldon P., 'Aumerle's Conspiracy', *SEL*, 14 (1974): 236–57.

Index